T0265192

Project: Execution

Strategic planning is the starting point for projects and often the primary reason for a project's success or failure. Project leaders and project-orientated organisations need to understand strategic planning to understand their position and environment, and make rational decisions when selecting and defining their projects and programmes.

The authors provide the reader with a straightforward, comprehensive understanding of the basics of project management, including the present status of the discipline, its history, and theoretical foundations. With emphasis on the project life cycle, it is designed to support the IPMA D, C, or B level qualifications, and IPMA Competence Baseline 4.0, providing you with all the information needed to pursue certification.

Project: Execution is also an ideal introductory textbook to progressive programmes on strategic planning, with a focus on collaborative work, open strategy, and an exploration of open strategic planning on a social level. It provides a wealth of learning tools and case studies to demonstrate best practice. This is the ideal guide to project planning for anyone that wants their planning decisions to be as wise as they are savvy.

Helgi Thor Ingason is a professor at Reykjavik University, a consultant, IPMA Certified Senior Project Manager, and Certified Stanford Project Manager. His background is industrial and mechanical engineering. He is the author of several books on management and his work has been published in the *Project Management Journal*, *International Journal of Project Management*, and *Journal of Metals*.

Haukur Ingi Jonasson is a professor at Reykjavik University, a consultant, and a Certified Stanford Project Manager. His background is in theology, philosophy, and psychology, which he applies to engineering and management. He is the author of several books on leadership and management.

Project: Execution

Helgi Thor Ingason and
Haukur Ingi Jonasson

Routledge
Taylor & Francis Group

LONDON AND NEW YORK

First published 2020
by Routledge
2 Park Square, Milton Park, Abingdon, Oxon OX14 4RN

and by Routledge
52 Vanderbilt Avenue, New York, NY 10017

Routledge is an imprint of the Taylor & Francis Group, an informa business

British Library Cataloguing-in-Publication Data
A catalogue record for this book is available from the British Library

Library of Congress Cataloging-in-Publication Data
Names: Helgi Thor Ingason, author. | Haukur Ingi Jonasson, author.
Title: Project execution / Helgi Thor Ingason and Haukur Ingi Jonasson.
Description: Milton Park, Abingdon, Oxon; New York, NY: Routledge, 2019. | Includes bibliographical references and index.
Identifiers: LCCN 2019010613 (print) | LCCN 2019013327 (ebook) | ISBN 9780429441530 (eBook) | ISBN 9781138338678
(hardback: alk. paper) Subjects: LCSH: Project management. | Strategic planning.
Classification: LCC HD69.P75 (ebook) | LCC HD69.P75 .H4475 2019 (print) | DDC 658.4/04–dc23
LC record available at https://lccn.loc.gov/2019010613

ISBN: 978-1-138-33867-8 (hbk)
ISBN: 978-0-429-44153-0 (ebk)

Typeset in Goudy
by Deanta Global Publishing Services, Chennai, India.

This book is dedicated to
our children

Contents

· ·

List of figures   ix

List of tables   xiii

Acknowledgements   xvi

Preface to the series   xviii

Foreword   xxi

1 Introduction   1
   Professional associations and certification
   Bodies of knowledge
   Structure of the book
   Bibliography

2 Projects, Programmes, and Portfolios (PPP): concepts, history, and context   13
   Definitions and concepts in Project, Programme, and Portfolio (PPP)
       management
   A brief history of project management
   Project characteristics and the project life cycle
   Project management in the context of the organisation
   Bibliography

3 Planning: definition and the environment   73
   Project planning
   Defining the project
   Scope and deliverables
   The project plan
   Project environment
   Combined environment analysis – example
   Bibliography

4 Planning: objectives, time, and the critical path   109
Objectives and their measurements
Master plan and work breakdown structure
Scheduling
The critical path
Bibliography

5 Planning: resources, management structure,
and role/task division   145
Resources and cost plan
Management structure and role/task division
Bibliography

6 Project start-up, co-operation, and information   171
Project start-up
Partnerships and agreements
Information management
Bibliography

7 Uncertainty and risk management   197
Types of uncertainty
Process of risk management
PERT
Decision-making and risk
Bibliography

8 The project manager and the project team   217
Methods of execution
The project manager
Teams and groups in projects
Bibliography

9 Project close-out   239
Organising the project close-out
Product delivered
Learning from the experience
Bibliography

Index   249

Figures

1.1 Definition of the ICB4 competence element structure   3
1.2 6th edition of the *APM Body of Knowledge* (APM, 2012)   7
1.3 6th edition of the *Project Management Body of Knowledge* (PMI, 2017)   8
1.4 Structure of the book and the division of the nine chapters   8
2.1 Cheops Pyramid   15
2.2 The dam at Kárahnjúkar   17
2.3 Projects, programmes, and portfolios   19
2.4 Tunnel at Indre Nordnes in Norway, built by IAV   21
2.5 Modern view of project management competences; the eye of competence   28
2.6 Project management as a principal activity within a project   29
2.7 Sliding scale of project character   32
2.8 Three dimensions of project characteristics   33
2.9 Project life cycle   34
2.10 Typical phases of a project life cycle   35
2.11 Accumulated work in the project life cycle   37
2.12 Phases as independent projects during the lifetime of an extensive project   37
2.13 Projects in the lifetime of an organisation, from the building of a project outcome until the demolition at its end   39
2.14 Life cycle of operation and life cycle of project   40
2.15 Influence of project management and the cost in regard to changes during a project life cycle   41
2.16 Spiral model of the life cycle of a software project   43
2.17 The Sydney Opera House   51
2.18 The labour requirements in a project during its life cycle   54
2.19 Organisation diagram in a traditional department-organised company   55
2.20 Example of an organisation chart in a project-organised company   56
2.21 Organisation chart in a matrix organised company   57

2.22 Declining influence of project management in safety matters
during the project life cycle   61
3.1 Project planning and project updating through the life cycle   75
3.2 The connection of a project with the direction and the vision
of the company   77
3.3 In the beginning, during project definition and initial
planning, creativity is essential   81
3.4 Framework for the content factors of a project plan   82
3.5 Visual presentation of the overall environment of the project   85
3.6 Analysis of the main outcomes of the project   87
3.7 A process for the analysis of project complexity   90
3.8 Typical stakeholders in projects   91
3.9 A process for the analysis of project stakeholders   95
3.10 Outline of consequences and likelihood in the evaluation
of risk   98
3.11 A process for the analysis of project risk   99
3.12 A visualisation of a combined analysis of the project
environment   101
3.13 Combined analysis of project environment for aluminium
dross recycling project   106
4.1 Iron Triangle showing categories of objectives in projects   111
4.2 Project management view of the Y2K phenomenon as a giant
project   113
4.3 Measurement of success relating to a particular objective   114
4.4 Success of projects and time frame   116
4.5 Main categories of objective in three dimensions   117
4.6 Structural guide to define a project goal hierarchy   119
4.7 Project life cycle and phases for the construction of an
office building   124
4.8 Project life cycle and phases for a concert   125
4.9 Work breakdown analogy – progression of building design
from initial perspective drawing to final detail   128
4.10 Breakdown of a project – traditional presentation   128
4.11 Breakdown of a project into two layers   129
4.12 Breakdown of a project into one layer   129
4.13 Analysis of the environment and related actions as important
factors in the breakdown of a project   130
4.14 Breakdown of the work parts in building a cabin   132
4.15 Breakdown according to departments   133
4.16 Possible time saving in regard to working on main tasks or
phases in parallel   135
4.17 Logical connection of work parts – finish/start (FS)   135
4.18 Logical connection of work parts – start/start (SS)   136
4.19 Logical connection of work parts – finish/finish (FF)   136
4.20 Logical connection of work parts – start/finish (SF)   137

4.21 Gantt chart to manage the production in a factory 137
4.22 Gantt chart of the same cabin building project as shown in Figure 4.14 138
4.23 The two main types of network diagrams 139
4.24 Example of a box grid (AON) 139
4.25 Example of an arrow grid (AOA) 140
4.26 Information that needs to be documented for the calculations of a critical path 141
4.27 Example of the critical path – calculations from start to finish 141
4.28 Example of the critical path – calculations from the finish to the start 142
5.1 Life cycle of a product – the costs during the life cycle 146
5.2 Evaluation of resources and links to the project breakdown 151
5.3 The calculation of the cost, based on the breakdown 153
5.4 A breakdown of a project according to cost factors (CBS) 156
5.5 Construction of a cost estimate from the perspective of the buyer 158
5.6 Graphical presentation of monthly outflow of cash and cumulative cost for a six-month project 161
5.7 Management model for a project which shows the main roles and their connections 164
5.8 Influencing factors in management organisation of a project 165
5.9 Example of a project organisation chart 166
5.10 Responsibility assignment matrix in a project – general representation 167
5.11 Responsibility assignment matrix – example of representation in a simple project 168
6.1 Project start-up 172
6.2 Joint venture – an example of a simple organisation 176
6.3 One example of many communication channels in a project 178
6.4 An example of a template form for recording minutes of a status meeting 181
6.5 Documentation gone over the limit 182
6.6 Example of internet usage areas and solutions in projects 185
6.7 Project meeting 186
6.8 An example of a simple process for change control 189
6.9 The House of Culture at Hof in Akureyri, Iceland (Menningarfélag Akureyrar, n.d. – photograph by Audunn Nielsson) 189
6.10 Pictorial representation of the main variables in the calculation of earned value 193
7.1 Risk associated with processes and the environment 200
7.2 Process of risk management in projects 201
7.3 Probability distribution for the time length of a task 202
7.4 Critical path example 204

7.5 Project selection   208
8.1 Simple representation of the Scrum method in project
     management   220
8.2 An overview of elements that need to be kept in mind in
     relation to the creation of facilities for projects   222
8.3 Main groups and key roles in projects   225
8.4 Development of project groups   227
8.5 A project team   229
8.6 The tendency to neglect project management in favour of the
     project work   231
8.7 The three main categories for conflicts in projects   233
8.8 Project sponsor   235
9.1 Reaching the final gate   240
9.2 Core elements of project close-out   240
9.3 Harpa, musical, and conference centre (Harpa, n.d.)
     (photograph by Vigfús Birgisson)   242
9.4 A framework for a schedule of a project close-out meeting   246
9.5 Project close-out   247

Tables

2.1   The differences between managing a project, a programme, and a portfolio – an overview   22

2.2   Technical classification of different project type categories   44

3.1   Scoring table to differentiate between routine work and projects   76

3.2   Evaluation of technical, resource- and organisational complexity of projects   89

3.3   Example of uncertainty factors in projects; they can involve various opportunities (+) or risks (–)   97

3.4   Analysis of project outcomes (scope) for aluminium dross recycling project   101

3.5   Stakeholder analysis for aluminium dross recycling project   102

3.6   Uncertainty analysis for aluminium dross recycling project   104

3.7   Complexity analysis for aluminium dross recycling project   105

4.1   Examples of objectives relating to the three project dimensions   118

4.2   Capturing impact objectives in a table format   119

4.3   Hypothetical impact objectives for Iceland in FIFA World Cup in Russia in 2018   120

4.4   Hypothetical project objectives for Iceland in FIFA World Cup in Russia in 2018   121

4.5   Hypothetical other objectives for Iceland in FIFA World Cup in Russia in 2018   121

4.6   Overview of phases in a project   126

4.7   Information in an example for calculations of the critical path   140

5.1   An example of a simple form to gather information about required resources   150

5.2   Types of budgets   152

5.3   An example of a cost estimate for a simple project   155

5.4   The cost estimate: evaluation of cash outflow and calculations of accumulated outflow   160

6.1   An example of a formal meeting system in relation to a simple project   180

6.2   Cost estimate: an example of a presentation which can also be used in the follow-up of the project   192

7.1   Evaluation of estimated task durations using PERT   204

8.1   Differences between traditional management and project management   223

Acknowledgements

Special thanks to our families for their encouragement, patience, and their contributions. Very special thanks to Jonathan Norman at the Major Projects Association Knowledge Hub for his unceasing support, guidance, dedication, and friendship. Thanks to Tim Morissey who read through the text and gave us some great suggestions for the content. We also thank Simon Vaughan for proofreading the book. Our thanks also go to Lara Jonasdottir, Jon Asgeir Sigurvinsson, Jane Appleton, Mary Frances Davidson, and Throstur Gudmundsson for their help with translations and to Olof Embla Eyjolfsdottir for her help in initiating the project with Routledge.

We also want to thank some of our friends and colleagues within the project management community for the many inspiring discussions: Bob Dignen, Beverly Pasian, Darren Dalcher, Mark Morgan, Miles Sheperd, Rodney Turner, Steven Eppinger, Sharon De Mascia, Tom Taylor, and Yvonne Schoper. Also, we extend our thanks to our co-workers in the Master of Project Management (MPM) programme at Reykjavik University: Asbjorg Kristinsdottir, Benedikt Arnason, Agnes Holm Gunnarsdottir, Gudfinna Bjarnadottir, Ellen Gunnarsdottir, Florence Kennedy, Greta Maria Gretarsdottir, Hannes Petursson, Yr Gunnarsdottir, Pall Kr Palsson, Pall Jensson, Pauline Muchina, Marta Kristin Larusdottir, Morten Fangel, Markus A Zoller, Sveinbjorn Jonsson, Thordis Wathne, and Thordur Vikingur Friðgeirsson. We want to thank the University of Reykjavik and all our co-workers there and our students for their ongoing support and encouragement. Special thanks to Aslaug Armannsdottir MPM and Iris Hrund Thorarinsdottir MPM and our co-workers on the Project Leadership and Project Management programme at the University of Iceland, Kristin Jonsdottir Njardvik, Kristin Birna Jonsdottir, Elin Juliana Sveinsdottir, and at the University of Akureyri, Elin Hallgrimsdottir.

We thank also Gudrun Hognadottir, Gunnar Stefansson, Kristjan Kristjansson, Kristinn Orn Vidarsson, Ingolfur A. Johanneson, Margret Bjornsdottir, Runolfur Smari Steinthorsson, Kristinn Orn Vidarson, and Tryggvi Sigurbjarnarson for their support.

Special thanks to CCP Games in Reykjavik, its CEO, Hilmar Veigar Petursson, and its SVP of Human Resources, Sophie Froment, for their help funding the translations. We want to thank JPV Publishing in Iceland, particularly our editor Oddny S. Jonsdottir and CEO Egill Orn Johansson, for their encouragement and co-operation.

Last but not least, we want to thank Halldor Baldursson for his wonderful illustrations and friendship and Amy Laurens and Alexandra Atkinson at Routledge for their patience, suggestions, and support.

Helgi Thor Ingason
Haukur Ingi Jonasson

Preface to the series

· ·

Transparent leadership and sustainable project management

This book is a part of a series of four that are written for anyone who needs to be able to lead and participate in different kinds of projects and the human, technical, and communication aspects of projects, programmes, and portfolios using a style and techniques adapted to the context and the environment of each one.

The series is tailored to help you strengthen four key proficiencies in a very creative way: strategy, leadership, implementation, and communication. Use the advice they contain to develop your personal leadership and managerial style and your ability to take ideas and advance them through planning and execution – with the transparency and accountability that successful project management today demands. We put equal emphasis on the technical and human elements of effective management. Success will require you to align the objectives of the project leader, team, and organisation within the project's social and environmental context.

We've written this series primarily for the next generation of project, programme, and portfolio managers. The models, techniques, and advice within the books have been taught for many years in the most popular and successful management education and training programme in Iceland. They reflect the integrated nature of this successful programme, which is designed based on the needs of those who want to lead well in both their professional and private lives. If you do that, then you will bring a degree of self-awareness and self-realisation to the leadership of businesses, public bodies, non-governmental organisations (NGOs), and society in general.

We have aligned the books to the most recent version of IPMA Competence Baseline ICB4. The idea is to provide a practical handbooks for anyone aiming to become IPMA certified.

We wanted to make sure the series will be of interest to an international readership since projects today are typically planned and operated across international boundaries and involve teams from different disciplines and cultures.

Our aim is to transform you into an international and transparent leader; someone who is intellectually and emotionally ready to manage others in a spirit of self-reflection; has the values and ethics to guide them in often complex and difficult environments; and has the flexibility and confidence to listen to and make use of criticism and communication in all its forms. Transparency implies leading in a way that shows constant, considered awareness of the project's content, context, and consequences for you, your team, your organisation, as well as the society and environment within which you live and work. The series is based on this vision.

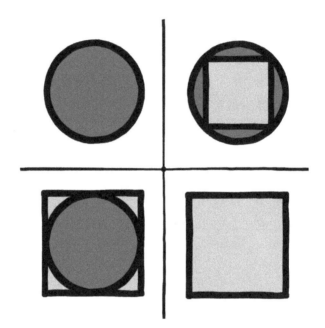

Foreword

Project management has been called the management method of the 21st century. New times call for new approaches; human knowledge has grown tremendously and continues to grow, the world has become one global market, and there is an ever-growing demand for diverse products and services. The challenges to be solved become more complex, there are demands for adaptability and response speed, and more and more people bring their expertise to solving complex problems. The pace of change in society is great and growing, and the need for interdisciplinary and cross-sectoral co-operation is high and growing as groups today deal with problems that were previously often solved by individuals. These multifaceted changes in the business and social environment call for new approaches and, indeed, project management began to evolve as an independent science field from the mid-20th century. Management by projects has become the most important driver of change within organisations and in collaboration between organisations. Hence, everyone must be familiar with the basic aspects of project management and be able to apply related skills – as a leader or participant.

This book is part of a series of four books that highlight different aspects of project management and demonstrate practical approaches to real-life problems. The series is meant to shed light on project management in a broad sense. It deals with the "Strategy" of organisations that prepare and execute projects in a rapidly changing environment and must coordinate their limited resources. It deals with "Leadership" – the individuals, their strengths and weaknesses, and their ability to self-reflect. It deals with "Communication," what can go wrong in communication and collaboration, and how these can be strengthened to achieve better results. Last but not least, it deals with "Execution" – technical methods to prepare and execute complex projects of all kinds.

Execution is the topic of the present book, which is intended to be a guide to project management from a very practical perspective and acts as an overview which outlines the fundamental components of the discipline. This book aims to provide the reader with a straightforward, comprehensive understanding of the basics of project management and its present status, as well as its history and theoretical foundations. The book is a somewhat traditional project management textbook. However, rather than take a very general approach, the book is heavily focused on project planning and execution, and revolves around the project life cycle. The book is designed to be especially useful for people pursuing their IPMA D, C, or B level certifications, and some of the concepts of the IPMA Competence Baseline 4 (ICB4) are discussed and put into perspective throughout the text. In particular, the book revolves around the so-called practice competences, and some basic methods, tools, and techniques that people involved with projects use to start, plan, execute, and close down projects. All the 13 practice competence elements of ICB4 are directly and indirectly defined and explained in this book. They are:

- Design
- Requirements, objectives, and benefits
- Scope
- Time
- Organisation and information
- Quality
- Finance
- Resources
- Procurement and partnership
- Plan and control
- Risk and opportunities
- Stakeholders
- Change and transformation

This book is primarily based on experience gained in Iceland, where the close interactions between the authors and different business sectors and students has led to the development of a unique knowledge base that has international relevance. We follow three key principles in our approach:

- Mental virtue – inventiveness and ability to solve problems wisely and properly.
- Moral virtue – the ability to detect the difference between what is right and not right and take a moral stand on issues and projects.
- Working virtue – professional awareness as part of a workforce that chooses the appropriate tools and approach for each task and applies them correctly.

These principles have formed the basis of the undergraduate training programme called Transparent Leadership and Sustaining Project Management which has been offered in Iceland since the year 2003 and has taken a fixed form, divided into four courses: Strategic Management Skills, Leadership Skills, Execution Skills, and Communication Skills. We have also developed a master's programme in project management – MPM – which was established in 2005 and continues to be a popular and successful educational choice for many professionals. The MPM programme is based on extensive experience built up in the industrial and other sectors in project management, business management, and human relations. The programme has benefited from our long experience of sharing our expertise with large and small groups of pupils with different professional backgrounds who have given us extensive feedback and the benefit of their own experience.

In recent years, we have recognised the need for high-quality teaching material to support the course and decided to write this series of books to assist students and interested readers alike. These were first written in Icelandic and have now been translated into English, as the material is considered to be of international relevance. We hope that this book will be useful and educational to our readers, and we wish them success in all their ventures and challenges, both at work and at play!

Helgi Thor Ingason
Haukur Ingi Jonasson

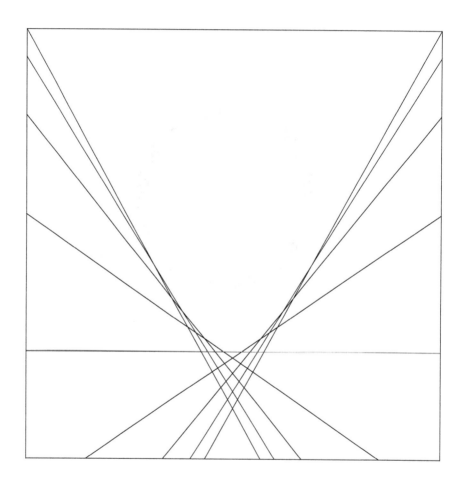

1 Introduction

∙∙

"By failing to prepare, you are preparing to fail." Benjamin Franklin's famous Universal Truth seems particularly apt for a discipline such as project management, where the planning and execution of projects require that the responsible individuals have a wide range of prior developed skills and experience. Whether the project is something as large scale and complex as the post-tsunami clean-up of the Fukushima nuclear power plant in Japan or, at the other end of the scale, the organisation of the annual Westman Islands Music Festival in Iceland, there are many different elements to consider in project management, and neglecting any of them can escalate potential problems and increase the chances of a negative outcome.

From our experience as project management course providers and business consultants, we recognise that people with a serious interest in project management have very diverse backgrounds, and this book is written with that diversity in mind. You may be a seasoned project management professional, a project management student, or someone who has a general managerial role or interest. You may operate as an individual, or as part of a larger public or private entity, and your current project could be described, in the simplest terms, as a cost-constrained operation to realise a set of defined outcomes to pre-defined quality standards and requirements. This, of course, can mean that you are responsible for organising anything from a school reunion to a new public health advertising campaign or repairing an orbiting satellite. Irrespective of the direction from which you have come, there are common elements that form the basis of successful project management, and we have identified four different areas of competence as being essential. These are: strategic skills, leadership skills, execution skills, and communication skills.

In this book, the focus is on planning and execution skills, and the aim is to guide the reader through an in-depth discussion of the various aspects of this topic using examples to illustrate, where applicable. In the context of this book, "execution" refers to the often complex interactions between the different elements or entities that constitute a project, their management and structure, whereas "skills" are considered to be learned capacities to carry out defined tasks successfully, efficiently, and effectively.

There are two principal foundations for this book. The first is the accumulated experience of the authors, acquired through a combination of managerial and teaching roles, and the second is the published literature of internationally recognised project management associations such as the International Project Management Association's Competence Baseline (ICB4).

Organisational skills are essentially multifaceted, even for relatively straightforward projects, and they will vary from sector to sector. To illustrate the scope of the subject, ICB4 lists 28 competence elements that are considered essential for a successful project manager, and each of these is given a detailed description. The competences are categorised into three areas: perspective, people, and practice. A summary of the elements is given in Figure 1.1. Throughout the book, there will be references, mainly to the elements of the practice competences, while other competences will be covered in the other books in the series.

Project management involves a complex process that weaves together a combination of many different elements. The book offers you a structured approach to achieving success and includes many examples that highlight various organisational skills in different environments. It aims to show that in order for you to be deemed a "skilful" planner, you'll need to have a deep working knowledge of projects and a high level of awareness of the requirements for project completion, both commercial and technical. By extension, this implies a good understanding of the relationships between all the different elements and entities within a project and the dexterity to break down a project into a series of manageable sequenced tasks, delegating when necessary. It also means, at all times, retaining responsibility for a successful outcome, leading by example, and having the flexibility required to react to circumstances as they arise. The ability to lead others and maintain a standard in quality control is not innate; you will need to acquire it through learning and experience. This is one of the areas of focus for project management methodology and leadership skills.

A reminder that even the most carefully planned projects can be derailed by simple human error.

In 1999, after nine months of space flight, the $125 million Mars Climate Orbiter reached the atmosphere of Mars, and NASA Mission Control was in the process of manoeuvering it into a stable orbit when contact was irretrievably lost, and the Orbiter presumably crashed. In the follow-up investigation headed by Art Stephenson, a director at the Marshall Spaceflight Center, reference was made to the need for periodic rocket

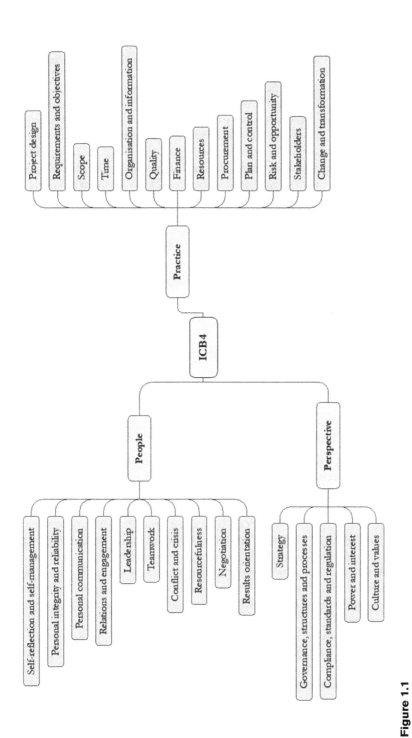

Figure 1.1

Definition of the ICB4 competence element structure.

firings during the outward journey to counteract deviations that had been caused by a combination of the asymmetry of the craft and the influence of the sun. Engineers on the ground calculated the size of the rocket firing using feet-per-second of thrust, a value based on English imperial units, while the spacecraft computer interpreted the instructions in newtons-per-second, a metric measure of thrust. This difference was significant, and the error built up, so that by the time the spacecraft reached the Martian atmosphere, there were indications that something was seriously wrong. "We were on the wrong trajectory, and our system of checks and balances did not allow us to recognize that," Edward Stone, director of the NASA Jet Propulsion Laboratory, said afterwards. Stephenson said that the problem was not with the spacecraft, but with the engineers and the systems used to direct it. "Sometimes the little things can come back and really make a difference," he said (Oberg, 1999).

Before we move on to a more detailed discussion of the various aspects of project planning and delivery, let's take a moment to introduce the professional project management associations that we reference, their key bodies of knowledge, and the outline structure of the book.

Professional associations and certification

There are three international professional project management bodies that we reference in this book, and a brief description of these is given below.

International Project Management Association (IPMA)

IPMA, headquartered in Switzerland, is a globally recognised, not-for-profit body that has been promoting standards in project management since 1965. The Association is a federation of about 70 member associations who each develop project management competences within their geographic areas of influence. IPMA works to introduce and promote project management methodology amongst individuals, companies, institutions, and organisations worldwide through its educational base and its certification system. A key feature of IPMA is the conceptual baselines it has developed, such as ICB4, which provide a strong foundation for the teaching of project management (Home – IPMA International Project Management Association, n.d.).

The IPMA awards certificates to individuals based on an assessment of their competences in typical project management activities that occur in their daily working lives. The certification system has four levels: A, B, C, and D, and a brief description of the standards that apply to these levels (also taken from their website) is given below.

Certified Projects Director (IPMA Level A) means that the person is able to direct an important portfolio or programme, rather than the management of a single project. To take on this responsibility, an advanced level of knowledge and experience is required.

Certified Senior Project Manager (IPMA Level B) means that the person is able to manage a complex project that satisfies certain criteria. Sub-projects are normal, i.e. the project manager is working with sub-project managers, rather than leading the project team directly.

Certified Project Manager (IPMA Level C) means that the person is able to lead a project with limited complexity, which signifies that s/he has demonstrated the corresponding level of experience in addition to the ability to apply project management knowledge.

Certified Project Management Associate (IPMA Level D) means that the person is able to apply project management knowledge when s/he participates in a project in any capacity, and common knowledge is not sufficient to perform at a satisfactory level of competence.

Project Management Institute (PMI)

PMI is a not-for-profit membership association for the project management profession that was founded in 1969 and is headquartered in the USA. As of 2016, it had over 470,000 members from 207 countries and territories (PMI | Project Management Institute, n.d.). It offers a variety of products and services to the project management profession in governments, organisations, academia, and industries, including overseeing a system of globally recognised standards and credentials, an extensive research programme, and professional development opportunities.

PMI developed the internationally recognised concept base PMBOK (i.e. *Project Management Body of Knowledge*), which is a key foundation of their certification process for project managers. This will be discussed in the following section and differs somewhat from the IPMA concept baseline. PMI has developed a certification system that consists of eight different independent certification types. The most common certification is PMP – Project Management Professional – where the competence of an individual to perform in the role of a project manager, leading and directing projects and teams, is validated.

Chartered Association for Project Management (APM)

This British project management association has been in operation since 1972 and now has more than 23,000 individual members. APM operates within IPMA and is the largest national project management association within IPMA. The goal of APM is to raise the profile of project management in all sectors of the economy, and their concept foundation is referred to as the APM *Body of Knowledge*. APM reached an important status in 2017 when it received its Royal Charter and became an officially chartered body (APM – The Chartered Body for the Project Profession, n.d.).

Bodies of knowledge

Each of the professional associations has their own published conceptual bases relating to project management. Of the three mentioned above, the ICB of the IPMA will be referred to frequently throughout this book, but we will give a brief outline of all three before proceeding. We'll provide detailed coverage of specific concepts and their context of live projects as we proceed, but the listing below is only intended to give an overview of these important concept bases.

IPMA

The IPMA's concept base, first published in 1999, was called ICB2. It formed the basis of the joint certification programme amongst the IPMA's associated countries and was focused on describing the knowledge and experience needed to deal with the various technical challenges of project management. The subsequent version, ICB3, was published in 2006 to meet the increasing importance of personal characteristics and behaviours for the project manager. It also considered the importance of changes in the business environment, as well as an increased focus on projects and their relationships to their environment, other projects, policies, and the business needs of the company. ICB4 was published in 2015 and is divided into three sections: Individuals working in project management, Individuals working in programme management, and Individuals working in portfolio management. The first, Individuals working in project management, consists of 28 competence elements divided into three areas: people, practice, and perspectives (IPMA, 2015). These elements are shown in Figure 1.1, and they are important reference points for this book.

APM

The concept base of the British Association for Project Management was first published in 1992. APM has a continually updated conceptual foundation with a longer history than ICB. In 2012, APM launched the sixth edition of the standard with a functional structure and comprehensive coverage of the disciplines of project, programme, and portfolio management.

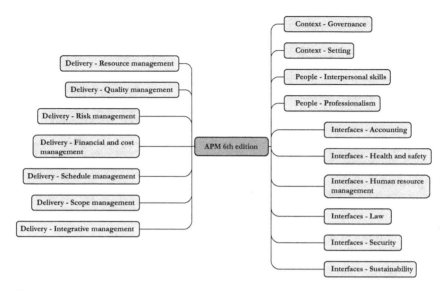

Figure 1.2

6th edition of the *APM Body of Knowledge* (APM, 2012).

The current version of APM defines 53 knowledge areas of project management and is an updated representation of the competences project management professionals need to know and be able to apply. The components of the APM are shown in Figure 1.2 (APM, 2012).

A seventh edition of the APM *Body of Knowledge* is currently in preparation for publication in 2019.

PMI

PMBOK (A *Guide to the Project Management Body of Knowledge*) 6th edition was published in 2017. PMBOK is a compilation of knowledge within the project management profession and – as such – is constantly evolving. PMBOK is intended to provide an overview of good practices within the project management profession, the knowledge and techniques that can be applied to most projects in most cases and where there are broad consensus and unity within the profession. In this most recent version, PMI has included information on agile practices in a separate agile practice guide. There are 49 PMBOK project management processes broken down into ten knowledge areas, and these are as shown in Figure 1.3 (PMI, 2017):

The three different concept bases (IPMA, APM, and PMI) identify similar traits and process knowledge necessary for being a successful project manager,

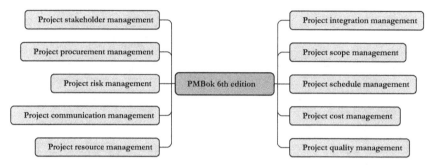

Figure 1.3

6th edition of the *Project Management Body of Knowledge* (PMI, 2017).

albeit in different ways. They describe the various requirements for a project role. There are, however, other concept bases that you will find useful, and we will cover them briefly later in the text.

Reflection points

- In what way is the case of the Mars Climate Orbiter an example of a project management problem?
- What is common and what is different between the three project management associations listed above, IPMA, APM, and PMI? You can visit the web pages of the associations to get a better idea about them.
- Based on the information above on the bodies of knowledge issued by the three project management associations, what seems to be common and what seems to be different?
- What is the significance of the chartered status of APM, and how do you think this will impact project management?

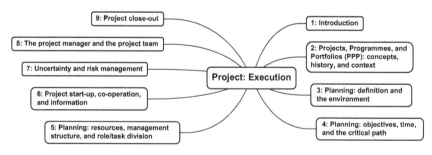

Figure 1.4

Structure of the book and the division of the nine chapters.

Structure of the book

Execution skills cover a wide range of knowledge areas and competences, and we have structured the book in a systematic way to help you break down the topic into manageable chunks and then to recombine them into a coherent whole. The ICB4 is a key reference point. A summary of the contents of the remaining chapters is given below (see Figure 1.4):

- Chapter 2 – Describes the key terms and concepts associated with projects. It discusses different project types and characteristics and how they relate to achieving strategic goals. It also includes an overall introduction to the concept of project management as a way to achieve those goals.
- Chapter 3 – Provides an overview of a practical method of setting up a project plan for both large and small projects. It covers the scope of projects, analysis of their environment, and the setting of milestones and goals.
- Chapter 4 – Covers the breakdown of tasks, presentation of the main work channels, and the preparation of detailed work plans.
- Chapter 5 – Outlines resource planning, procurement, and the management structure for projects.
- Chapter 6 – Discusses how projects should be initiated and the management of communication and information.
- Chapter 7 – Deals with the management of uncertainty in projects.
- Chapter 8 – Outlines the key roles and management techniques as they apply during the project's lifetime to ensure that the project plan will be successfully implemented.
- Chapter 9 – Deals with the finishing of a project: the sign-off of the project to the project's investor(s) or client(s), including related settlements, and the lessons learned, reporting on how the project was prepared and executed, for future reference.

Bibliography

APM – The Chartered Body for the Project Profession. (n.d.). Retrieved from www.apm. org.uk.

APM. (2012). *APM Body of Knowledge* (6th ed.). Princes Risborough: Association of Project Management.

Home – IPMA International Project Management Association. (n.d.). Retrieved from www.ipma.world.

IPMA. (2015). *Individual Competence Baseline for Project, Programme & Portfolio Management*, version 4. Zurich: IPMA.

Oberg, J. (1999). Why the Mars probe went off course. *IEEE Spectrum, 36*(12), 34–39.

PMI | Project Management Institute. (n.d.). Retrieved from www.pmi.org.

PMI. (2017). *A Guide to the Project Management Body of Knowledge (PMBOK Guide)* (6th ed.). Newtown Square, PA: Project Management Institute.

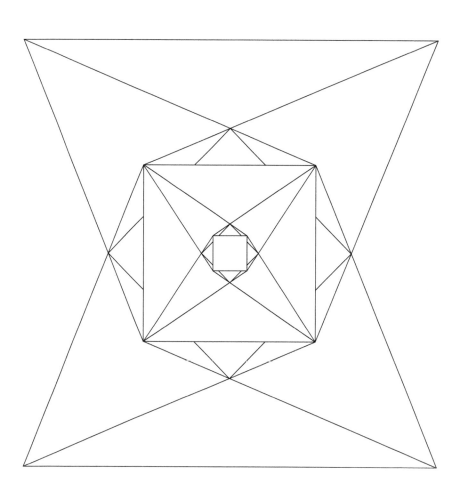

2 Projects, Programmes, and Portfolios (PPP): concepts, history, and context

· ·

Definitions and concepts in Project, Programme, and Portfolio (PPP) management

Projects

What is a project? The question is simple, but the answer is maybe not so simple. In everyday language, the term is used freely, although it can often be confused with other terms. For example, if we take the car to a service station to wash and wax it – or if we go to the mall to select and buy a gift for our best friend's birthday – we call these tasks. If, on the other hand, we decided to clear out a cold and untidy attic and put in new insulation, proper flooring, and storage units – then we would call this a project. The differences in real life can be subtle, but tasks are considered to be expected actions that one takes, based on recognised norms, whereas projects have more of a one-off or special element to them. Upgrading the computer hardware system of a business or constructing a new electricity line are not routine tasks and require special consideration, planning, and financing, and have separate definable goals from normal operations, i.e. they are considered projects. It is useful to note how ICB4 defines a project:

> A project is a unique, temporary, multidisciplinary and organised endeavour to realize agreed deliverables within predefined requirements and constraints.
>
> *(IPMA, 2015)*

Another definition is given in the ISO 21500 standard, where a project is defined as follows:

> A project consists of a unique set of processes consisting of coordinated and controlled activities with start and end dates, performed to achieve

project objectives. Achievement of the project objectives requires the provision of deliverables conforming to specific requirements.

(International Standards Office, 2012)

This definition includes a few general conditions that need to be fulfilled in order to apply the term project.

An example of a dictionary definition of "project" is as follows:

- *A planned undertaking: as a) a definitely formulated piece of research, b) a large, usually government-supported undertaking, c) a task or problem engaged in usually by a group of students to supplement and apply classroom studies.*
- *A usually public housing development, consisting of houses or apartments, built and arranged according to a single plan.*

(Definition of PROJECT, n.d.)

The dictionary definition is a more generalised definition and is maybe not so clear on what differentiates a task from a project. It can be said that projects are special challenges that have a defined beginning and a defined end – reflecting the fact that the objectives have been achieved – and are challenges that require special administrative measures. A recent trend has been to define the term project as an inherently temporary organisation – a group or groups of people who share/divide their roles, that work on a specific temporary subject, according to an approved organisational structure.

Each project is unique in the sense that it has never been done before in the same manner, in the same context, by the same people, and in the same environment. Projects may be divided into work streams and then again into tasks. Each project has a defined beginning and a defined end that we can visualise at the start of the project. In light of this viewpoint, we should return to the everyday tasks that were considered at the beginning of this section. The act of washing and polishing the car can be quite a challenge and certainly has a defined beginning and end. However, there is no substantial difference in the way we go about this task each time we perform it, and the tasks are not many, maybe only one. The goal is also simple. The same goes for buying a birthday present at the mall; we go straight at it, even though sometimes it can seem a bit complicated. These everyday challenges bear a partial resemblance to projects, but in a textbook on project management it is better to regard these as tasks rather than projects. They are relatively simple actions that we repeat in a similar fashion again and again and do not call for special administrative measures.

It is important to also emphasise the concept of a beginning and an end as defining a project. For example, a state or local authority may instigate a project to take over the running of schools from other non-governmental bodies, but once the new administration structure has been established, the "project" would be considered complete and the day to day running of the schools would be described by the term "operation."

To create a strong image of how we may think of a "project," let us travel back in mind to the year 2528 BC and a plain next to Cairo in Egypt. We see a long row of people dragging enormous rocks on rolling logs, which are constantly being replaced under the rock at the front. About 15 people are working on moving each rock, which probably weighs more than two tonnes. Ropes are drawn over the rocks, and some of the people pull the ropes, while others push on the rocks and others move the rollers. Where are these people going? We look in the direction of their destination and we see a spectacular sight. We see the Cheops Pyramid reaching up towards the sun. It is almost fully finished. The last stones are being pulled up ramps that have been built off the sides of the structure. The people work extremely hard at raising the rock into its final resting place, but they rest from time to time to drink water and eat. It seems well coordinated, and nothing appears to be done at random. Around the pyramid, we see a much smaller group of men distinguishable by their different dress. They keep a close eye on proceedings, peering from time to time at stone tablets which contain drawings and symbols. Sometimes they beckon the men standing next to them and say something to them. This message is then transmitted to the various groups at work via intermediaries. It is a hierarchical structure whereby large groups of workers are performing tasks under the command of a smaller group of technical overseers and foremen, and all to complete a special project conceived by a distant, controlling entity.

Project management is practised by almost all types of entities in one form or another for a broad range of reasons, and this variety should be apparent while reading this book. These entities will each have their own unique project management structures that may or may not represent best

Figure 2.1

Cheops Pyramid.

practice in their area. Examples can be extremely diverse, ranging from schools putting on plays to salvaging a foundering vessel on stormy seas, but there are broadly recognised project management conceptual elements that can be widely applied in all cases, which are explained in more detail in later sections.

Programmes

While the term "project" can relate to a wide range and scale of individual special undertakings, it is useful to use the term "programme" to describe a combined group of special undertakings that together constitute a directional or strategic change. ICB4 says the following in relation to this:

> A programme is set up to achieve a strategic goal. A programme is a temporary organisation of interrelated programme components, managed in a coordinated way to enable the implementation of change and the realisation of benefits.
>
> *(IPMA, 2015)*

A programme would therefore often have a larger scope and longer time scale than individual projects and provide more significant benefits than individual projects. A programme may also have quite different overall success characteristics, and its success is measured by the extent to which it satisfies the needs for which it was undertaken. These needs may change during the programme, and this must be taken into account in the management of a programme. An example of a programme within an organisation might be a bank that needs to drastically reduce its operational cost and launches a programme to change the culture of the organisation and implement a culture of continuous improvement. Such an undertaking is not one project, it is a programme of projects with one mutual future vision. In this case, one of the first steps would therefore be to develop a change or transformation strategy for the bank. This strategy would then be implemented through a series of projects, focusing on building up new infrastructure, training staff, and raising awareness among employees. Another example might be an organisation that wishes to modernise its systems or to carry out new product development. Such programmes would normally be controlled by higher-level management in line with overall strategy priorities. A government-driven awareness campaign to reduce population obesity and consequent public medical care costs would be a good example of a programme. It may be the case that all projects implemented were not defined at the outset, as it is common for the later projects within the programme to be dependent on the results of previous projects. The strategic goals of an organisation are achieved through programmes and projects.

A good way to illustrate this concept is to discuss the construction of the Kárahnjúkar hydropower plant in East Iceland. In this example, the main controlling entity was the energy company, the National Power Company (Landsvirkjun), which was required to embrace large-scale programme orientation in order to achieve its strategic goals. The planning component alone was very extensive and involved sub-dividing the programme into a series of discrete projects involving many domestic and foreign consultants working in tandem to get to the point of producing the necessary approval and tender documents. Added challenges were the remoteness of the area, the harsh climate, very short winter days, and a range of potential hazards, including glacial flash floods, earthquakes, and the effects of volcanic eruptions from the nearby active volcanic zone. In terms of construction, this was not a single project but many large-scale projects. The main project was the construction of the 730m long and 193m high dam across the Jökulsá á Dal river, one of the highest dams in Europe. This dam, together with two other large dams, formed the main reservoir – Hálslón – which has a capacity of 2.1 km³. Large diameter tunnels were bored from Hálslón to Fljótsdalur where the hydroelectric plant and tail race system is located. In total, about 73 km of tunnels were constructed during the Kárahnjúkar programme.

The main contractor responsible for the construction of the Fremri-Kárahnjúkur dam, as well as the extensive tunnel system, was the Italian company Impregilo. The construction of the Ufsarlón and Hraunaveita reservoirs was in the hands of the Icelandic company Arnarfell. The joint venture company Fosskraft executed the construction of the power station in Fljótsdalur. This involved four separate contractors: Icelandic companies IAV and ÍSTAK; German company Hochtief; and Danish company Pihl.

The supervision requirements of the construction programme were extremely extensive and necessitated the use of advanced programme

Figure 2.2

The dam at Kárahnjúkar.

management methods implemented by the National Power Company. This involved a complex system of work stream division with many internal and external technical consultants, both domestic and foreign, to oversee this. The overall work was divided into a large number of projects, each with its own critical path, and their relationship to the overall programme critical path was determined in order to achieve economies of scale and avoid costly delays (Vefsíða Kárahnjúkavirkjunar, n.d.).

It has been shown that a programme is similar to a project in that, for example, both are temporary. But they are also very different, and the components of a programme could be other programmes or projects. Each of these components has its own management, and the management of a programme is thus the coordinated management of all the different components of the programme. Typically, this means that in the management of a programme, one is dealing with more complexity than in managing individual projects. Furthermore, for programme management, the emphasis is typically on a common vision, implementation of principal change, and the realisation of general benefits. This typically calls for a collaborative approach, where strong leadership can be of even more importance than in the case of project management.

Portfolios

A collection of projects or programmes may also be termed a portfolio. In this case, they are not linked through any specific strategic direction change but instead represent parallel undertakings that are controlled by higher-level management, often as part of a much larger overall strategy. ICB4 puts this in the following way:

> A portfolio is a set of projects and/or programmes, which are not necessarily related, brought together to provide optimum use of the organization's resources and to achieve the organization's strategic goals while minimizing portfolio risk.
>
> *(IPMA, 2015)*

Figure 2.3 explains the concept of a portfolio. General vision and mission are set out in the direction setting of an organisation. Programmes have been defined to achieve the vision at any time. There are also ongoing operation projects that do not belong to any particular programme. Each project and programme involve the use of standard management which the organisation has implemented. The different projects and programmes are united under the portfolio and controlled in the same manner.

The management of portfolios is a frequent research topic in project management. Consensus prevails that in order to be successful, general procedures need to be defined that can be applied to each project within a portfolio to

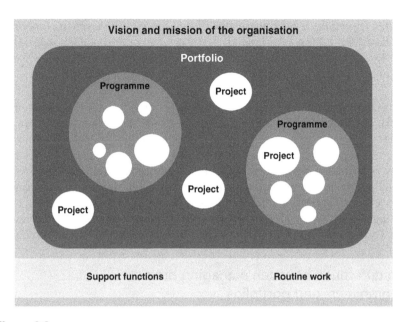

Figure 2.3

Projects, programmes, and portfolios.

determine whether it conforms to the conditions set by the company at any time for their projects.

The Icelandic company IAV (previously mentioned in relation to Kárahnjúkar) – a subsidiary of Marti Holding AG in Switzerland – is one of the largest prime/general contractor companies in Iceland. The works of such contractor companies are normally carried out as projects of different sizes, and together they form the project portfolio of the company. Holistic management of this portfolio is carried out at the headquarters of the company, and this includes, amongst other things, the provision of necessary resources and the distribution of them to the different projects as required and the specifying of coordinated procedures to ensure that all work is carried out to company standards. IAV projects would be considered large according to Icelandic standards but not large enough to justify a pure project-organised structure for the company. Some IAV projects are actually big enough to be defined as programmes, for example, the East Harbour development in Reykjavik, which IAV worked on for the development company Portus Ltd. This development was divided into three main works or projects. The first was the demolition of existing structures, including a large warehouse building and petrol station, and the laying of all the necessary utility piping and cablework. The second was the construction of the iconic Harpa concert and conference hall on the cleared site. The third was the construction of a series of related facilities, including a large underground car park. Another example of programmes in

IAV's portfolio is the construction of a silicon metal production plant on the Reykjanes peninsula in Iceland. The total area of the buildings was 6.0 m². An example of a single project in IAV's project portfolio would be the 5.8 km tunnel at Indre Nordnes in Norway (IAV, n.d.) (see Figure 2.4.).

The management of a portfolio is not a time-bound activity; it is a part of the regular operations of the organisation. The purpose of portfolio management is to enable the organisation to use its limited resources in an optimal way – on those projects and programmes that are most important for achieving the strategic goals of the organisation, while at the same time minimising the risk to an acceptable level. Portfolio management is thus, in essence, establishing and maintaining an overview of all projects and programmes, and running a very dynamic decision-making process, where all the projects and programmes are continuously evaluated. Portfolio management will be addressed in more detail later in this chapter.

The difference between managing projects, programmes, and portfolios

We have shown that projects, programmes, and portfolios are different phenomena, yet related. A project has the principal goal of producing deliverables, while a programme has the goal of achieving strategic change. A portfolio, on the other hand, has the goal of giving an overview of many projects and/ or programmes, and coordinating and optimising them. The managing of a project is thus different from the management of a programme, and even more different is the management of a portfolio. Some of the differences between managing projects, programmes, and portfolios are summed up in Table 2.1.

To understand how the world looks from the different perspectives of a programme, project, and portfolio manager, we can imagine the aforementioned contractor company IAV. One of its programmes was Harpa, the conference centre and concert hall in Reykjavik. This was a large programme and organised as a special department, quite visible in the organogram of IAV during the limited life cycle of the programme. The scope of delivery for this programme was a concert hall and conference centre in full operation, with various benefits to many stakeholders, including the cultural scene and the growing tourist industry in the country. The main management tools for the programme manager were high-level schedules, based on individual projects. The projects changed through the life cycle of the programme; some of them were in fact never executed due to changes in the external environment. The main priority of the programme manager was the performance of the individual projects, delivering the new business capability, and all the different benefits mentioned above. Looking at this from the perspective of the manager of a specific project within this programme, we can, for instance, look at the car park project, an integrated part of the Harpa programme. The scope of delivery for this project was a set of specific deliverables defined originally by detailed technical documents. The focus of the manager of this project was the performance of the individual tasks

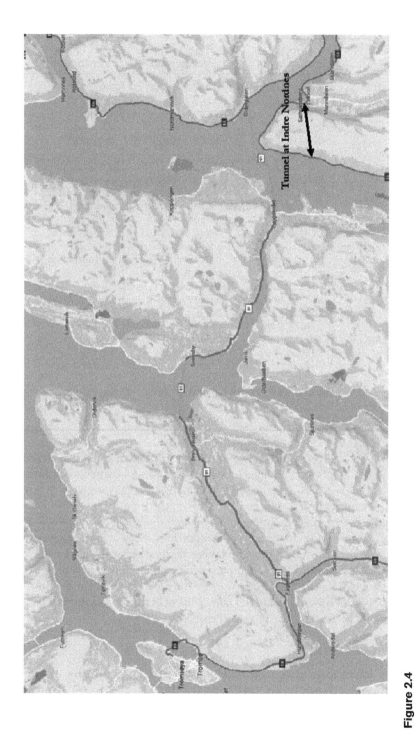

Figure 2.4

Tunnel at Indre Nordnes in Norway, built by IAV.

Table 2.1 The differences between managing a project, a programme, and a portfolio – an overview

	Project management	Programme management	Portfolio management
Key principle	To do things right	To do things right	To do the right things
Scope of delivery	A set of deliverables that has been specified	A business opportunity or a business problem	Strategic objectives of the organisation
Main focus of management	Performance of the project tasks	Performance of the projects included in the programme	The aggregate performance of the portfolio elements
Management tools	Detailed schedules and cost baselines based on tasks	High-level schedules and cost baselines based on projects	Control variables that indicate aggregate performance
How success is measured	On time, within budget, according to specification	Broadly defined, typically by benefits delivered to stakeholders	Long-time value to the organisation
Temporal nature	Temporary, has a defined start and end	Temporary but with a longer time frame than for a project	Permanent activity of the organisation
Typical competences emphasised	Management skills	Leadership skills	Analysis and decision-making

of the project and delivering this project on budget, on time, and according to specifications. His tools were detailed schedules, according to which work packages were delivered according to the original plan. The last perspective is that of the portfolio manager of IAV. His concern is to do the right things and choose the right projects that are appropriate and likely to bring the most value/benefit to the organisation. The management of this portfolio focuses on the aggregate performance of all of the programmes and projects, and they are balanced, using indicators that measure risk, financial parameters, performance, and progress, and other variables for each and every project and programme in the portfolio, enabling the portfolio manager and the management of the organisation to keep a good overview of everything that is going on.

Reflection points

- Three definitions of a project are given at the beginning of this chapter. Compare the definitions by the International Project Management Association (IPMA) and the International Organization for Standardization (ISO) – what is different and what is comparable?

- Explain the difference between a project and a programme. In what way is this difference quite clear, and what – if anything – is not so clear regarding the difference? Use examples if you can.

A brief history of project management

The definitions of the last section belong to the present. To view the methodology of project management in times past, one needs to provide historical context. When the story of the construction of the Cheops Pyramid in Egypt is examined in the light of the definition of project management, it can be argued that its construction was carried out by coordinating human and material resources to achieve the specified objectives. The men in the distinctive dress issuing orders who were mentioned at the beginning of this chapter were the project managers of their time and used the latest technologies of that time to achieve their goals, both in regard to the management of the project and in regard to the work itself. If one views the genesis of project management as something which happened when it became a defined methodology, however, it is easier to examine developments that have occurred since the middle of the last century.

Project management in the modern sense first appeared as a distinct, recognised phenomenon around 1950, in association with the Cold War. At that time, there was a race between Russia and the USA with regard to sending craft into space, and Russia had developed a considerable advantage. In 1957, the entire world watched as they sent the dog Laika into orbit around the earth. Unfortunately for Laika, it was not the intention of the Russians that she should return. It was a different story with the astronaut Yuri Gagarin, who the Russians sent into space in April 1961, and thereby became the first to send a man to orbit the earth. Meanwhile, the Cold War between Russia and the USA was escalating. The key to victory in that war, in the opinion of the Americans, was to develop and produce weapons of mass destruction and deter the enemy from attacking. During this time, the Americans put particular emphasis on the development and production of long-range bomber aircraft, nuclear missiles, and nuclear submarines.

It is said that senior figures in the American defence had come to the conclusion that traditional management approaches and methods could not be used to deal with the enormous challenges associated with the Space Race and the Cold War. There was a need to increase efficiency in managing projects, reduce development time, and build up more capability in establishing, planning, executing, and controlling increasingly complex projects. Systems project management emerged, with an emphasis on boundaries and interfaces, holism, and hierarchy. This was initiated through network planning and the introduction of the "Critical Path Method," or CPM, by DuPont, an activity-orientated tool for the planning and controlling of construction projects and PERT (Program Evaluation and Review Technique), an event-orientated network scheduling system, as a part of the Polaris programme in the USA (Morris, 2013). In PERT, statistical calculations are applied to assess uncertainty in the total time of the project by highlighting the uncertainty in the times/timing of individual tasks and how these are linked together. In CPM, the focus is on the longest chain of sequenced events that is necessary to complete the project and on ensuring that there is no unnecessary delay, as the required activities are coordinated in such a way that the next task within this chain can be commenced straight after the previous task. The set of tasks that form this chain is commonly referred to as the critical path – it is their individual outcomes that tie the project and determine its duration. The PERT and CPM methods will be explained in more detail later in the book.

There was increased concern for people at work, and project management as a profession started to gain recognition. Peter Morris (2013) calls Brigadier Bernard Schriever the father of modern project management. Mr. Schriever led the Atlas programme, in which the first intercontinental ballistic missile was developed and tested in 1956. He applied concurrent engineering and defined the role of the project manager as a person with both technical and budget authority for the project. Gaddis (1959) wrote an important paper entitled "The project manager" in the *Harvard Business Review*, where he shared his thoughts on this recent and important role.

Lenfle and Loch (2010), have pointed out that the projects associated with the space travel programme of the Americans – and which marked the beginning of project management as a modern discipline – were characterised by enormous uncertainty, as not only was the intention to create results that were poorly defined in the beginning, but people did not recognise any known methods to generate these results.

There were other, earlier important developments though, such as in the early 1900s, when the American engineer Henry Gantt developed a method to make production management easier by simple visual presentation (Wilson, 2003). This was the famous Gantt chart, which is widely used today to outline the sequencing of tasks. Although it has its limitations, it is nonetheless very useful, and there are a number of examples given later in this book.

If we return to the topic of the genesis of project management as we understand it today, we can debate whether project management did not exist before the PERT and CPM methods were developed and before Henry Gantt drew his first schedule chart. For example, how did people build the Brooklyn Bridge over the Hudson River in New York, dig the Panama Canal, or build the Pantheon temple in Rome? It is obvious that all the above structures were based on extensive projects, and these projects were indeed managed by applying all the knowledge and technology of their time. One can assume that plans based on a detailed technical design were made in regard to the building of these structures, and that the plans were followed by ensuring that the necessary resources were available – people, materials, and equipment. Without a doubt, these projects would have had a recognisable management strategy, although this may have evolved during the course of the project as major challenges were encountered, rather than being laid out beforehand. This was certainly the case with the Panama Canal, where there were several major changes in approach during the US-led construction period between 1904 and 1913 due to unforeseen circumstances. Other notable projects that predate the PERT and CPM era include the building of the temporary Mulberry harbours at Omaha and Arromanches in France by the Allied Forces as part of the Normandy landings in WWII. This project required special coordination on a very large scale and had to be planned and executed in total secrecy and to very strict and demanding timelines.

To conclude the historical discussion, it is perhaps correct to say that it is the choice of the present to assign the beginning of project management to the mid-20th century. Building on this foundation, practical experience and academic development have helped to broaden the scope and field of application of this earlier methodology into the very diverse field that is evident today across many sectors and which is constantly adapting to new challenges and information.

The Icelandic herring industry was a very significant element of the Icelandic economy from the early 1900s through to the 1960s, when it collapsed spectacularly due to overfishing and environmental shifts. Alongside this larger story were the rise and fall of many individual fishing towns in the north and east of Iceland. The largest of these was Siglufjördur, which underwent a major boom in this period, with catches landed and processed there accounting for more than 20% of Iceland's total exports for a number of these years. Another smaller but important fishing centre that experienced a similar rise and fall on the back of this industry was Djúpavík at the head of Reykjarfjördur in Northwest Iceland. This area was first settled in 1917 when Elías Stefánsson built a herring-salting factory there, but this early venture went bankrupt in 1919 due to an economic depression. In September 1934, the Djúpavík Corporation was established at Hotel Borg in Reykjavik with the aim of building and operating a herring factory in Djúpavík, with the construction of a new factory beginning that same year.

Helgi Eyjólfsson, a builder from Reykjavik, oversaw the building of the factory. The building of the plant was a complex and extensive project, and its preparation would have called for planning on a considerable scale, not least because of the need to transfer all of the resources to this remote area by sea, as no road was laid in this area until 1965. Short rail tracks were used to transport rock and aggregate material from a hand-worked quarry at the base of a nearby mountain for the foundations. The workers involved in the construction of the factory lived in the South Land, a decommissioned ship that was dragged up onto the beach. This was also done to control sediment in the local river and protect the harbour. The herring factory was operational within a year, in 1935, and was the largest building that had been built of concrete in the country, equipped with the most advanced technology of the day. Various innovations to cut costs were tried at Djúpavík, including a landing crane, which was the first of its kind built in Iceland, and conveyor belts and large storage tanks built into the factory for efficient transport of the herring.

In the following decade, plentiful herring catches in Húnaflói (the nearby large bay) meant that the fish oil and fish meal processing enterprise boomed, bringing improved financial status and living standards to the whole region. There were about 60 full-time factory workers and more than a hundred people worked in the salting. In 1944, however, herring catches started to decline, with a sharp drop in 1948 and, despite attempts to keep the enterprise running by processing other fish besides herring, eventually the venture came to an end and the machines at Djúpavík became silent in 1954. After this, the residents moved away, and the settlement was abandoned again. In 1985, Hótel Djúpavík was established in the old women's quarters, and conservation of the factory and other buildings began (Arnadottir, 2013).

In view of the fact that Iceland was a rather poor country with weak infrastructure in 1934, the achievement of builder Helgi Eyjólfsson and the owners of the herring factory is impressive from a project management perspective.

Contemporary project management

The increasing development of computing power and scope in the last few decades have had a significant effect on how we approach project management as we can now build up complex models or systems to help guide decision-making, make plans, and monitor developments and outcomes. Modern project management has thus evolved from its beginnings in the middle of the last century, but there is also much which has remained essentially the same. There is no substitute for a project manager having to think carefully through all aspects of the project. As part of this process, there are numerous technical methods to set goals and make plans and follow them through. For instance, systematic planning for scope, cost, and time is a key prerequisite for the success of projects, and project management therefore puts a great emphasis on strategic planning. Once a project has been defined, it is broken down into manageable units. There are several known methods of making detailed schedules and evaluating capital investment and cash flow requirements in this process, and this is looked at in more detail in the following chapters. Project management also involves a high level of interpersonal communication, however, and these non-technical aspects of project management can be just as important in achieving successful outcomes. The person who controls the project needs to have the power to speak to people, encourage them and strengthen them, tell them what to do, gather information and distribute information as necessary. Therefore, they need to have control over strategies that could be useful in developing and enhancing interpersonal communication.

We have shown how the origins of project management as a discipline can be traced to the development of technical methods to deal with complex projects, but the underlying forces are changes in societies and industries.

The technical methods were mathematical algorithms, where information about the duration of individual tasks was used to calculate the duration of the total project. The individual project was seen as a system, and operation research was applied to understand the system, optimise it, and manage it. Using mathematical methods to identify the critical path and calculate the duration of a project based on the duration of individual activities is good, so far as it goes. Those familiar with project management know, however, that the most serious problems in the management of projects are typically not related to underestimating the project duration. Projects are a special type of system; they are social systems consisting of people, not machines. To understand projects – and how to succeed in their management – it is necessary to have insight into human behaviour, the forces which drive people, and to understand the interaction between individuals and problems in these interactions, what increases people's happiness and joy, and what causes concern. This is, of course, true for management in the broadest sense. A modern business environment is characterised by the complex interaction of companies and teams. Departments of modern knowledge companies work together to strengthen the infrastructure or to create value for customers. Increasingly, companies need to work together to create products or services for demanding customers where the scope and technical content of the outcome is such that a collaboration of more than one company is required to supply all resources, produce the outcome, and make it all happen. In these complex projects, there is the need for leaders who understand the nature of human collaboration and communication and can motivate people to do good work in a positive way rather than using traditional authority, which delivers limited success in modern knowledge-based companies.

It is of enormous importance in modern society that projects are prepared and implemented in a professional manner. There is an urgent need to increase awareness in the community about professional project management. So, what does it mean to be a professional project manager in the 21st century? Modern representation of the content of project management is reflected in the aforementioned conceptual baseline ICB4 with its Eye of Competence, which represents the three basic domains of basic competences in modern PPP management, namely people, practice, and perspective (see Figure 2.5) (IPMA, 2015).

The three domains include the skills that modern project managers should possess. This is no small list of skills, and in this book we are focused on analysing the different elements and how they relate to the required practical skills for successful project management, as well as providing examples of tools and methods that are directly relevant.

A project manager is someone who applies professional project management techniques to manage projects to deliver certain results at the right time and at the right cost. He needs to be organised and have a good grasp of human relationships, which is often a governing factor rather than direct authority. He must have a good understanding of the business strategy of the

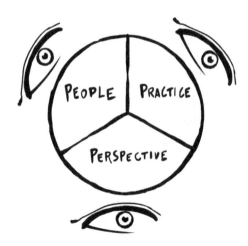

Figure 2.5

Modern view of project management competences; the eye of competence.

organisation, the processes, organisational structure, and culture in order to understand the context of the project and the company. Project management is undoubtedly a profession one can specialise in, both by studying the subject at school and by gaining experience and learning systematically from it.

There are clearly a large number of factors involved in being a successful project manager, and different authors/institutes may organise these differently and emphasise some aspects more than others, but there is a general consensus as to what these are. Linked to this is the term methodology, which is a structured approach to dealing with challenges and usually involves specific components such as phases, tasks, and various techniques and tools.

Project management methodology, therefore, relates to structured approaches and techniques to prepare for, manage, and complete the tasks that together comprise a project and focuses on achieving the various goals that have been set for the project. Various scholars have tried to better define what is involved in project management since the very rapid spread of its application across many disciplines as a method of control in recent years, and these new application areas necessitate a re-evaluation of the term.

Project work and project management

When a project is considered successful, it is commonly due to the fact that the objectives that were defined have been met. When a project is considered a failure, it is often due to the fact that it went beyond its budget and took longer than planned. The key to successful management of projects, therefore, involves preparation and planning, together with focused and effective communication throughout the life cycle of the project. These can be called the necessary conditions for success in the projects, but it is hardly sufficient (see Figure 2.6).

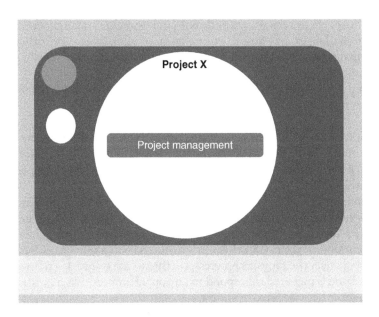

Figure 2.6

Project management as a principal activity within a project.

Looking back at the simple model of an organisation with its portfolio of programmes and projects, we can look at an individual project. The individual projects may be of different types, different scopes, different complexity, and the activities in a particular project reflect what is being produced in that project; a unique outcome – either a product or a service. But what is true for every project is that, in addition to the technical work being done, the project must be managed. We can thus make a distinction between two principal activities that are going on in every project: the project work and the project management. Realising this difference and being able to separate the technical work in a project from the project management is a prerequisite for understanding project management as a profession and as a management discipline. Furthermore, it can be said that success in the management of a project is a prerequisite for success in the project itself. It is difficult to imagine a project delivering the right outcome, on time and at the right cost, if the management of that project has not been successful. It is, however, possible to carry out successful project management for a project that is terminated due to some unforeseen changes in the external environment. Successful project management is thus a necessary condition for project success, but it alone is not enough.

Separating project management from project work is the first step to understanding project management and also the first task for a professional project manager in every project. Each project is a unique undertaking, and the way a particular project is managed must be based on the characteristics, special aspects, internal and external environment, stakeholders, and the special challenges and obstacles in that particular project. In other words, the management for a project needs to be designed according to the needs of that project.

Some general key points in project management – which specifically relate to planning in projects – are as follows:

- *Goal and scope.* Emphasis is placed on setting the goals of the project correctly at the outset and defining as accurately as possible what the product of the project should deliver. With this, the scope of the project is defined within certain parameters.
- *Environment of the project.* Detailed attention needs to be paid to the environment in which the project operates, both from the perspective of the project's impact on the environment and the impact of the environment on the project. In this way, the focus is on a number of factors that could affect the project's progress, i.e. threats are responded to in advance, and one is prepared to respond to any opportunities that may arise which might otherwise have been lost.
- *Continuous planning.* At any given time, plans are made that respond to the information that is available on the project at that time. This is a process that occurs over the entire life of the project. Part of the planning process is to choose the appropriate methods that retain flexibility in the project so that realisation and corrective action can be taken in a timely manner once new information becomes available.
- *Governance.* A special project administration is created to suit the project. This entails defining the roles of key individuals involved and establishing two-way communication channels so that everyone associated with the project is informed about what is expected of them and how they are succeeding in regard to meeting the expectations placed on them, as well as having an input and a sense of belonging.

Turner and Müller (2003) argue that the main features of project management as a management approach are in response to three main driving forces from the internal and external environment of the project, outlined below:

- In all projects there are uncertainties. It is, therefore, difficult to predict with certainty that the plans made will eventually lead to the product or planned modifications that the project aimed to achieve.
- In projects, there is a need for a variety of coordination, for example, in regard to the resources required for the project, between the different parts of the project, and between the project and the company in which the project is run.
- The project is initiated due to some kind of pressure; a product needs to be delivered or the outcome of the project is required within a certain time frame.

Reflection points

- The beginning of project management as a scientific field is often ascribed to the mid-20th century. Why?
- What was the main project management challenge of Helgi Eyjólfsson, who oversaw the building of the herring factory in Djúpavík?
- What is the main difference in our contemporary view of project management as compared to the view of the field in the mid-20th century?
- Why is it important to understand the difference between project work and project management? Explain by using an example.

Project characteristics and the project life cycle

Project character

An important area in project management studies is identifying common factors between different types of projects in order that successful management methods can be transferred from sectors where they have demonstrated success to other, less mature sectors. Part of this process is outlining the characteristics of different undertakings, and this requires breaking them down into their constituent work elements and analysing their administration needs.

In order to effectively apply project management and achieve project success, the nature of a project must be understood and the appropriate project management and leadership styles chosen. In other words, we can consider the essence of a project as an aggregate of characteristics and attributes that form the character of a project. Already in the early stages of the project, it is necessary to profile this character of the project, as this can indicate what will be the appropriate project management processes and leadership style for that project. There are several different systems to classify projects, some of them based on different project types, and we will come back to that later in the chapter. Hauksson et al. (2012) gave an overview of different classification systems. Some of them have the purpose of assessing whether an undertaking has the basic characteristics of a project, while some of them have the purpose of helping to make decisions about projects and how they should be run. Some of the systems focused on evaluating projects based on their results and the way they were managed. Some had the purpose of identifying project leadership skills or indicating the required approach for planning and control in particular projects.

In this paper, a graphical tool was presented to assess project character; "the sliding scale of project character" (see Figure 2.7). The spectrum extremes are on the left-hand side of the scale – operational projects – predictable projects typically associated with operational change. This is where a prescriptive approach can be applied, or "management as planned." In software development, this would be referred to as a waterfall approach. On the right-hand

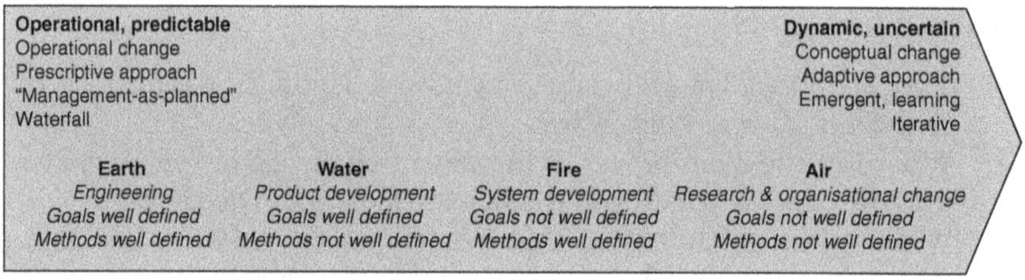

Operational, predictable			Dynamic, uncertain
Operational change			Conceptual change
Prescriptive approach			Adaptive approach
"Management-as-planned"			Emergent, learning
Waterfall			Iterative

Earth	Water	Fire	Air
Engineering	*Product development*	*System development*	*Research & organisational change*
Goals well defined	*Goals well defined*	*Goals not well defined*	*Goals not well defined*
Methods well defined	*Methods not well defined*	*Methods well defined*	*Methods not well defined*

Figure 2.7

Sliding scale of project character.

side of the scale, dynamic uncertain projects are shown, typically operational change, where an adaptive iterative approach is needed.

The sliding scale of project character is in line with well-known conceptual models from the literature, e.g. the earth, water, fire, and air model by Payne and Turner (1999) and the carpenter, builder, mission, and inventor model by Zurich (2011). The project character, being an aggregate of the project characteristics, can be used to help to determine the appropriate project management approach and leadership style for a project.

When is an activity a project?

When is an activity a project and when is it a regular operation or a miniature task? This question is of importance for a number of reasons. Primarily, we would choose the tool based on its purpose. In other words, project management would not be applied to all activities. We would apply project management to activities that we categorise as projects. Other types of activities would call for different management approaches. For instance, running a regular operation in a company, on shifts all day round, is clearly not a project. So, applying project management for such activities is not appropriate. In addition, looking at the project and assessing how it fits typical project characteristics helps us to assess the project in the beginning to start building up some kind of a perception of its content and how to deal with it. The question "is it a project?" is not a simple question with one variable and one answer. We have to look at different aspects of the activity to understand if it can be seen as a project. We find it useful to look at this in three different dimensions or perspectives: demarcation, participants and execution, and finally, interaction with the environment (see Figure 2.8).

From the perspective of demarcation, a project would typically be time bound – there would be pressure to conclude it within given time limits. A project would also be unique in the sense that it isn't something that is carried out again and again with minor changes. Yet another example of demarcation would be that a project has a defined scope and a defined frame in terms of how much it can cost. We would thus be expecting to see various examples of demarcation in a project. When it comes to execution and participants in

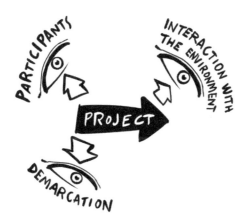

Figure 2.8

Three dimensions of project characteristics.

a project, we would typically expect that there is a need to create a specific project organisation, a description of roles and responsibility for the project, as a temporary organisation. In a typical project, there is a need to search for knowledge and information because all the knowledge required to plan and execute the project is not at hand within the organisation. It would also be a symbol of typical project characteristics that people with different backgrounds come together to form this temporary organisation, people with different perceptions and professional backgrounds, who see things differently. It is also typical for projects that the participants come from different units, different departments, and different organisations, and sometimes project teams consist of people of different ranks. These participants typically have a number of projects going on, in addition to routine work, and the coordination of all work can be a difficult challenge for people. Finally, it is one of the characteristics of projects that they interact with their environment in different ways. To begin with, projects are often associated with risk and opportunity; much is unknown at the beginning of a project and this is a reality that the project team needs to deal with. A project leads to change in the environment, either tangible change or change that is not so tangible. But typically, when designing the project approach, it is necessary to take the environment into consideration and adjust the project accordingly. This is a standard project characteristic. Finally, it is typical for a project that there are many stakeholders, both within the organisation and outside it, and these stakeholders or interested parties must be taken into account during the project life cycle.

We will not necessarily find out that a particular activity fulfils all these criteria. But we would expect a project to fit the profile above in a number of ways. Having said that, it is obvious that the description above is quite general, and a wide range of activities can fall under it.

The description would therefore not be very useful if, e.g. an enterprise wanted to assess how large a part of its activities is project work. Such a measure can, however, be developed, and recent research of the share of project work in western economies used the following definition of a project (Schoper et al., 2018):

- A specific target has been defined for the project.
- The project is limited in terms of time (start and end).
- The project requires specific resources (e.g. financial, staff, …).
- An independent project organisation exists, which is defined as different from the standard organisation in the company.
- The projects work on non-routine tasks.
- The project has a minimum duration of four weeks.
- The project has at least three participants.

This definition is rather specific, and it should be noted that projects can, of course, have a shorter duration than four weeks, and direct project participants can be fewer than three.

The project life cycle

One of the characteristics of projects is that they have a defined beginning and end (see Figure 2.9). A project is never a journey without a promise – when you start your journey it is already known when you intend to be home again. Equally, it can be said that all issues have a beginning and an end – a company which is established may have its golden period but then may experience terminal decline if the market disappears or if the owners lose their relationship with the market. When we talk about a project, we narrow the horizon. Business operation is not a project, but during the life cycle of an enterprise, there are many challenges that could be considered as projects. Establishment of an enterprise is one example of a project that begins with a decision of

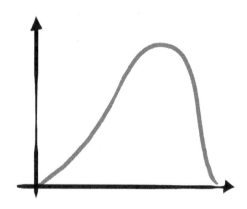

Figure 2.9

Project life cycle.

the owners and ends when the required formalities have been completed and operations have begun.

Normal human life is full of undertakings which can be considered as projects, such as going through high school, getting married, arranging a family reunion, building a cabin, etc. These are all examples of projects, some of which take a short time, others longer. The life cycle of projects can be divided into several phases where, in each phase, the focus is directed on specific challenges that must be completed in order to commence the next phase. As a project manager, it is useful to try and visualise the phases of each project and how they will begin and end, as the focuses and priorities of the project will vary between phases.

Whether or not there are several phases involved depends on how large and extensive the undertaking is. In simple tasks, we can speak of two phases, preparation and execution. This could, for example, refer to an event such as a wedding, which most people would look at as a project. Planning starts a few months, or even a few years earlier with the proposal – a positive answer is given, and the date is decided. Prior undertakings then involve compiling a guest list, choosing a venue, finding a celebrant, choosing music performers, arranging refreshments, sending out invitations, and overseeing the related procurement, all in order to execute the extensive preparation in anticipation of the big day. The actual execution takes place on the wedding day – the marriage ceremony, the celebration afterwards, and everything that goes with them, and finally the clearing up after the guests have left.

Building a cabin is an example of a rather more complicated project, where four main phases can be described (see Figure 2.10). These are definition (I), planning (II), execution (III), and commissioning (IV). These phases can often be seen in simple construction projects where the outcomes of the projects are built structures.

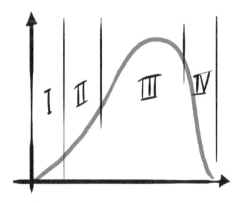

Figure 2.10

Typical phases of a project life cycle.

The definition phase (I) is when the scope or outlines of the project are drawn up. If the project is large enough, a project plan is made, the main objectives are defined, and a rough estimate is made on whether it is considered feasible to continue. It may well be that the result is that this is not the case, and then the project will not go ahead. If it is deemed feasible to continue, then a systematic planning phase (II) starts. It is often said that a project is initiated at this point, and this initiation of a project will be discussed in detail at the beginning of Chapter 6 of this book. Systematic planning can include design, followed by a detailed cost estimation and time plan. For the certain types of projects that require it (often those above a chosen monetary value), a formal tendering process would be considered part of the planning phase, i.e. the preparation of tender documents, the bidding process itself, and then the choice of contractors and the finalising of contracts made with them. Upon completion of the planning phase, the execution period itself takes over; the period of physical work to create a product of the project.

The execution period (III) can be long or short depending on the nature of the project. Towards the end of the execution period, the end product of the project takes on an increasingly well-defined aspect, and finally it is ready for use. The last phase (IV) is then started when the finished product is handed over to the client and the product is brought into service or commissioned. At the early stage of this phase, the project buyer would commonly draw up a snag list which can be either short or long and easy or difficult to remedy. The project normally ends when it has been demonstrated that the product is built to the required standards and equipped with the features that were intended. It is not uncommon, however, for problems to emerge at a later date after a buyer has expressed satisfaction, which can sometimes lead to litigation proceedings, such as when foundations subside over time. Such an aftermath would, of course, be related to the project, but would not be considered as part of the project itself.

The life cycle of a construction project as described above may be represented in a simple way in graph format where time is indicated on the x-axis and workload is indicated on the y-axis. Labour requirements, measured in man hours, are small in the beginning, when the project is defined, grow somewhat once systematic planning has begun, with the bulk of the work taking place in the execution phase when the actual building is carried out. The last phase is the handover of the project to the buyer, when some further work will often be needed to fix issues as actual usage takes place. The decline in labour requirements is completed when the project is closed and the operation of the product begins.

One can also draw up a project life cycle cumulative work chart, and this is shown in Figure 2.11. Little work (involving few people) is done in the definition period, but more work (involving many people) is done in the execution period. The curve is steepest when the actual execution takes place, as the greatest amount of work is performed at this stage of the typical construction project life cycle.

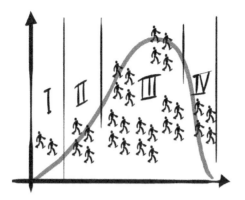

Figure 2.11

Accumulated work in the project life cycle.

Generally, the life cycle of extensive construction projects can be viewed in the same manner as explained in the previous figures. However, each step in the execution of major projects can be so large and complex that we can look at them individually as independent projects within the overall project. This is explained in Figure 2.12. We can see the model of the organisation with its portfolio of projects and programmes. We look specifically at one of the programmes and we narrow down our perspective to one of its individual projects. That particular project consists of a definition, planning, execution,

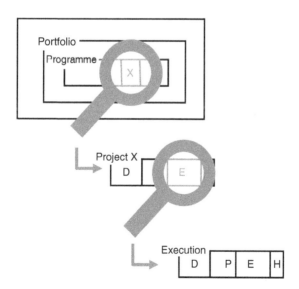

Figure 2.12

Phases as independent projects during the lifetime of an extensive project.

and commissioning phase. We can narrow our perspective further and look at one of the phases, for instance, the planning phase. That phase can be seen as being an independent project in itself comprising the same four characteristic phases. These are as follows: (1) a definition phase, when necessary information is collected and the baselines are laid out; (2) the planning phase, involving the establishment of a detailed design plan, where the division of labour and responsibilities are defined, amongst other things; (3) an execution phase that involves the technical design and preparation of drawings and a quantity list; and (4) the handover phase, involving the finalising of all the information and delivery of this to an entity (often a contractor) that will carry out the building works in the subsequent main execution phase. If one or more contractors or suppliers are chosen to execute the project, the procurement options, routes, tender documents, and selection criteria must be agreed on, and, in this case, such activities would take place as a part of the design phase. Alternatively, some of the procurement routines could be the general responsibility of a special department within the organisation.

The interfaces between single phases of a project such as described above are often referred to as milestones, which will normally have a set of previously defined deliverables that signify the end of that phase, once achieved. In large construction projects, each new phase can often be recognised with the arrival of new personnel in the overall delivery team, and these will often be new independent consultants and/or people working for external contractors who have been successful in the tendering process.

Depending on one's perspective, the same phase may be seen differently by different participants in a project. If you are the project originator and owner, then you will view the execution stage of a project differently than, say, a contractor who has just become involved after submitting a winning bid. They will consider this time period to be the beginning of their project, even though they may have had to carry out a significant amount of work during the tendering process. When analysing the different elements in these large construction projects, the larger context should always be kept in mind.

The concept of a life cycle can also be viewed from an even more general perspective than has been described above. We return to the model of the organisation with its portfolio of projects and programmes, support functions, and routine work. The organisation may make a strategic decision to build up its infrastructure and introduce new ability to do its routine work. This strategic decision leads to the definition of a project, and its outcome can be, for instance, new production equipment. The original project has been concluded, and the organisation runs its routine work as "business as usual" – which is not a project-based activity. Again, the organisation may make a new strategic decision to enhance its infrastructure and extend its production capacity. A new project is defined in the portfolio, it is executed and concluded, and delivers the required extension of the production capacity. Again, the daily operation of the organisation – "business as usual" – continues. In other words, running the daily operation – e.g. some specific production equipment – is "business as usual." This is not a project but rather a continuous process. However, various ideas or challenges may arise during the life cycle of the production equipment. For example, there may be a desire or need to expand the production. Then, a special project is defined for this expansion, and that undertaking has its own life cycle, which is divided into phases. Finally, the structure may become abandoned and derelict or go out of date, and its operative life cycle finishes. Then, one potentially has to tear down the equipment (see Figure 2.13). A specific project is defined around this, which could be called a demolition project.

Another way to demonstrate this graphically is illustrated in Figure 2.14. The outcome of the original project can be a production facility that is put into operation. During the life cycle of this operation, different projects take place: a maintenance project, an extension project, and finally, a demolition project. Everything happens within the context of the organisation and in accordance with its vision and mission.

Lake Myvatn, in North Iceland, is situated in a volcanically active area and is a popular tourist destination, renowned as an area of outstanding natural beauty. Its name means "midge water" due to the large swarms of midges that occur there in most years. The area is historically known for its very productive agriculture and fishing and its range of birdlife. In the 1950s, the area first became a focus for commercial interests in the mining of diatomite, a deposit formed from layers of tiny diatom skeletons deposited over a long period of time. This has many industrial uses, particularly in filtering applications. In 1964, the Althing – the Icelandic Parliament – granted special permission to

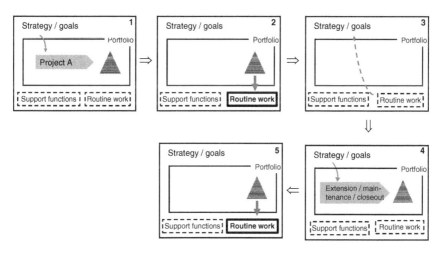

Figure 2.13

Projects in the lifetime of an organisation, from the building of a project outcome until the demolition at its end.

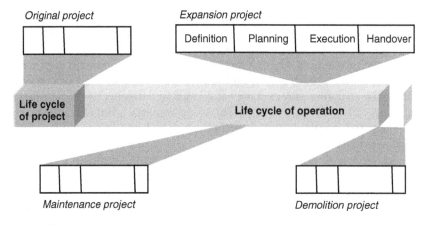

Figure 2.14

Life cycle of operation and life cycle of project.

the company Kísilidjan (part-owned at the time by the US multinational Johns Manville Corporation) to mine the deposits in the shallow lake-bed by dredging. A specialised dredger arrived from the Netherlands in 1965, and the first deposits were taken ashore that year. Two more years of development work followed, including the building of a factory, and commercial operations began on a small scale in November 1967.

Various projects were undertaken alongside the building work, including optimising the processing methods – cleaning, filtering, and drying. This factory was also part of a larger programme, which included the building of Iceland's first geothermal plant in 1969 – the 3MW Bjarnarflag plant – which used steam from the Námafjall geothermal field to drive a turbine to create electricity. This steam source was also used to provide the heat energy to dry the wet diatomite, and water separated from the steam was used to heat fresh water for district heating in the area. A number of houses were also built to house the extra workers associated with the new plants.

Phase 1 of the Kísilidjan diatomite works was considered complete when annual production reached 12,000 tons, which was achieved in 1970. Phase 2, involving a large expansion of the facilities, quickly followed, so that in 1971, over 21,000 tons were produced, which were almost all exported. Over the following three decades, production levels remained relatively stable, with a maximum close to 30,000 tons, and during this time routine upgrades were carried out, including the installation of a new cleansing mechanism for the exhaust gases in 1998.

Since inception, however, the project had raised environmental concerns as the lake is a fragile ecosystem, and experts were concerned that the dredging works could upset the ecological cycle. A number of research projects carried out over the years pointed to the dredging as a significant source of disturbance that was affecting previously abundant fish stocks, amongst other things.

Growing environmental opposition and a worldwide oversupply of diatomite in the early 2000s led to the closure of the plant in 2004 and the demolition of the factory buildings in 2005. In the same year as the Kísilidjan diatomite works were closing, a new geothermal spa that derives its heated waters from the Bjarnarflag plant – Myvatn Nature Baths – was opened and is now a popular tourist destination.

Turner et al. (1996) argued that every project needs a preparation period where success indicators are defined, the main objectives are determined, the work of each task group is outlined, and lines are drawn in regard to procedures and management. Without this structure, it can be difficult to achieve the desired results in a project, regardless of the type of project, but it is also important to realise that while they are important, these conditions are not the only ones that matter. The life cycle of a representative software project is shown in Figure 2.15. Time passes from left to right.

As can be seen, the influence of project management on performance is greatest in the first stages of the project when decisions are made and the product is defined. At the same time, the cost of making changes to the project is not great. When we come to the actual execution phase, however, this is reversed. Then, all the major decisions have been taken and all aspects defined. The cost of making changes at this level can be very high, much higher than it was in the beginning, and the figure reflects a general truth about most projects. One difference between projects is that some will have more information to start off with, while others may have very little. In all

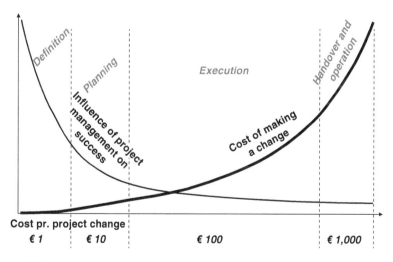

Figure 2.15

Influence of project management and the cost in regard to changes during a project life cycle.

cases, the aim is to make a coherent picture of the subject at the beginning on the basis of the available information.

Some managers say that making a schedule for a project is unnecessary, as scheduling never matches up as planned anyway. The second part of the claim is not far from the truth – few things go completely as planned in the beginning. The first part of the claim is meaningless. A project schedule that is made in the early stages of a project is not a holy scripture that cannot be changed. It is a living instrument for the whole project. It helps the project team to focus on what matters, and it provides guidance on what changes need to be made on the project due to impending problems in their environment so that they can achieve the objectives.

In software projects, this method of phase division has been called a *waterfall model*, where the project is seen as a series of work phases where each phase should be completed before the next one begins. One of the main challenges involved in this approach is that the work that takes place in the first part of the project might be flawed, but this might not appear until near the end of the project or in the test phase of the software. At worst, this can lead to the need to revise the design and all the consequent tasks, and the cost of this can be very high. It is quite common – and not only in software projects – that the needs of the customer are vague at the beginning, to both themselves and the other parties concerned, but evolve and take shape as the project progresses. This causes the lifetime of a software project to look different from the traditional simple exposition of the waterfall model, which assumes that the full needs analysis can be finished before the design begins and that the design can be fully finished before the execution begins. This has led to the development of project management approaches that can deal with this need for adaptability, and a synonym for these approaches is agile project management. We will come back to agile project management later in the book, but at this point we present a predecessor to this iterative management mindset. Boehm (1988) presented a model for the lifetime of a software project that takes this particular form and calls it the *spiral model*, as shown in Figure 2.16. In Boehm's model, the beginning is in the middle and the project plan undergoes an iteration process, which involves deciding upon the following aspects: definition and assessment of needs, planning, design, and construction. With this repetition, the final product is developed from concept to prototype to final product.

In all projects that aim to follow the spiral model, it is first necessary to define at the beginning which way the project is heading, the project budget, and how much time can be used. Even in research projects, where the researcher begins with a very unformed idea of what the final materialised outcome of the project will be, it is necessary to define these parameters. Such a plan will be the guiding light for the researcher through the project, and it helps him or her deal with inevitable changes that will occur in the project, for example, due to changing circumstances and assumptions. The same, of course, can apply to other projects, including those that lead to tangible

Figure 2.16

Spiral model of the life cycle of a software project.

results, such as construction projects. For this reason, great emphasis is placed on planning in this book.

Reflecting on "the sliding scale of project character" presented earlier in the chapter, we see that the spiral model is well suited for projects that lean towards the right-hand side of the scale, dynamic uncertain projects, where an adaptive iterative approach is needed.

Different project types

Projects are as diverse as they are numerous and vary greatly depending on the nature of the controlling entity. There are a number of ways to classify them into several broad types, which can be useful in a number of ways, for example, in making portfolio selections or deciding which administration structures to use to manage them. One such classification may be based on whether they are internal or external to an entity, or whether they are local, regional, national, or international in scope. This may not be a particularly useful classification in terms of deciding upon project management methodologies, however, and there are many alternatives. Another type of classification system for project types, which provides more by way of technical description, is outlined in Table 2.2, and we will give a brief description of each of the project types listed in the following sections. Based on the information at hand in the initial stages of a project, e.g. the project classification and/or based on the sliding scale of the project character, a high-level project definition can be issued – a project blueprint or a high-level project architecture. The appropriate general project management approach can then be chosen that has the highest probability of success. This general approach is, of course, subject to change during the project life cycle and must be defined more specifically in view of the project analysis.

Table 2.2 Technical classification of different project type categories

Category	Project type description
Construction projects	The planning, design, and building of civil structures.
Software projects	Introduction of new systems software and everything that involves, including need analysis, design, execution, and implementation.
Product/service development projects	The development of a product or service, including need analysis, design and planning, and the product/service development itself, including testing.
Structuring projects	Changes in the structure of the company or an institute, reorganising, merging of companies.
Improvement projects	Projects that are a part of continuous improvement activities, e.g. process implementation and process optimisation.
Research projects	Research, commonly in the university environment.
Social projects	Reform of welfare, protection of vulnerable population, overcoming the effects of natural and social disasters.
Event projects	The preparation and staging of a particular event.

Construction projects

These types of projects relate to construction in one form or another, e.g. structures of all kinds, including buildings, housing, roads, utilities, etc., and this is the area which would be traditionally most associated with project management methodology. There are numerous examples of these project types given in this book.

Software projects

Examples of software projects are large systems projects, such as the upgrading of accounting and human resource systems used by the public service/services, as well as smaller projects, such as a simple web design. In between these, there are projects of all sizes that involve the development and implementation of a software system. "The Book of Icelanders," for example, is an online system that allows Icelanders to trace their ancestry back to the early Viking settlers, if applicable, and involved the transfer of genealogical information from extensive written records to digital format and search and information display functions. Another example is the computerisation of banking services, which has been executed in a series of periodic upgrade projects over the last few decades.

There are various arguments for considering a software project as a specific type of project. The progress in projects will be intangible, and systems may not function as desired until the project is 100% complete, which can take a long time and may involve costly recoding if glitches occur. This requires a particular type of understanding from a senior management perspective, as it is not possible in such projects to demonstrate progress in the same way as pointing to a half-built building and saying that your construction project is half complete. It is also well known that in software projects, it can be particularly difficult to define the outcome of the project and the objectives at the beginning, as the buyer's preferences and criteria are lacking at that moment and will develop as the project evolves.

Product/service development projects

Bringing a product or service to the point where it is customer-ready can be a very lengthy process and will involve a number of different units within a company working in tandem. Aspects to cover are wide ranging and include marketing, technical development, and legal issues. There are many risk factors involved, including the often unpredictable nature of markets, whereby opportunities may disappear through competition and/or from a loss of customer interest. This means that these development projects should be carried out rapidly, but this may not be possible in some sectors. Early stage customer interaction needs identification, and ongoing customer feedback is of major importance in this process, as is careful management of the entire product development process. Companies that specialise in product development need to develop strategies to manage their product development projects. These strategies need to reflect the nature of the products that are to be developed, as well as the culture and the structure of the companies, not to mention the specialities of those markets where the companies operate. The best-known model of the product development life cycle is called the stage gate model (Cooper, 1994). The model was designed to facilitate and speed up the delivery of products to market, and the product development process is divided into phases and gates. At each phase, certain tasks/work parts are worked on, and at the end of each phase there is a gate where managers make decisions about the continuation of the project.

A number of Icelandic companies that have achieved good success in business and who get most of their income through export markets are inherently product development companies. For example, one can mention Marel and Össur, which work in different fields but are quite progressive companies. Product development projects can be very varied; they can involve the development of a new production line for chicken processing at Marel and a new type of computer-controlled artificial leg at Össur. In fact, both Marel and Össur have become international companies even though they have their roots in Iceland. One could also mention the development of a new tourist attraction, service and product lines associated with this, e.g. at the Myvatn Nature Baths.

Structuring projects

Many projects involve planning components in one way or another. What makes structuring projects unique is that the products of such projects are not really tangible, at least in comparison to the products of a construction project. For these reasons, it can be difficult to get a sense of success and progress. Structuring projects can involve adjusting or changing the structure of an organisation or business or merging or dividing companies. It is crucial in such projects to assess the adaptability of the organisation to change, and to develop a change strategy to address the envisioned transformation. Such a change strategy should take into account the ability and/or willingness to carry through the transformation. Structuring projects can also deal with changing the image of companies, and they are usually all carried out under the premise of increasing efficiency. Political campaigns could also be considered as particular types of structuring projects.

An example of a structuring project in Iceland was the merging of a previously distinct water supply entity and a heating and electricity supply entity to form Orkuveita Reykjavíkur or Reykjavik Energy – the main energy supplier of Reykjavik. Another example of a merger is when Disney and Pixar merged in 2006, an example of a successful structuring project.

A structuring project of a different type is a change in the public administration structures of an area or region, and these types of projects can be contentious and are very political in nature. An example of this in Iceland was the amalgamation of two previously separate communities in North Iceland, Siglufjörður and Ólafsfjörður, to form a new local authority – Fjallabyggð. Both towns had witnessed ongoing population decline for years, but in 2006 it was approved in an election to combine the two communities. This was done with a very narrow majority, or 51% of voters. It should be kept in mind that, in times past, the driving distance between the towns was 66 km across Lágheiði in the summer but 236 km across Öxnadalsheiði in winter. The opening of the Héðinsfjörður Tunnel in 2010 changed this dramatically, as the distance between Siglufjördur and Ólafsfjörður became 17 km, and thereby created the possibility of a much wider range of co-operation and sharing. The tunnel was in fact a prerequisite for the integration of the two communities. At the micro level, the merging of the two communities involved a lot of consideration and planning. Among the tasks that needed to be done was an overhaul of the local authority organisational chart involving new delegations of responsibility for the staff involved. A range of services such as waste collection and schools and kindergartens had to be transferred to new administrative structures and coordinated, including harmonisation of rules and fees. Also, a range of policies had to be agreed and formulated, including those relating to culture, human resources, employment, education, and development of a regional master plan. Last but not least, this project involved the integration of two communities with their own distinct cultural and economic characteristics.

Improvement projects

Improvement projects are typically a part of the continuous improvement activities within an organisation. Sometimes they are originated because of a singular problem in the operation. They can involve implementing new procedures or rethinking segments of the operation, usually to increase efficiency, reduce waste, and improve general customer satisfaction.

An example of an improvement project could be an accounting service company that decides to reduce its processing time for annual reports of small companies by mapping the process for this activity and improving it. Another example would be extensive process improvements of an international engineering consultancy as a part of the implementation of quality system standards ISO 9001 and ISO 14001.

Research projects

Research projects are often difficult to deal with from a management viewpoint. The reasons for this are primarily due to the fact that, in the case of fundamental research, it is not possible to define the outcome in advance, except in the most general terms. For example, a doctorate project within an engineering university might be set up to investigate whether it is feasible to use the crystal structure of molecules of a certain metal to store hydrogen. The results from such a project will be a peer-reviewed document that contains the results of the study, and the time to complete the project may be three or more years. It is not possible to say beforehand what the conclusions will be, as they will be based on the results obtained, so there can be risks involved for sponsoring entities. In general, undergraduate, masters, doctorate, and post-doctorate projects can be useful ways for companies to get information relevant to their business objectives in a cost-effective manner, as governments are usually also willing to significantly fund research in the university system.

An example of a publicly sponsored university research project, which led to a successful high value-added business, is the case of the company Marel. In 1977, a project was instigated at the Science Department of the University of Iceland related to the study of manufacturing processes in the fish industry, and this in turn led to the founding of Marel in 1983. Marel is now, after years of steady expansion, a large multinational company focused on food processing technology, with a workforce of over 4,600 people and an annual revenue of 819 million EUR in 2015. The ethos upon which the company was founded is still evident in the fact that between 5% and 7% of income is reinvested each year in research and development projects, and this is exceptional for this sector.

Many large companies have well-resourced in-house research and development departments that are focused on the delivery of future products and innovations in existing operations, although there is an increasing trend to rely on university collaboration in this regard, particularly for smaller companies, as the required equipment and technical expertise in these environments can be very expensive and difficult to budget for.

Social projects

This category includes community service projects, i.e. projects that are typically done by a group of people that benefit others. One example of this is a specific course in the Master of Project Management (MPM) programme at Reykjavik University that continues throughout a whole semester. The students design, plan, execute, and evaluate a project that is supposed to have a social dimension, to be for the benefit of the greater good, and deliver benefits to society. Social projects can also be organised within a municipality or a state and focus on the reform of welfare in society and on the protection of vulnerable population/people in a society. They can also revolve around overcoming the effects of natural and social disasters. For example, following the financial collapse in Iceland in 2008, the state, municipalities, and some aid organisations planned and executed a number of projects to deal with the aftermath of the collapse.

Event projects

The last category of projects is so-called event projects. Here, the outcome of the project involves running a certain event or events, the preparations for which are often extremely dynamic. The special thing about event projects is that their actual execution often takes a very short time compared to the preparation.

As an example of such a project, we could mention the Live Aid concert, held on July 13th, 1985 and organised by Bob Geldof and Midge Ure to raise funds for relief of the then-ongoing Ethiopian famine. This concert itself lasted for a few hours, but the preparation took months and required major logistics and personnel planning.

There are numerous examples of events run on an annual basis in Iceland, including Cultural Night in Reykjavik, the Night of Lights in Keflavík, "I Never Went South" in Ísafjörður, and the National Celebration in the Westman Islands. As these events are run annually, they each have an established organisational framework, although the following year's event will always be different in a number of ways to the current one, bringing fresh challenges for the organisers.

Project success, as seen from different perspectives

When it comes to defining success, there are differences between projects, programmes, and portfolios. Whereas a project is more of a singular undertaking, both programmes and portfolios can consist of many projects, and if one of these proves unsuccessful it may not be so important. It is understandable, therefore, that project and portfolio managers may have different mindsets, for example, with a portfolio manager possibly having more of an appetite for risk and a greater need for strategic awareness, whereas a project manager needs to maintain consistency and avoid risk as much as possible. The focus of a project manager is more likely to be on getting a defined job done in the short term as opposed to defining and executing business strategies in the face of fluctuating environments in the longer term, which is the focus of a portfolio manager. A programme manager can be somewhere in between, in that success in the short term with individual projects may not be critical, provided one can learn from experience and eventually deliver successful projects and an overall satisfactory programme outcome. For the remainder of the discussion here, we will focus on success in both projects and in project management.

Having a clear vision of project success is important for a project manager in order to achieve project goals. Having said this, there may not be universal agreement on what defines success in any particular project, as each stakeholder will have their own views, and these may be different from those of neutral observers. From the project manager's perspective, the focus is on the previously defined completion goals of the project, i.e. in terms of time, cost, and quality, and the success of the product of a project may be of less concern. A construction project manager working for a primary contractor may oversee a very successful construction of a hotel, for example, but there is no guarantee that the hotel will attract enough business to remain viable. At this stage, the construction manager is likely to be working on another project and to have been paid for his work, so he may not be too concerned with this. If, in this example, the primary contractor is heavily reliant on the hotel project owners for repeat business, there would be more concern about the longer-term outcomes of individual projects.

In professional project management success, time and cost are closely linked, and clear objectives are usually set in this regard, either for completion of a project or for milestones within the life cycle of a project. If the objectives set by the project owners are not met by some margin, then the management of the project may be considered as unsuccessful, even though the product may turn out to be very effective and popular with users. Other issues can relate to factors like quality and external costs. A project may be completed on time and within budget, but if the resulting structure or work shows serious signs of degradation within a short period, this can be hugely problematic. An example would be where pyrite is found in structural concrete, leading to widespread cracking. Another example concerning external costs might be where a sub-contractor in charge of waste removal dumps toxic wastes related to a project illegally in sensitive areas in order to cut costs. Again, this may only come to light at a later date, after the life cycle of a project.

In larger projects, with design specialists working with project owners in projects executed by primary contractors and a host of sub-contractors, assigning the responsibility for a lack of success can be very complex and can lead to legal proceedings in particular cases. In this case, contract negotiation is a very important part of the project manager's skill set. A project manager also needs to ensure that all payments are made in relation to a project, and this will involve producing the necessary evidence of completion, and in some cases, this can be in the form of detailed reports.

In publicly funded projects, the notion of success is often more closely related to outcomes as opposed to how things were executed, and taxpayers are likely to be less exercised by a major project cost overrun than a private enterprise with limited funding. All these concepts can get mixed up in public debates about projects and their successes or failures. A common scene in Iceland is groups of people meeting up in the hot tubs at the swimming pools, and this can often end up in lively discussions about projects where public money was wasted. It is a feature in most societies that although many projects are successful, and the people closest to the project are satisfied with the outcome and how it was executed, these will merit little mention in the media. Projects with negative outcomes, on the other hand, are far more likely to appear in the media, and this can influence opinions in the hot tubs and their international equivalents.

There has been much research done on what distinguishes those projects that do not go according to their original plan and do not achieve their objectives. Professor Bent Flyvberg and his associates have studied large infrastructure projects in this context. In the paper "Cost Underestimation in Public Works Projects: Error or Lie?" from 2002, they say:

> It is found with overwhelming statistical significance that the cost estimates used to decide whether such projects should be built are highly and systematically misleading. Underestimation cannot be explained by error and is best explained by strategic misrepresentation, that is, lying.

Icelandic researcher Dr. Fridgeirsson (2015) has yielded similar results, finding that there is a lack of discipline in public projects and that projects are not only going beyond their planned budget but also their initial time frames. The questions remain: What is a successful project and what is an unsuccessful project? What causes one project to be successful and another not? Does the reason lie in the implementation or is it in the outcome?

The Sydney Opera House (see Figure 2.17) is one of the most recognised structures in the world. It has long been a symbol of the city and an important element in the image of Australia. The unprecedented design, consisting of multiple arched and curved roof sections, was the winning entry by Jørn Utzon, a Danish architect, in a 1957 competition amongst 230 entries, including many well-known international architects. In many ways, the design was ahead of its time, and when it came to the execution phase that began in 1959, there were many problems encountered in terms of the detailed structural engineering design to support the large roof sections. This began to lead to major

Figure 2.17

The Sydney Opera House.

cost and time overruns (the original plan was for it to take four years and cost 7 million AUD). Moreover, the arrival in 1965 of a new regional government, who were not supportive of the project, did not help. Utzon resigned in 1966 after not getting approval for a range of requests and left the project with most of the roof shells complete and the costs running at 22.9 million AUD. Other architects took over, and the final construction costs at the time of the official opening in 1973 were 102 million AUD, which were mostly covered by lottery funds.

With this history in mind, should the Sydney Opera House project be considered a success? And what about the management of the project, if it eventually took 16 years to build from initial concept and became about 14 times more expensive than planned?

Reflection points

- Look at the spectrum extremes in Figure 2.7. Can you give examples of earth, water, fire, and air projects? Explain.
- Look at the definition of a project as put forward in the research project led by Schoper et al. (2018). Reflect the projects you are working on in this definition. Do you agree with the definition?
- Pick one of the projects from the reflection point above and draw a general figure showing accumulated work in the project life cycle. Does it look similar to Figure 2.11 or is it different? How?
- We presented an example of projects in the lifetime of an organisation (Figure 2.13). Would you say that the project manager in project A needs to take into account that in the future there might be a demolition project? Why? If you think so, in what way could that be done?
- Is there any category of project types missing from Table 2.2? If you think so, explain and give examples.

Project management in the context of the organisation

The permanent organisation

Behind individual projects or programmes that may have a temporary organisational structure lie controlling entities that can have their own permanent organisational structure. How this permanent structure views project management can vary greatly, depending on what overall approach is taken. Projects cannot be adequately carried out without the involvement of resources contributed by the permanent units of the organisation. The product/results of the project will typically be used and maintained by the permanent organisation.

As a business or other entity gets larger, the type of corporate governance and management structure it employs will become more and more important if it is to run its operations effectively and achieve strategic goals. We will discuss three types of organisational structures for such entities (here referred to as companies for simplicity, but they could be associations, etc.) and how these may embrace project or programme management methodology. Over the years, a huge amount of practical knowledge has been built up on how best to plan and execute projects. Projects are highly variable. Some are simple, while others are extensive and complex, although people of different knowledge and experience levels may disagree on what constitutes a simple or complex project. All projects in some way begin with a future vision, an analysis of strengths and weaknesses, and an outline of future opportunities and risks. To undertake a certain set of tasks can exclude another set of tasks, so it is important to predict the costs and opportunity costs, benefits and risks, and then evaluate the most favourable option.

We will now discuss some of the basic elements of a permanent organisation, the interfaces between those elements and projects, and the management of projects. We will divide the discussion into two main sections; on one hand we will talk about the infrastructure of the permanent organisation and on the other hand we will discuss its environment.

Infrastructure

Systems, products, and technology

Systems of different types are an integrated part of each and every organisation. Some systems are based on technology, other systems are set up to plan, control, and manage the activities of the organisation, both activities that create value through the production of services and products, and also a range of supporting activities. The vehicles to implement systems, create or change products or services, and develop technology are projects, and the decision to execute projects is a result of the strategic management of the organisation.

An example of a project involving systems and technological change may be when a decision is made to use electronic payment systems and to use the electronic data generated through this system to obtain useful market information to streamline advertising services. Online purchases of products and services now take up a sizeable portion of many markets, and there are operational efficiencies for companies in this approach as well as many recognised ways of using this information to enable rapid and accurate market research and subsequent targeted advertising. A project like this will involve a number of different departments within a company, including the Information and Communication Technology (ICT) department and Sales and Marketing departments, and will also be closely overseen by the executive management.

Other types of projects may revolve around product development and the full scope of enabling work required to realise this. This may, for example, include extensive technical product testing, satisfying legal requirements including licensing, the setting up of new manufacturing lines, and/or the setting up of new sales and distribution channels, pilot testing, etc. The concept of a life cycle is important in this regard, and in each case tailored project and programme management methods will be required.

Human resource management

Getting the right people, in the right organisational structure, with the right resources and the right motivation is a key concern in Project, Programme, and Portfolio management (PPP management). Various aspects of human resource (HR) management are crucial – the management of projects and programmes, such as planning, recruitment, selection, training, retention, performance assessment, and motivation. In many projects and programmes, the major cost revolves around salaries and other personnel-related expenditure – for instance, external consultants, etc. Healthcare projects and programmes would be good examples of where personnel management is very important in order to deliver the required objectives, and particular challenges may be evident in public healthcare delivery.

Personnel management in projects will often require a different approach to traditional human resources management in permanent organisations, as it must factor in the fact that projects will end and new ones begin. Typically, many projects are taking place simultaneously, with people being routinely co-opted from individual departments. In a small company, this can create significant continuity problems, with difficulties in guaranteeing a smooth transition for workers between projects, particularly if there are unavoidable gaps in requirements. A typical outline of labour requirements for a project through time is shown in Figure 2.18 and shows the gradual build-up in numbers to a peak followed by a gradual decline.

The figure shows that the need for labour can be extremely varied depending on where in the project's lifetime the project is located. This is dealt with through in-depth planning, where the labour required is closely assessed and the most efficient staffing of the project is determined. Sometimes it is useful to try to even out resources within a project or between projects. That can

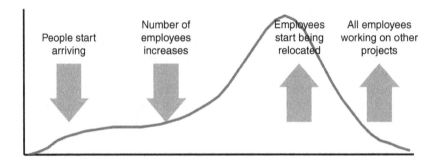

Figure 2.18

The labour requirements in a project during its life cycle.

affect the work time and may extend the total project life cycle, but it may lead to higher overall efficiency when everything is taken into the picture. Project-orientated companies plan their activities based on this reality, but there you will also find traditional aspects of personnel management; work development, planning and follow-up, training, performance evaluation, and employee evaluation. Companies that operate projects that can be influenced by external factors such as weather need to factor this into their overall schedules. A simple example would be a painting and decorating firm running both indoor and outdoor jobs simultaneously in order to be able to remain productive on rainy days. Another example might be a big budget movie shoot which has lined up several indoor and outdoor scene locations to avoid the same problem on a bigger scale.

Organisational structures

Different organisational structures are discussed in our book *Project: Strategy* in this series, and some examples can be found in that book of traditional and more modern organisations and the way they are structured. But for the present discussion, it is necessary to present some basic traditional models for organisational structure to explain the context between projects and the organisation and typical problems that may occur. Figure 2.19 shows a common arrangement in companies whereby they are split into separate divisions, each with their own specific tasks and responsibilities, and individually reporting to executive management through a division head. This arrangement is also called a functional structure. An example might be a production company with a development department, production department, finance department, and technical department. The departments are a kind of a home of expertise within the company. Departmental structures can make tasks more easily manageable while they are limited to individual departments. Often challenges emerge in such companies that may originate within a specific department but require a cross-departmental approach to address them.

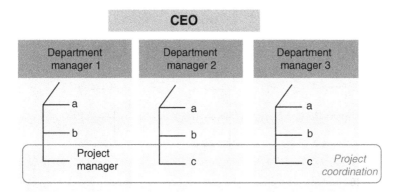

Figure 2.19

Organisation diagram in a traditional department-organised company.

Such challenges are treated as a project, but it can often be difficult to find a place for them within the organisational structure. Usually, a project manager is appointed – commonly from the division in which the project originated – and along with the project manager a task group with representatives from other departments. There can be benefits in this arrangement – the same group members can participate in many projects and so their knowledge and experience can be used widely throughout the company. Technical expertise is retained within the department, which is also the "home" of the knowledge after the project ends. In this way, it is ensured that the knowledge flows between projects.

There can also be problems with such a structure. Participants in a project will have primary responsibilities within their departments, and their bosses are the department managers – not the project manager. As a result, the project can be left on the back-burner, as it is lower down on the group participants' priority list, and the project manager gets left with the challenge on his own – one that he may have little chance of getting to the bottom of. Specific problems can arise when one division starts with a task or project and later gets assistance from team members in other departments. Here there is a risk that the best people will not be called on to participate in the project due to the entrenched legacy structures. Another drawback is that the components of the project that do not belong to a particular department might get less attention than the ones that do. Also, in the case where a customer/project buyer may be remote from the principal department, there is a risk that their needs may not be addressed promptly and effectively.

Finally, communication between departments can often be formal and cumbersome, and that can affect decision-making in tasks or projects where important decisions have to be made at short notice, often in reaction to received news or results that can be unexpected.

Some companies are structured first and foremost to look at each business challenge as a project and therefore seek to build up expertise in project

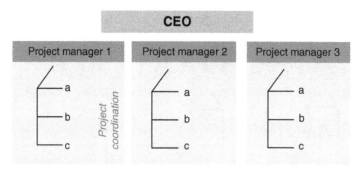

Figure 2.20

Example of an organisation chart in a project-organised company.

management. These companies are structured differently from the department divided ones, and Figure 2.20 shows a typical organisational structure that would apply in this case.

The objectives of these companies are often seen as a series of projects, and these individual projects can be large and involve an extensive project team. They can be so big that they could be seen as separate companies within the larger companies, each with their own management system which takes care of their own finances and human resources as well as relations and communications with suppliers and customers. The strength of this arrangement lies precisely in the fact that the management system is dedicated to each project individually, and the project's interests are paramount. This can mean that workers will be well utilised with the use of temporary contracts, preventing overstaffing. Members of the project team will each be answerable to a single manager, communications distances will be short, and the project team can develop a strong commitment and strong team spirit. It can also mean that personality clashes that can have detrimental effects within departments in department-organised companies can be more easily avoided due to the possibility of transferring incompatible personnel into separate projects.

A potential weakness of this organisational structure is that while it may work well for large projects, it may not scale down well and, as projects get smaller, a risk arises that resources, both people and equipment, will be poorly utilised. For example, it may be that a particular project does not need a full-time finance manager, or that a specific piece of machinery is only required for short, intense periods of activity, while otherwise remaining unused. Also, there is a risk that the direction and objectives of the overall management may get forgotten or that technological knowledge does not flow from one task to another. Another potential negative factor is that members of a group (particularly if on temporary contracts) may not have sufficient professional support, and this can create serious problems. Reallocating people to new projects after completion of older ones can be a difficult task, and loyalty issues may also arise with workers more likely to jump ship at that point. This can

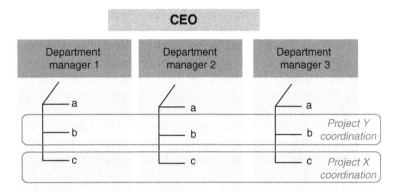

Figure 2.21

Organisation chart in a matrix organised company.

lead to a serious loss in project knowledge and knowledge transfer that will affect future projects.

Finally, we introduce the matrix structure. This type of hybrid organisational structure is designed to retain the combined advantages of the department-organised company and the project-organised company whilst avoiding the disadvantages. Figure 2.21 shows this arrangement. Here we also have professional departments, but they are primarily service departments, and their bosses have the role of coordinating resources in the relevant professional field between multiple projects that are managed in a special task division in a coordinated manner.

There are many benefits with this arrangement – chief among them being the cost-effective allocation of resources and the clear designation of responsibility and accountability. The projects are at the forefront in a matrix organisation. In order to explain the inner workings of this management structure regime, the figure shows project X and project Y, which are being worked on in the company. Project X has perhaps a need for four and a half work units from Department 2 and a half work unit from Department 1. Related department managers are responsible for providing these employees and ensuring that they have the knowledge and skills needed. Furthermore, they are responsible for maximising the use of their employees. For example, a half employee in project X in Department 1 is possibly useful as well in project Y. The knowledge base has a professional support structure within the company, as well as participants in the projects and, therefore, they do not need to worry about their future when the project is completed. At the same time, it is ensured that work is done in accordance with the direction and objectives of the company as a whole. Last but not least, the knowledge base for project management also has a professional support structure within the company. It may be called programme management, project management office (PMO), project department, or something else. The responsibility and authority can be very different from one company to another. Sometimes, this department would be managing all projects, in other cases, the actual project management would be in other departments. But, typically, this base would be responsible for developing and continuously improving the organisational project management competence for project management organisational learning; making sure that lessons learned are gathered from concluded projects and applied in present projects and providing support to projects and project managers in relation to organisation, planning, reporting, meeting management, and documentation.

A drawback of the matrix organisation is that the management system can become very complex and employees can have multiple bosses, which can cause difficulties. The progress of projects can be dependent on the flexibility and ability of the senior managers, and a wide range of skills and experience are needed by them to ensure successful outcomes.

The matrix organisation structure can be implemented in different ways and has been sub-divided by some commentators into weak matrix organisations, strong matrix organisations, and matrix organisations in balance. In a weak matrix organisation, the project manager has the role of balancing resource priorities – although they do not have much direct authority or responsibility. In a strong matrix organisation, the opposite is the case, with the primary role of departments being to provide staff for the projects, while the daily management of the projects is within the remit of the project manager(s). In a balanced matrix organisation, there is a policy of keeping a balance of power between the project managers and the department managers, and the department managers are then partly dependent on the projects to ensure the most efficient use of their employees.

It is good to keep in mind that, while this can be a challenge, most companies competently handle both special projects and routine tasks and create a management structure that is adapted for the most effective overall functioning of the business. Usually this would be a combination of the approaches that have been mentioned here, for example, a mixture of matrix organisation and department organisation, or a mixture of matrix organisation and pure project organisation. A company that focuses on the professional development of project management competence and that wishes to preserve that knowledge and experience in a conscious manner may vote to set up separate organisational units for this purpose, which are often called project management offices (PMOs). It is common for project management offices to support the project manager of the company and provide various administrative and managing services. They also collect information from projects, analyse it, and transfer the knowledge to those that need it within the enterprise. Finally, the project management office keeps track of work procedures that have been built around previous project management experience. Project management offices within companies are ever-changing entities that adapt to the needs and culture of the company, have the support of, and provide support to the senior management. Key criteria for the success of the start-up and operation of a project management office is that it is considered to help with realising the objectives and strategic direction setting, and thereby bring value to the organisation.

HSSE – Health, Security, Safety and Environment

The issues of HSSE – Health, Security, Safety and Environment – have become a centre of attention in all societies, with increased emphasis on corporate responsibility and increased awareness regarding the environment, health, and public safety. Health considerations apply not only to the project team members but also to those who will use the product of the project or those that could be affected by this product. The possibility of litigation has made it necessary to ensure that organisations have the appropriate level of knowledge and experience on these issues. Major project issues regarding HSSE are covered by regulations and standards. Furthermore, many organisations run operating procedures that minimise risk to an acceptable level, e.g. for the organisation, the public, the employees, and the legal system.

These issues can manifest themselves in a variety of ways across different project management sectors. Invariably, they require serious consideration by enterprises and represent essential aspects of professional project management competence. Those who manage projects need to know the ins and outs of all the general rules and regulations that apply to their particular project area.

Across the full range of projects, factors like excessive work-related tiredness and stress and bullying can occur in poorly managed projects and again may require that the project manager has broad experience of such phenomena and can spot symptoms early and deal with them before they become more serious. Allowing employees to engage in full and frank discussions without fear for their position can be an important part of building trust in this regard.

Security risks can vary among different projects and may require the services of external contractors for their duration if this is felt necessary. Insurance issues also need to be considered in order to mitigate overall risks in projects. For example, it is not uncommon to hear of expensive compensation cases where a building site with poor security measures was entered by children who subsequently injured themselves on some form of hazard.

Increasingly, issues of sustainable development and environmental concerns are becoming a factor in projects, and the assessment of the impact of a project on the environment and society is crucial in many projects as well as the subsequent actions – to limit or compensate negative consequences. A failure to identify the environmental concerns at an early stage in project development may prove costly if regulating bodies decide at a later date, after a lot of money has been spent, that the project poses unacceptable environmental risks. The professional assessment of such risks and the need for ongoing monitoring, sometimes over decades, to alleviate the concerns of stakeholders can be expensive and need to be considered early on in the project development path.

A good example of very high standards in project management practice today is the airline construction industry, where the consequences of overlooking problems can quickly lead to disastrous outcomes. Here, strict regulation is applied in terms of ensuring the fitness of the aircraft and its vital systems, and in ensuring personnel are suitably qualified and experienced to carry out their functions. In this, an advanced system of checks and balances has been developed to mitigate risks, and features such as mandatory reporting of faults and incidents are an important aspect of the control system.

One of the key areas where things can go wrong in projects is the area of health, safety, and environment. While it is impossible to eliminate all risk in projects, poor work practices and a lack of foresight can lead to accidents that may have effects ranging from small to devastating. In this regard, international standards have come a long way in the last century, as hard experience has led to more stringent requirements, although cost factors and cutting corners are always still a threat to doing things the correct way. Some project managers may operate under intense pressure from the project owners to save time and money, and this will often require them to remain strong in the face of such pressure.

HSSE factors are taken seriously in Iceland, and the construction of the recent Alcoa Fjardaál aluminium plant in Reyðarfjörður is a good example. This was a large-scale international project that is linked to the Kárahnjúkar hydropower development. The groundwork had been underway for several years when Alcoa got involved in 2002 and made a contract with the engineering contractor Bechtel to plan, design, and build the aluminium plant. Bechtel is one of the largest companies in the world in their field and has extensive experience managing giant projects. Soon after Bechtel began construction in Reyðarfjörður, it attracted attention in Iceland that the HSSE guidelines of the project were quite different and stricter than had been previously known. For example, no one went onto the Bechtel construction site to work without a prior two-day seminar on health and safety matters and general behaviour – with regard to the environment, machinery, equipment, or people. If anyone deviated from the rules on health and safety, the employees ran the risk of being fired after a prior warning. Examples of deviations from the rules in this regard include not wearing protective clothing or driving too fast within the work area. There was also a lot of emphasis placed on respecting the environment, such as decreasing the pollution of machinery on the site and minimising pollution from all the working/workers' camps/accommodation. Bechtel's motto in health and safety matters is "zero is possible," which refers to the fact that it is a realistic goal to complete the project without injury.

To reach that goal, Bechtel works through a well-defined methodology where the emphasis and operations in HSSE are outlined in the context of the project plan from the beginning and regularly upgraded at each phase of the project. This involves everything down to the smallest tasks and is based on a philosophy that managers have the greatest positive impact for HSSE matters in the early stages of a project when decisions are made in regard to how various

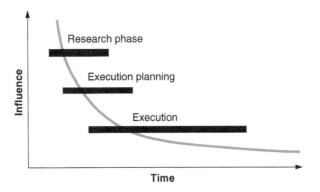

Figure 2.22

Declining influence of project management in safety matters during the project life cycle.

executions shall be conducted. This concept is illustrated by simple means in the context of time in Figure 2.22.

The line shows the effect that management can have on HSSE matters. This is highest initially but decreases as the project progresses. During the initial research and planning stages, the work is organised with regard to the hazards in the working environment where the aim is to exclude them as far as possible and to use safety and protection devices when it is not possible to rule out the dangers. For example, the potential hazard of frequent very strong winds in Reyðarfjörður (up to 140 km/h) was considered at a very early stage by Bechtel, and they decided to minimise high cranage requirements by doing a lot of ground level and off-site assembly, with erection in benign conditions. Once construction begins, the basic framework is at hand – not least regarding procedures and staff attitudes to safety – and the influence power of the management has become less than in the beginning. Feedback and reviews of performance efficacy are, however, an important aspect of HSSE management so that it is possible to learn from the experience.

Bechtel's heavy emphasis on health and safety has yielded rich results, and the recorded statistics for the Fjardaál project, with rates of 0.12 and 0.04 injuries per 100,000 worked hours in 2005 and 2006, attest to this. These are very low in comparison to others, and the good performance of Bechtel in Reyðarfjörður has had an effect beyond the construction site of the aluminium plant, as Icelandic primary contractors IAV have adopted the philosophy and methods of Bechtel for their projects.

Business environment

Business

The business of the organisation has, of course, an impact on all of its projects, and the projects may have an impact on the business. It is very important that required information on both sides is available to ensure that all issues are addressed and that the results from projects, programmes, and portfolios are aligned with the needs of the business.

Being in business means being involved in the provision of goods or services, and this may be through a for-profit or not-for-profit enterprise. In either case, there are external factors at work as the environment around the business is constantly changing, requiring the business to be able to adapt quickly. For example, this may be the arrival of new competitors in the market, an increase in the return of faulty products, an imposed significant increase in rent and/or rates, or the impacts of new legislation. The concept of adaptation is derived from the natural world, and biologists and ecologists have learnt a great deal about the adaptations of different animal and plant species and how successful they have been in recent times. A common theme in this work is the understanding that increasing size and complexity is not necessarily a good thing, and simple and robust adaptations may be better. An exception in the former case, however, may be an entity like an ant colony, where there are exceptional and successful organisation and division of labour.

The emphasis in this case is on the two-way relationship between business objectives and plans and PPP management. Projects form a core element in business development and particularly so in the start-up phase where the whole enterprise could be referred to as a project or programme. An example might be the early research work and development that is carried out in universities across the full range of sectors that can gradually be turned into some form of consultancy service or product-based business. In this case, the early development work might involve obtaining proof of concept, building up useful knowledge, attracting investment, analysing all the business risk categories, developing business networks, etc.

In mature enterprises, projects and programmes will take a different shape but are no less important. They run alongside normal business operations as reflected in the permanent organisation management structure and could be viewed as having an outcome that is either short-term, medium-term, or long-term. A long-term project or programme might, for example, be one that identifies long-term potential risks and gives the enterprise advance warning of this, allowing them to adapt in time. Companies routinely undertake this approach, although it can be a significant drain on resources and thus requires careful management to maintain relevance. An example is the approach of car manufacturers to the fuel efficiency of their cars. In the 1990s and early 2000s, when oil prices were historically low, some companies had extensive programmes for developing new, fuel-efficient engines in anticipation of a major change in the market and were well placed to take advantage of consumer shifts once higher oil prices became established.

Short- and medium-term projects and programmes in mature enterprises that have a two-way interaction with the business objectives can vary widely in scope and scale. Food companies, for example, will often undertake projects in the form of market research and controlled trials to identify new opportunities and test new ideas in order to retain their competitive edge, and these will also change depending on market reactions once products are launched. Another different example is when companies decide to embrace new nationally and internationally recognised standards for their products or services. This can require intensive project management and will also have a two-way interaction with business objectives. In each case, a particular type of project management organisational structure might be called for that will have the necessary senior management support, expertise, and resources to carry out its work, and we will refer back to this in later sections.

Law and contracts

Examples of contractual regulations of a project may be duties, rights, and processes – and they all have their basis in law. The requirements are typically contained in specific bodies and legal systems, particularly corporate and contract law, commercial law, employment law, and health and safety. A variety of other laws may also be relevant; laws on data protection, building regulations, intellectual property, and copyright law, as well as patents and royalties. Furthermore, laws relating to discrimination on the basis of gender, sexual orientation, disability, age, race, or religion may need to be considered.

A responsible organisation will maintain a reputation for conducting business within the law and in an ethical manner. Such behaviour will limit the organisation's legal exposure by reducing the risk of someone taking legal actions against it.

Having a broad-based knowledge of the laws relevant to the area of operation (and experience of legal proceedings) is important for a project manager and can help to avoid damaging legal confrontations which can be costly, both in financial and reputational terms, even if cases are won. Legal risks in projects need to be identified early and particularly during contract negotiations, where small oversights may eventually prove very costly further down the line. Given the increasing complexity of legislation, it may be necessary to engage external expertise, but also not to overdo this and waste scarce project funds. Accurate record keeping can also be an important aspect of this if a legal conflict situation arises and past activities are open to detailed questioning.

One important responsibility of a project manager is to manage – or participate in the management of – contracts made in the project with customers, vendors, partners, and employees. This includes negotiating the terms and conditions, but also ensuring compliance with the terms and conditions, and last but not least documenting and agreeing to any changes that may arise during the execution of a contract. Contract management can be summarised as the process of systematically managing the creation, execution, and analysis of contracts for the purpose of minimising risk while maximising financial and operational performance.

Finance

The financial management of the organisation is responsible for making the necessary funds available for the project in a responsible and timely way. In most organisations, the project financial management, including financial reporting, is closely linked to the accounting and controlling processes of the organisation. Arranging project finance so that there is always sufficient cash flow to enable the smooth running of a project or programme is another key competence for a project manager and requires a broad range of skills covering investor relations, cost estimation, negotiation, cost control, and accounting. Again, there can be major differences between large and small enterprises, with the former likely to have a wide range of expertise to deal with the often-complex financial structure of large projects. In many projects, there can be a structure whereby milestones are used to define funding allocations which will each have a specific set of deliverables that may or may not influence the decision to continue or discontinue a particular project. This can be a method of reducing unnecessary expenditure but can also lead to discontinuities in projects if review periods take an overly long time.

The genesis of projects

One way to classify projects is to focus on their genesis. Shenhar et al. (2001) describe two types of projects: projects as part of regular business/operations and projects as part of planning and direction setting. We could also add a third category to this; projects that have their genesis in independent ideas. We will give examples of each of these project types below.

Projects as part of regular business/operations

We can further classify controlling entities in this category into those that generate income from the execution of projects and those that use projects to assist in general business/operations rather than income generation.

In relation to the first of these, it is normal for service companies to generate their income by working on projects for external buyers. Consulting companies are good examples of such companies, as are engineering firms and contracting companies who may perform designing, building, or operating services or a combination of these. There is no long-term ownership involved on the part of the contractor in this relationship. Other examples of service companies that operate in a similar vein would be independent media production companies or advertising companies that operate on a project-by-project basis, providing content to client companies and large broadcasting or publishing organisations. The selection criteria for projects, in this case from the perspective of the service supplier, will be very different from that applied to internal projects within companies. Their first concern will often be about whether they get paid appropriately for the services that are supplied in a timely manner, and if there is potential financial exposure due to, e.g. litigation risks, etc. Other concerns may revolve around health and safety risks or reputational risks, and these should all be covered during contract negotiations, although sometimes project buyers can be in a position to dictate terms that are unfavourable to project suppliers.

A recent study on projectification in western economies showed that about 80% of all projects are internal projects like marketing, sales, ITC, R&D, or product development projects, and only about 20% of all projects are external customer-based projects (Schoper et al., 2018). In the internal operations of companies or large public entities, many problems or challenges can arise which require quick solutions and knowledge accumulation to avoid recurrences. In a company with a certified quality system, the response to such issues should be established as a series of procedures to define the problem, plan a solution for it, and follow it through until there is a successful outcome. Examples of projects of this kind are:

- A customer of an accountancy firm makes a complaint about having received a wrong bill. To see what went wrong, the particular details of this case are investigated and are dealt with, but equally, actions are taken to prevent the recurrence of similar mistakes.
- A public organisation exceeds the financial resources that had been made available to it through voted expenditure, and the issuing governmental body decides to investigate the cost overruns in order to reduce present and future financial commitments.
- An employee of an industrial company is injured at work. The causes of the accident are identified, as well as the response which took place at the scene. If necessary, the emergency plan is reviewed, and action is taken to ensure that the accident will not recur. These measures may include, for example, changes in the work practices or the purchase of safety equipment.

Projects as part of planning and direction setting

All modern companies/organisations and institutes use planning and direction setting as a means to define their purpose and role in the present and future. An example of this is the Icelandic company Eimskip, which for a long time was a shipping company but redefined its role in the late 20th century and now operates as a one-stop transport and distribution company, with a wide range of onshore facilities and services in a number of international locations. As part of company planning and direction setting, a number of separate or linked projects can be created, which are used to gauge the effectiveness of changing business/operational methods and objectives. Examples of such projects are market research studies or pilot programmes which aim to ensure that there is convincing evidence that a new direction or venture will be successful before a significant investment commitment is made. These projects are bridges to the desired future, and it goes without saying that they can take many forms, big or small, long or short.

Some examples of planning and direction-setting projects are:

- An engineering company decides to implement a management system according to the ISO 9001 standard and to become certified within two years. To manage the implementation process, a schedule for time and cost will be set up and a project manager appointed.
- An investment company that has specialised in fisheries has identified an interesting business opportunity and decides to begin participating in the telecommunications industry. The company begins by appointing a person responsible for this aspect of its business and they, in turn, build up a team of people with knowledge in that field. Connections are made in the areas of technology and finance, and investment options available to them are examined in detail, promising opportunities are taken up, and deals are done.
- A local authority in a rural area decides to redefine its role in such a way that, in addition to its traditional role of public service provision, it will additionally build an image based on culture, a healthy lifestyle, and sports. In line with this new vision, the authority sponsors a number of new related projects such as the opening of a cultural history museum, an expansion of existing sports facilities, and supporting efforts to promote healthier lifestyles among the population.

In this context, it is interesting to reflect on the Giza pyramid project (2550–2530 BCE); the tallest structure until the completion of the Eiffel Tower in Paris. This project had enormous technical challenges. Kozak-Holland (2011) points out that ancient Egypt is recognised as the first nation-state, and the Giza pyramid project helped unify it by the economic returns it provided. This state-sponsored project employed a vast workforce of up to 20,000 at any time.

Projects in the form of independent ideas

Ideas to improve existing business operations or to create new ventures often pop up which are not attributable to special planning and direction setting. Such ideas can arise among employees in a company or organisation, its customers, or independently from unaffiliated groups or individuals. Within companies, for example, people can be encouraged to contribute suggestions, and many will be familiar with suggestion boxes at their place of work where people can put pen to paper and their ideas are submitted for review. Examples of independent ideas formed by individuals or groups may be the following:

- An Icelandic entrepreneur gets the idea of holding a concert with the band Guns and Roses in Iceland. He contacts their agent, makes an assessment of the costs and revenues, and decides to start the project.
- Colleagues at a university get a business idea in relation to undertaking joint research. They set up a business around the idea, develop business relationships, raise funds, and start operating.

- A guest at a popular restaurant in London puts a simple suggestion into the restaurant's suggestion box proposing a new arrangement for the registration of orders to improve accuracy. The management of the restaurant agrees with the suggestion and decides to implement a new ordering system based around it.

In Autumn 2005, a couple and their family living near Akureyri in North Iceland were facing an uncertain future due to the fact that their livelihood was threatened by a forced retirement from work at sea because of an accident. According to Agnes Sigurdóttir, one evening she happened to see a documentary on Icelandic television about a microbrewery in Denmark, and she was immediately fascinated with the idea and discussed it with her husband. They decided there and then to have a go and started researching how practical it would be to establish such an industry in their home at Árskógarströnd.

A week later, they arrived in Denmark to see the microbrewery featured in the documentary. After that, the wheels spun quickly, and a new company was established in December. The couple found themselves a connection in the Czech Republic and hired a brewing master from there. Purchasing of equipment from the Czech Republic was finalised, and a factory premises was designed in haste and built on site in the spring and summer of 2006. An early decision was made to use entirely Czech traditions, yeast, and hops, and the pilot project went incredibly quickly and smoothly, according to Agnes.

The couple got early investors around the table without too many problems, but it was more difficult to get banks involved in the project as the idea was considered rather innovative and not everyone had faith in the viability of the company. At that time, there were two beer makers in Iceland, Egill Skallagrímsson and Vífilfell, and the banks very likely thought that there was little scope to compete with these big companies.

Financial backing for the venture was eventually obtained through a regional bank, Sparisjodur, construction was completed and production began in the autumn of 2006. At that time, the entrepreneurs had managed to realise a 120 million ISK investment (equivalent to approximately 1 million GBP at that time) with hard work, some risk-taking, the participation of several small investors, and borrowing.

The resulting beer – Kaldi – immediately achieved great popularity since it was unique in the market: quality Czech beer, made in Iceland with pure Icelandic water and sold only in dark 330ml glass bottles. Today, Kaldi is one of the best-selling beers in its category, and the Bruggsmidjan brewery facilities have been expanded several times and further expansions are expected.

Projects and organisational strategy

Strategy

Competition between projects is a recognised phenomenon in all companies and institutions. The need for new projects is usually many times greater than what can be achieved with the available resources. In addition to this, the overall focus and motivation of an organisation are shaped by the attitudes of management at any one time. Some of the challenges encountered may require urgent attention, with clearer short-term outcomes, whereas other challenges may have less defined, long-term outcomes. Normally, the latter will then need to wait for a better time to be dealt with, although the danger is that this might never happen or be too late when it finally does, leading to some form of crisis in the medium to long term. Other considerations involve risk spreading, where companies navigate their way through uncertain waters by spreading the risk of their ventures. There is a need to constantly work on an analysis of the best projects to undertake, but what tasks are best and how can one abide by this choice? In this context, it is common to talk about strategy, and the following definition captures well the meaning of that concept (Johnson et al., 2008):

> Strategy is the direction and scope of an organisation over the long term, which achieves advantage in a changing environment through its configuration of resources and competences with the aim of fulfilling stakeholder expectations.

This topic is covered in more depth in the book *Project: Strategy*, which is part of this series of books. In that book, we discuss the methodology of direction setting and strategic management. It also includes a detailed discussion of practical methods to develop strategies for organisations. Readers are encouraged to familiarise themselves with the contents of this book.

A company can be managed so that its strategic objectives are achieved through the planning and execution of projects or programmes and the operation of a project portfolio. This can involve the achievement of longer-term strategic goals, often obtained in an iterative process over a less defined time frame or having more easily defined goals from the outset and a more defined time frame. Implementing PPP management in an organisation is the result of a strategic decision and should be followed up by building up infrastructure, knowledge, competence, and skills in PPP management.

Alignment with strategy

Direction setting derived from strategic objectives and/or general business methodology defines much of what is important in the planning and execution of projects and is guided by data and background knowledge that has already been compiled and made available to the controlling entity. An example of this is the legal framework of the project and the impact of laws and regulations on the projects and programmes of the company. Further references to these factors will be discussed when the environment of projects will be covered in more detail later. Similarly, the company may have taken public positions on a variety of issues, and this can make things simpler when working on the implementation of individual projects. An example of this may be a company that has promoted itself as a green or environmentally aware company, so that each time it implements projects it knows that these have to have solid justification in terms of sustainability.

Last but not least, every project must be aligned with the strategy, mission, vision, and values of the organisation. In that context, project selection methods will be discussed in Chapter 7.

Reflection points

- Would you say that human resource management in a project-orientated organisation is different from a traditional functional organisation? Explain the difference and any extra challenges.
- It is stated that the rules of sustainable development and environmental concerns are becoming a factor in projects. Give an example that sheds light on this from more than one perspective.
- In the section on the genesis of projects, we listed three categories. Can you find examples of projects that fall outside these categories? Is there a fourth and perhaps a fifth category?

Bibliography

Arnadottir, O. (2013). Endurgerð og umköpun gamalla bygginga: Síldarverksmiðjan í Djúpavík. BA thesis, Reykjavik, Iceland: Listaháskóli Íslands. Retrieved from http://hdl.handle.net/1946/15436.

Boehm, B.W. (1988). A spiral model of software development and enhancement. *Computer*, 21(5), 61–72.

Cooper, R.G. (1994). Perspective third-generation new product processes. *Journal of Product Innovation Management*, 11(1), 3–14.

Definition of PROJECT. (n.d.) Retrieved from www.merriam-webster.com/dictionary/project.

Flyvbjerg, B., Holm, M.S., & Buhl, S. (2002). Underestimating costs in public works projects: Error or lie? *Journal of the American Planning Association*, 68(3), 279–295.

Fridgeirsson, T.V. (2015). Improvement of the Governance and Management of Icelandic Public Projects. Doctoral dissertation, Reykjavik, Iceland: Reykjavik University. Retrieved from https://skemman.is/handle/1946/23278.

Gaddis, P.O. (1959). The project manager. *Harvard Business Review*. May–June 1959, Harvard University.

Hauksson, T., Ingason, H.T., & Jonasson, H.I. (2012). Project profiling: Adaptive project management using project character clues. In: *26th IPMA World Congress – Integrating Project Management Standards – Therapeutic Way Forward in Times of Economic Challenges*, p. 312. Hersonissos, Greece: IPMA.

IAV. (n.d.). Retrieved from www.iav.is/en/.

International Standards Office. (2012). *ISO 21500:2012. Guidance on Project Management*. Geneva: ISO.

IPMA. (2015). *Individual Competence Baseline for Project, Programme & Portfolio Management*, version 4. Zurich: IPMA.

Johnson, G., Scholes, K., & Whittington, R. (2008). *Exploring Corporate Strategy: Text & Cases*. Harlow: Pearson Education.

Kozak-Holland, M. (2011). *The History of Project Management*. Ontario: Multi-Media Publications.

Lenfle, S., & Loch, C. (2010). Lost roots: How project management came to emphasize control over flexibility and novelty. *California Management Review, 53*(1), 32–55.

Morris, P. (2013). *Reconstructing Project Management* (1st ed.). Chichester: Wiley-Blackwell.

Payne, J.H., & Turner, J.R. (1999). Company-wide project management: The planning and control of programmes of projects of different type. *International Journal of Project Management, 17*(1), 55–59.

Schoper, Y.G., Wald, A., Ingason, H.T., & Fridgeirsson, T.V. (2018). Projectification in Western economies: A comparative study of Germany, Norway and Iceland. *International Journal of Project Management, 36*(1), 71–82.

Shenhar, A.J., Dvir, D., Levy, O., & Maltz, A.C. (2001). Project success: A multidimensional strategic concept. *Long Range Planning, 34*(6), 699–725.

Turner, J.R., Grude, K.V., & Thurloway, L. (Eds.) (1996). *The Project Manager as Change Agent: Leadership, Influence and Negotiation*. London: McGraw-Hill.

Turner, J.R., & Müller, R. (2003). On the nature of the project as a temporary organization. *International Journal of Project Management, 21*(1), 1–8.

Vefsíða Kárahnjúkavirkjunar. (n.d.). Retrieved from www.karahnjukar.is.

Wilson, J.M. (2003). Gantt charts: A centenary appreciation. *European Journal of Operational Research, 149*(2), 430–437.

Zurich Insurance Group. (2011). *Supporting Change Management*. Zurich, Switzerland: Author.

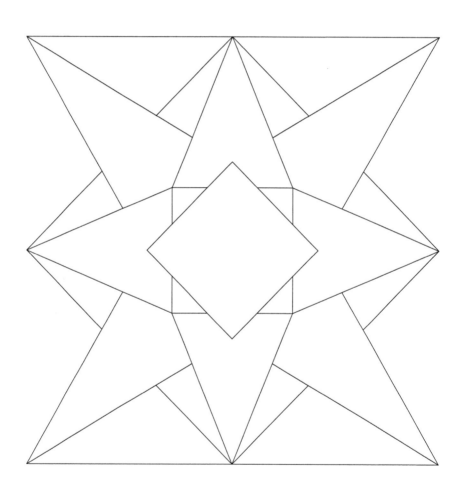

3 Planning: definition and the environment

••

Project planning

Why?

Project management without planning could be called "retroactive" project management. In this case, the project is started without the existence of a clear idea of how it should be executed, and there is probably no developed idea of what should come out of the project either. Such a philosophy and approach are not conducive to successful outcomes – although they are maybe not that uncommon – particularly when project managers have little accountability and are not directly affected by a negative outcome. Without a worked-through plan, a project manager will soon face a range of problems. To begin with, he or she will possibly manage to solve them, but no sooner will he have fixed them, then a few more may crop up that are even more difficult to deal with. In this way, the project manager will soon lose control of the project amidst an increasing number of problems. He will find it difficult to concentrate on what matters, and the people under him will sense insecurity and uncertainty. Most likely, a project, as just described, will spiral out of control in one way or another.

This book defines a proactive approach to managing a project and to planning not only the project but also the management of the project. It is generally understood that a project begins with a definition, followed by planning, execution, and, finally, the finishing of the project when the outcome of the project is put into use. This simple model of the life cycle of a project describes quite well certain types of projects such as simple construction projects. The model does not apply as well to various other projects, as has been mentioned in the previous chapter. There, we pointed out that such representation assumes that the environment and the needs are known and stable at the beginning of the project, but that is not always the case. Regardless of the type and characteristics of a project, it is necessary to put hard work into planning and preparing at the early stages or the preparation phase of projects, and there are times when this may require multiple iterations.

The scope of this preparatory work is dependent on the information available, but the preparation work also serves a wider purpose: it helps to form relationships between people and to build up trust between those who will work together on a project. It is worth noting that the purpose of planning is not, in itself, to create documents, fill out forms, and write reports. Indeed, it is best to keep all such things in moderation and to focus on documenting the most important elements. What matters most in the end is the process itself – the working through of ideas during the planning and the building of relationships and trust that occurs in that process. The positive correlation between planning and performance in projects might be self-apparent, but it can also be overlooked and, for those in doubt, there are many studies that confirm this correlation. The success of a project depends on various factors. In general, there is a good relationship between the planning of projects and performance, in particular, the original definition of the outcome of the project, as well as the planning and management of internal resources of the project and change control through the project life cycle. Other key factors include the experience of the project managers where greater experience is associated with better performance. Numerous other factors, however, affect performance, and later in this book we will talk about success in projects and methods for measuring this.

What?

In many places, one can find a discussion of the contents of a project plan. Meredith et al. (2016) say that each project plan should include several factors: basic purpose, description and overview of the project, more detailed objectives, schedules, resource requirements, personnel and stakeholders, risk management, and evaluation methods. Kerzner (2017) lists the elements of a project planning and control system, including such elements as goals/objectives, work descriptions and instructions, network scheduling, master/detailed schedules, and budgets.

Mikkelsen and Riis (2017) suggest that a project plan contains, amongst other things, a general overview of the project and its aims, an analysis of the environment, the division of tasks and time schedules, a description of the management organisation and communication paths, and a list of necessary resources, as well as the processes that the management of the project should be based on. Fangel (2013) wrote about the main approaches to project management and the importance of starting the project in a decisive manner. In this book, we will outline a simple model for performing the different stages of project planning.

It is generally assumed that project plans are set out at the beginning of the project and are the guiding light for the project's entire life cycle, being regularly consulted, for example, at important times such as the transition between phases. This relationship between project planning and the project's life cycle is shown in Figure 3.1.

In the beginning, little or no information is available about the project, but the idea or concept is developed until the project is properly defined. This is

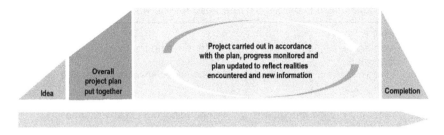

Figure 3.1

Project planning and project updating through the life cycle.

followed by formal planning of individual elements, and together these com-bine to form an overall project plan. Once this is in place, the project should be carried out in accordance with this plan, although there is a continuous need to monitor the project's external and internal environment, as well as the project progress, and possibly to update the plan to reflect the realities encountered and new information received. The organisational requirements may change, and changed requirements, risks, and opportunities need to be identified and acted upon. The project plan is therefore under constant review and, in the end, with all the changes documented, can be further used as a future guide for later projects as it documents the experience gained in the current project.

Defining the project

Assessing the "project fit"

Not everything is a project, and project management can therefore not be applied to everything that is going on in an organisation. And yet the question of whether an initiative is a project or not is not always easy to answer. Based on ideas put forward in lecture notes by Dr. Morten Fangel, we offer a simple scoring table to differentiate between routine work and projects through the assessment of three dimensions; namely demarcation, implementation, and environment (see Table 3.1).

Here, numerical answers are given to a series of questions in three cat-egories – demarcation, implementation, and environment. The scoring from 1 to 10 is shown below, and an explanation of each of the different questions and how they relate to the differentiation between tasks and projects are given below:

- Is the time frame in which we have to deal with the issue ample or nar-row? If we consider the time frame quite ample, we give it a low grade, for example, 2. If we consider it quite narrow, then we give it a high grade, maybe 8.

Table 3.1 Scoring table to differentiate between routine work and projects

Demarcation	
Ample time frame	Narrow time frame
Repeated	Unique
Takes place in a part of the total life cycle	Takes place over the entire life cycle
Implementation	
Following routine procedures is sufficient	Additional organisational measures necessary
Similar background of participants	Many types of participants
Necessary knowledge in one place	Need for broader co-operation
Environment	
Tendency towards security and predictability	Potentially multiple risk categories and/or opportunities
Should not lead to major changes	May lead to major changes
Environment has limited effect on the outcomes	The outcomes are dependent on the environment
People associated with the initiative are few and known	People connected may be many and not all are known
1 2 3 4 5	6 7 8 9 10

- Are the challenges something that we have to deal with repeatedly and with little change? Then we give it 1. Or are we looking at a unique challenge that has never been dealt with before? Then we give it 10. We could also think that similar projects were carried out in the business a few years ago, and so we might therefore grade it as 5.
- Are we talking about a task that extends only within a particular part of the lifetime of an overall undertaking (low grade), or does it last the entire life cycle of the undertaking (high grade)?
- Can the existing management of the company or organisation perform the issue directly, without special organisational measures, or is there a need to create a special management system to address the challenge, e.g. appoint a project manager? In the former case, a low grade would be given, with a high grade in the latter case.
- Do the participants have a similar background (low grade), or are they different and with a variety of backgrounds (high grade)? If the group is a mixture of both, a grade of, e.g. 5 could be given.
- Is all the necessary knowledge to deal with the task in one place (low grade), or does the subject call for a wider co-operation with other individuals (high grade)?
- Is the environment characterised by security and predictability (low grade), or is there a wide range of risks or possibly opportunities in the environment (high grade)?
- Will the results lead to small changes (low grade), or will it lead to significant changes (high grade)?
- Does the environment have little effect on the outcomes (low grade), or are the outcomes highly dependent on the environment (high grade)?

- Are the people concerned few and well-known (low grade), or are there many who are linked to the challenge, some of whom are lesser known (high grade)?

When a considered answer has been given to all these questions, the scores are added together. The resulting sum gives an indication of how strongly the undertaking resembles a project. This analysis gives the user a feel for the nature of the undertaking, and if the sum is less than 60, then the undertaking has weak characteristics as a project. If so, one could conclude that it is not feasible to apply project management as a managing method as it is a task that only requires that standard management procedures be followed. Please note that through the application of this simple scoring table, some important observations regarding the project characteristics have already been made and the project analysis has already started.

Primary definitions

It is important that the project has a secure anchor in the company. This means that it has the support of the management, which will ensure that it has the necessary resources, and that the workers in the project are aware of the importance of the project and its context in the wider challenges that the company faces. The decision to initiate a project is taken by authorised managers, and their initial role is to ensure that the project is in line with company strategy or policy and to judge that the likely outcome will be good for the company in one way or another. Figure 3.2 shows this context, and readers are

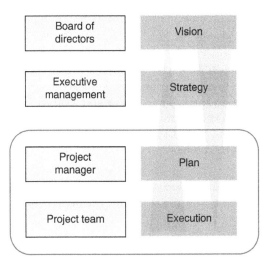

Figure 3.2

The connection of a project with the direction and the vision of the company.

advised to study the book *Project: Strategy* in this series of books to learn more about strategy and direction setting in the context of organisations.

A company that has undertaken strategic planning has a future vision and has adopted a strategy to achieve it. The projects that the company undertakes are the means by which to follow this strategy. A project manager operates under the authority of the chief executive officer (CEO) and a board of directors, and they need to understand the whole context of the project within the company and share that understanding with the project team. The arrow on the right side of the figure reflects this context. On the other hand, the project team and the project manager are required to provide information about the progress of the project to the executive management, who may convey this information on to the board of directors. Information which is communicated in such a manner to the senior management can have an impact on the strategy of the company, as the arrow on the left side reflects, and in a way this can be considered as a type of continuous circuit.

The project will therefore be defined in part in the policy/strategy document agreed upon by the executive board, executive manager, or other administrators/managers in the upper layers of the decision chain of the business. It is possible to look at this event in the context of the life cycle of the project. It is common to have projects where an idea for a project has been incubating in the company for a while and, after a period of time, this project is formally defined as an interesting idea or *business case*. At that point, the idea of the project has become sufficiently mature for the company's management to want to formalise the project and document it. Then it is defined and put in a formal framework. The definition of the project involves presenting a formal statement about crucial key factors. The presentation of this initial definition of the project depends on the traditions that have been built up in the business and the processes that are followed. Examples of topics covered in the definition might be:

- Who is your project for – who will fund and otherwise support it?
- Who will be responsible for the project – the project manager?
- Who are the main participants, direct and indirect?
- List of the products expected to come from the project.
- Target time for the project.
- Target costs for the project.

More items may be included, such as known risk factors, the impact of the project on regular operations in the company, the main reasons for it, and more.

Reflection points

- It is stated that this book defines a proactive approach to managing a project. Do you know of a case where a reactive approach was applied? Describe that approach. How did the project go?

- Is the question "is it a project?" a simple "yes" or "no" question? What are the most important characteristics of a project and why?

Scope and deliverables

The definition of the *scope* of a project, also called the *demarcation* of a project, is one of the basic factors of planning, and hence effective project management. Scope description defines the boundaries of the project, it describes the outcomes, the outputs, and benefits of the project, and the work required to produce them. A scope description can also define what is not contained in a project.

It is important that the project manager knows the scope of the project and its environment and can thus clearly define the project. Projects that do not have a clearly defined scope tend to expand and may spiral out of control. Defining the scope is the first step in formulating the deliverables in a project.

It is common at the early stage of project planning for there to be a long wish list of desired outcomes or deliverables that are a normal result of trying to get "more bang for your buck." This can include tangible and intangible assets created in the project that are to lead to expected effects and benefits, and this is typically the basis for judging project success. It is most often the case, however, that resources – be they time, money, personnel, equipment, or facilities – are limited, and prioritisation has to take place in order to focus on the most important outcomes. There are many different ways to do this, with some preferring a numerical prioritising system that is based on formulae involving multiple parameters. Other simpler methods, for example, can be to classify different deliverables as "essential," "beneficial," or "of possible benefit." Once agreed upon by the interested parties, the deliverables will be formally defined in the project documentation and systematically organised in a process often referred to as "Manage Scope Configurations." This will include documentation around approval procedures. As the project progresses and new information is received, the scope of the project may change, and it may be necessary to modify the configuration to account for this. Scope configuration management has the purpose of ensuring that the scope is aligned with the agreed needs and requirements and that everyone working on the project is working with the same version of the product. The purpose of scope configuration management is also to minimise deficiencies and errors and unintended scope creep.

Project definition is the first stage in attracting investment and support for a project, as people need to have a concrete idea of what the project is intended to achieve before making a commitment. As an example of this, consider the rebuilding of a small hydropower plant (32 kW) which has been neglected in recent times and is beginning to show clear signs of degradation. The project group (HydroPower Co-op) decided to apply for financial support to fund essential maintenance, so it may be possible to save the plant. The group agreed on the following in regard to the project definition prior to preparing a formal grant application:

Definition of a small power plant project

Date:	1st March 2018.
Project title:	Rebuilding of hydropower plant.
Client:	HydroPower Co-op.
Project manager:	John Doe
Key players:	Management of HydroPower Co-op, community, parliament.
List of tasks:	Foundations strengthened, rebuilding of penstock, dam wall to be repaired.
Demarcation in time:	The first phase – reinforcement of foundations – must take place no later than the autumn of 2018.
Containment of costs:	It is expected that the overall cost will be about 100,000 GBP.

After reading this short definition, it is possible to get a clear idea of what the project is about, who will manage it, who it is likely to affect, how much it should cost, and an indication of the timeline. This abridged version of a full project plan is sometimes called a *project charter*. A charter would typically also include a formal decision to launch the project and it would define the role and authority of the project manager.

The project plan

When it has been decided to initiate a particular project, it is time to consider the making of a detailed project plan. This describes the objectives of the project and how they should be achieved. It should answer the following questions:

- What will be done in the project?
- Why this project?
- How will the project work?
- Who will do what?
- When will the project be worked on, including individual parts?
- How much is allocated to the project in regard to various resources?

The definition of a project and the making of a project plan are milestones in the life of the project where, amongst other things, there is a need for creative thinking. At this time, it is essential that most options are on the table so that a decision in regard to them can be made.

The need for creative thinking exists throughout the whole of the project life cycle but most especially at the beginning. Here it is important that the views of the project team and external consultants are respected and ideas on what directions to take are listened to. This can be seen in Figure 3.3.

As Figure 3.3 shows, initially there is a focus on gathering information so that as many aspects and opinions as possible can be taken into the picture, and on making sure that nothing is missed in the definition of the project and the planning process. At the end of this, the processing of information takes over, and the actual detailed planning begins. If the lead-in preparation phase goes well – see the upper part of the figure – there is less need for new data in the actual planning – see the lower part of the figure.

It is right to look at strategies that encourage creative thinking and help the thought flow in a working group which seeks to understand the nature of the project, its environment, and breakdown. One technique that has become quite widespread is to draw up a so-called *mind map*. From the very beginning, people have used graphical representation for mapping out the context of information. The mind map – as it is known today – can, however, be traced back to 1970 or so. A mind map is a way to gather information, and it relies on the use of the natural function of the brain. A mind map is actually a drawing used to formulate words, ideas, tasks, or other factors that are linked to and arranged around an idea or a key word located in the centre of the mind map. In the context of projects, a mind map can be used to give an overview of the project, making teamwork more efficient, helping the definition of tasks, and facilitating decision-making.

Previously, there has been a brief discussion generally about planning and the components required for the project plan. This book is based on a framework plan, and the framework is divided into a number of sections as shown in the mind map in Figure 3.4. In the compilation of a project plan, it should be emphasised that the key factors for the project are summarised at the end of the planning when all necessary information is available. These can then be conveniently placed on a single page to highlight the essential elements

Figure 3.3

In the beginning, during project definition and initial planning, creativity is essential.

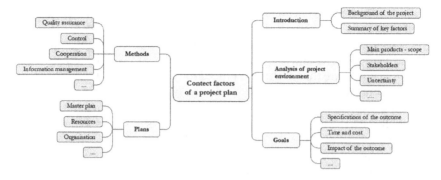

Figure 3.4

Framework for the content factors of a project plan.

and outcomes of projects. Detailed analysis of the project's environment is the main task involved at this stage and is a prerequisite for all types of plans, as is a discussion about objectives, goal setting, and performance measurement. Detailed planning will include a breakdown of all tasks and work streams, an evaluation of resources/supplies, and all costs, including management. In Chapter 5 and Chapter 6, we will discuss working methods, which relate to the methods to be applied in the project, including those relating to control, management, steering, and follow-up. Also included in these chapters is a discussion of the forming of partnerships and how to handle storage and distribution of information.

It should be emphasised that Figure 3.4 is only a guide, and other factors may be included. The execution of the project plan must take into consideration the type of project and its scope. In a small execution project, it may be considered unnecessary to make a detailed plan, and it may suffice to briefly mention the key factors as outlined. In a large construction project, it will be necessary to make a detailed plan and discuss all the aspects in the table "Definition of a small power plant project" in detail.

Project environment

One of the main characteristics of projects is the multifactoral relationship between them and their environment. Projects cause changes in their environment, as is most often their intention, but at the same time, the environment has impacts on the project, and those impacts need to be mapped out, analysed and, where appropriate, responded to. Analysis of the project's environment is therefore a key aspect of planning. An obvious example would be the construction of a harbour, where the walls projecting into the sea might have a major effect on local erosion and deposition of sands, leading to a much-altered environment from that documented in baseline studies.

Another less obvious example might be when a new IT system is installed in a company, requiring the staff within that company to acquire new information in order to be able to work with the new system, and the possible changing of work practices as a result.

Classification of environment

The environment of a project can refer to the surrounding physical landscape, people, and objects, or the non-physical settings and conditions in which a particular project is carried out. The range of different environments related to projects is therefore as diverse as the range of different project types that have been discussed in the previous chapter. It is important, then, to classify these environments so that project managers can quickly assess the relevant environmental factors for their project. A financial project manager, for example, might be more concerned with the interest rate environment than the natural environment, whereas an event project manager might be more concerned with the weather than interest rates.

Proper environmental classification involves looking at projects from a number of different perspectives. The *general external environment* of a project may include lots of intangible elements, such as social factors, inflation, legislation, taxation, the role of the state and local governments, etc. It can also refer to technical factors such as developments in computer technology. The *professional environment* may refer to many different aspects, such as codes of conduct, organisational structures, and qualifications. The *business environment* encompasses aspects, such as competition, marketing, research, and development, and all manner of risks, including those associated with changing regulation. The *consumer environment* refers to the desires, habits, and reactions of people that form the target market for a product or service. The *internal environment* encompasses the administrative aspects of an organisation, its history and culture, and its main strengths and weaknesses.

As discussed previously, the important aspects of the general project environment should be identified and analysed at the beginning of the planning process. If the project environment is viewed in an organised manner, important information can be revealed that is integral to planning assumptions. There are a number of methods for this, and two of these that are complimentary but emphasise different aspects will be discussed separately in more detail here before we take a combined look at them.

PESTLE analysis

To begin with, we discuss a well-known method for classifying and analysing the environment, the PESTLE analysis. This method is explained in more detail in our book *Project: Strategy* in this series. The acronym refers to the following key categories: Political, Economic, Sociological, Technological, Legal, and Environmental. PESTLE analysis is essentially an audit of an organisation's environmental influences designed to provide information that will guide strategic planning. This includes both the internal and nearby environments, over which an organisation may have full or partial control, and the wider environment, over which an organisation has little or no control. PESTLE analysis can be used as an "orientation" tool in the early stages of planning and is a very useful approach to take so as not to overlook important elements that can feature later in the project. A brief description of the different environment headings and how they relate to projects is given below.

Political: This category refers to a large class of matters involving politics of all sorts, both internally within a project or a company and externally with outside individuals or groups. Internally, for example, can refer to disputes that arise in projects due to personality or ideological clashes, or strategic and priority differences that result in battles over limited resources. Externally, a project may have different effects on different people and groups of people, and this category covers their reaction and influence that they can bring to bear on it. This can be at the individual, local, national, or international level, depending on the scope of the project, and can cover a wide range of aspects, such as business clashes or environmental concerns. This environmental category is not all potentially negative or concerned with risks, however, and some projects can receive wide political backing, and opportunities can occur as a result.

Economical: This category relates to the financial environment within which a project operates, both at present and in the future, and covers a wide range of aspects. In terms of project planning, the main concerns are cash flow during all stages of project development and the ability to meet requirements. Many factors can have a direct impact on this, from fuel prices to interest rates, currency exchange rates, taxation rates, market rates, money supply, and consumer confidence, etc. In addition, potential financial issues and conflicts can arise that are influenced by the external environment, and these should be assessed in the early planning stages. For example, delays in receiving official permission to undertake a project can have major implications on the viability and profitability of a project, as can legal action taken by others in relation to a project. Another factor may be when external contractors or suppliers who are important to a project encounter financial or operational difficulties, which mean they cannot perform their role.

Sociological: All projects operate within some form of societal environment that is formed from many different elements, including social stability, traditions, culture, religion, social class, and social mobility, etc. These can be important elements for certain types of projects in order to pursue opportunities and avoid unnecessary clashes. The element of religion can, for example, be crucial in certain parts of the world, where projects can be the subject of a scrutinised view based on religious perspectives before any kind of approval is given.

Technological: Different sectors within which projects are undertaken will have their own technological environment, and this is a category that can be of key importance in certain types of businesses such as software development and telecommunications. This includes other external technological developments that may have a disruptive effect on the products of a project. An important part of this environment can be technological standards that need to be adhered to, and knowledge of these should be kept up to date.

Legal: Laws and regulations that need to be taken into account are an important aspect of project planning, execution, and follow-up, and can overlap to some extent with the technological environment outlined above. Project managers need to understand the relevant laws that apply to their field and put systems in place to follow the correct procedures that they might entail. This environment can undergo significant change over time, and project managers need to be aware of these legal changes. Technical standards need to be considered, and codes of conduct that exist within a professional association need to be followed, as do good business practices, which can be formally defined or regarded as unwritten law.

Environmental: This last element relates to the physical or natural environment of a project, e.g. climatic and geological conditions. It is often of major importance in construction execution projects. Increasingly, it overlaps with legal and regulatory elements, as requirements such as an "Environmental Impact Statement" – EIS – or an "Environmental Impact Assessment" – EIA – become mandatory for projects above a certain scale.

It is common in PESTLE analysis to join the political and sociological categories together, as well as the technical and environmental categories, to produce a chart as shown in Figure 3.5. In Figure 3.5, there are four quadrants

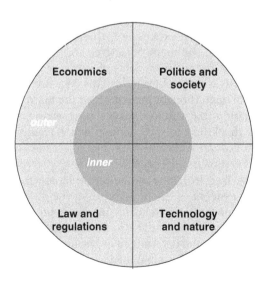

Figure 3.5

Visual presentation of the overall environment of the project.

shown, each representing the different category groupings. In one quarter is economics, in another is politics and society, in the third is technology and nature, and in the fourth is law and regulations. There is also an inner and outer circle, representing the internal and external environments of a project. This visual aid can be useful in project orientation, and an example of its further use in conjunction with other methods is given later in this chapter.

Figure 3.5 can be used in a simple way as a kind of checklist to highlight those aspects in the environment of projects which are most relevant to their preparation and execution. The first step is to list those factors, events, and stakeholders that are important in the environment of the project. Each of these items is reflected as a small number in the figure and explained very briefly to the side of it. In this manner, a list of items is created that can be short or long, depending on the scope of the project, which is available as a basis for further analysis.

More specific project analysis

More specific diagnostic tools are necessary to analyse the environment of a project from different perspectives. In the following text, four important perspectives are discussed: (1) Products and scope, (2) Complexity, (3) Stakeholders, and (4) Uncertainty. These perspectives and the tools used for analysis are each explained in more detail in the following sections.

Project products and scope

A necessary part of project planning and environment classification is to define clear boundaries for the project by listing the key products or outcomes and outlining the scope. If this is not done, there is a tendency for a project to become bigger – and more expensive – than was initially planned, and the chances of achieving the main objectives are often reduced. Carrying out a simple analysis of the main products of a project as part of the overall environmental analysis is a useful exercise. This does not refer to actual goal setting, but an initial open thought process about the main products that can yield useful information that will assist actual goal setting. It is also the case that an analysis of this kind can shed light on which elements of the project will most require follow-up and control by the project manager. An example of such an analysis is shown in Figure 3.6.

The process described in Figure 3.6 is self-explanatory. The second step reflects a general assessment of the importance of the different outcomes, as well as the perceived uncertainty in achieving these outcomes. Assessing the importance of the different outcomes for project success is based on a prioritisation of the requirements and determined by the project sponsor, top managers, or external customers. When combined with the uncertainty assessment, this should give an indication of the necessary project management priorities for the project. The total results from the process are documented in a table format as shown in step 4.

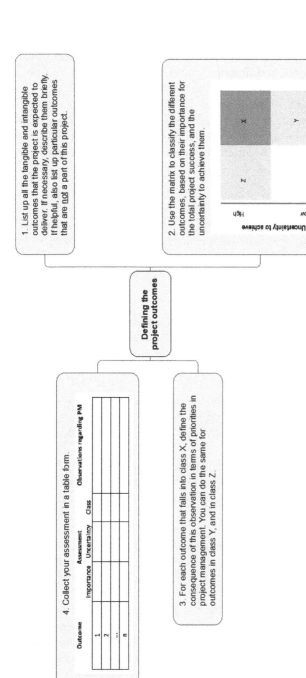

1. List up all the tangible and intangible outcomes that the project is expected to deliver. If necessary, describe them briefly. If helpful, also list up particular outcomes that are not a part of this project.

2. Use the matrix to classify the different outcomes, based on their importance for the total project success, and the uncertainty to achieve them.

Uncertainty to achieve

High

Z

X

Low

Y

Low   High

Importance for the success

Defining the project outcomes

4. Collect your assessment in a table form.

Outcome	Assessment		Class	Observations regarding PM
	Importance	Uncertainty		
1				
2				
...				
n				

3. For each outcome that falls into class X, define the consequence of this observation in terms of priorities in project management. You can do the same for outcomes in class Y, and in class Z.

Figure 3.6

Analysis of the main outcomes of the project.

Project scope can be defined as the work that needs to be accomplished to deliver the project product or outcome. If not already evident from a project definition, scope description can be undertaken in various ways, and listing the products of the project and describing and prioritising them can be a good basis for this. This will often require further consideration, however, as the scope of a project can be much wider than the products or outputs. In research projects, for example, it is often necessary to study a wide area around a subject – the subject environment – even though the final results may not reflect this, as elements in the wider environment studied are not considered to be relevant to these results.

Project complexity

One way to identify project characteristics and their context within the project environment is to assess the complexity of a project. Complexity is a combination of many factors, and it can be assessed in different ways. Here, we follow a simple approach where project complexity is assessed under three main headings:

- *Organisational complexity* – Number of people, departments, companies, countries, languages, cultures, and time zones related to the project.
- *Resource complexity* – The scope of resources needed for the project; this is sometimes estimated from the rough budget/financial plan that is available.
- *Technical complexity* – Describes how much innovation exists in the product of the project or the method used for its completion. Also, the potential for innovation, connectivity, and co-operation in tasks.

For each factor, the complexity is assessed as low, medium, or high. This scale is, of course, quite subjective and dependent on the experience of those that evaluate it. As more projects are evaluated in this manner within the same company, a tradition is formed in regard to how evaluation should take place.

Assessment of complexity can give a good indication of the management challenges in a project and is one way to compare projects. A worked-through example is shown in Table 3.2, where the company in question has to assess two potential projects and has developed a standardised approach to project selection, preparation, planning, and execution to enable this.

The comparison in Table 3.2 shows that the development project is considerably more complex and calls for effective communication and dissemination of information. The new shop project is simpler, but the management challenges there will involve controlling costs and monitoring the success of the new enterprise and the return on investment. Scale in projects is not necessarily an indicator of complexity, as it can often involve more repetition of tasks. For example, installing a new 50 km long water pipe across agricultural

Table 3.2 Evaluation of technical, resource- and organisational complexity of projects

Factor in project complexity	Project 1: Open a new store	Project 2: Develop new product
Organisational project complexity	The opening affects mainly one department of the company and the staff are few. The organisational complexity of the project is low.	The development calls for co-operation and synchronisation with developers in China. The project involves quite a large number of individuals with different backgrounds. The organisational complexity of the project is therefore high.
Resource complexity of a project	The opening of the new store calls for quite a lot of resources, both in starting costs and in relation to the operation of the 12-month trial period which is considered part of the project. The resource complexity is medium.	Resources which are needed for the project are relatively limited, the designers of the company are working on it, and there is no need for additional workforce. There is no additional cost related to the co-operation in China. The resource complexity is medium.
Technical complexity of a project	This will be the fourth outlet of the company and good information about how to do this is available. The technical complexity of the project is therefore low.	Here the aim is to develop a new product within the company's product line which involves innovation design and iterative testing. In addition, there is a requirement to further develop co-operation with the Chinese producers. The technical complexity is high.

land may require a lot less management input than installing a 5 km long water pipe in a built-up area.

A four-step process for assessing complexity is presented in Figure 3.7. It is important to make the best use of the information obtained in steps 1 and 2. This is reflected in the simple process model shown in the figure.

In the first step, the possible sources of complexity are listed. They fall under one of three complexity areas: technical, organisational, or resource complexity. Furthermore, they can be linked to the PESTLE classification and they can be a part of the inner or outer project environment. In the second step, the level of complexity for each of the different sources is assessed as low (C), medium (B), or high (A). The third step looks deeper into sources of complexity that fall into categories A or B, and some appropriate project management actions to deal with this complexity are defined. In the fourth step, all the information is collected in a table format.

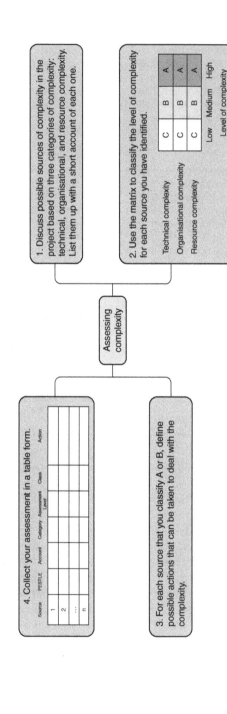

Figure 3.7

A process for the analysis of project complexity.

Stakeholders

The terms "stakeholders" and "interested parties" in project management both refer to individuals or groups of individuals that are either involved in a project, are interested in the progress and outcome of a project, or are bound in some way to a project. They can be internal or external to the project organisation and have an interest in its success and in the environment in which it operates. Typically, the most important stakeholders include executives and sponsors and representatives of the owners of the project, and these are sometimes called primary stakeholders. Figure 3.8 illustrates the range of stakeholder types that can be found in many projects and is a useful template to use when working on project planning and seeking to understand the broad environment in which a project operates. It is also worth adding that, much like in a play where a few actors may perform many roles, individual stakeholders can have different roles, and their overall approach to a project will involve some kind of balanced viewpoint that accounts for this. For example, it is not uncommon for industrial development in previously undeveloped areas to divide a community into those that see the possibility of business and employment opportunities and those that are concerned about the long-term effects on the local environment, with many people's views somewhere in between. This community will involve local representatives as well as, maybe, direct investors, who could be the same individuals in a project, and the resulting decision-making process can become politically complex.

Figure 3.8

Typical stakeholders in projects: Project team, suppliers, buyers, competitors, consumers, owner, authorities and creditors.

Another way to understand who the stakeholders in a project are is to use a simple questionnaire:

- **Who is the buyer?** The buyer is the one who funds the project and agrees on its time frame and budget frame and will probably enjoy the profits of the product that the project will deliver. The buyer is sometimes called the owner of the project. A project may have one buyer or multiple buyers in partnership. An example of the latter would be the community amalgamation project in Fjallabyggd in North Iceland, referred to in the last chapter.
- **Who provides information, knowledge, and expertise?** Projects require a variety of information and knowledge in preparation and execution, and this may come from within or externally. In the latter case, these external providers are a particular type of stakeholder. They may be paid or unpaid, and have different interests regarding the project. Examples of external information, knowledge, and expertise providers can be consultants in the field of technology and business, engineering consultants, and legal consultants. These would normally be paid for their services regardless of project outcomes. Other examples of stakeholders in this category could be suppliers of materials and equipment.
- **Who provides the labour and other resources?** Projects will most commonly require labour and other inputs, such as machinery, tools, and building materials. In projects in the business field, these inputs are paid for, and the cost of them is often a crucial part of the total cost. Contractors and sub-contractors commonly fulfil this role in projects where they will be paid on agreed terms. Less formally, casual workers can offer themselves for hire in a variety of projects, such as in market research or construction. In other projects, the labour is not paid for, and examples of these include voluntary work of various kinds, e.g. concerts to support international relief and construction of walkways in tourist areas.
- **Who uses the results?** The product of the project will be exploited in some way, and potential users should have an input at the early stages of a project in some form. Users can provide information regarding needs and requirements, and how the project outputs will be used. If we are talking about a construction project, the product could be a house. If we are talking about a research project in a Master's degree, the product will be research results, which are documented in a report. In all cases, someone will exploit the results – people will walk around the house and other researchers will utilise the research report.
- **Who approves the execution?** Often, the actual execution of a project is done in such a way that authorities must give their consent for it. A good example of this is in house construction, where the local authority must give consent for building. Another example would be a project that involves collecting some kind of personal information about individuals,

which has to be cleared first with the public bodies assigned to oversee data protection in different jurisdictions.

- **Who approves the result?** When the execution of the project is completed and its results can be seen, then the act of agreeing upon them takes place. Often it is the project buyer who accepts the result. In a construction project, this happens only when the buyer or their inspector conducts an assessment of the structure and confirms that the contractor has submitted it according to the contract. Sometimes it is the user who ultimately accepts the results, for example, in an organisational change project within a company. In this case, the project buyer can make a significant investment to implement such change, but it can be to no avail if the users, staff, and middle managers do not give consent, even if it is in an informal manner. Analogous examples can also be seen in some construction projects. There are examples of structures that are delivered on time and within budget, but users are unhappy because they consider them to be unsuitable. It can happen that such structures never come into full operation, which equates to the result never actually being approved.
- **Who does the result concern?** Those who are directly or indirectly affected by a project can be many or few, depending on the situation. It can be important to take the time early in the project planning stage to write down who these people are and what their possible viewpoints will be, as it is possible that they can influence the progress of the project. Examples of stakeholders that fall into this group are nature conservationists who object to roads on untouched land and owners of shops in a village that will be bypassed if a new road construction project goes ahead.

When stakeholders are examined in more detail, and their potential attitudes towards the project are analysed, it is good to take into account the following questions:

- What is the interest field of each stakeholder in question in regard to the project? Is the level of interest low or high? Are they connected to it as a whole or to a particular phase? Do they have an interest in specific inputs or in the results that will come out of the project?
- What is the influential power of the stakeholder? Are they in a position to affect the project in a good or bad way? In what way could that occur?
- What inputs do they bring to the project, if any? Do these inputs regard work, knowledge, or experience, or do they take part in important decisions in the project?
- What is the relationship between what the stakeholder brings to the project and what they gain from the project? What are the needs and requirements of the stakeholder? Where do their motivations lie? Do they get paid for the hours worked or a fixed amount? Do they perhaps not get any direct financial rewards? Does the project lead to a worsening in their circumstances in any way?

- What is the attitude of the stakeholders to the project? Are they positive, negative, or neutral towards it? Is this position directed towards the project itself or does it perhaps relate to other stakeholders in the project?
- What are the reasons for their position or lack of position? Is it due to values, financial interests, political interests, or something else?
- How can we expect the stakeholder to respond to the project? Will there be particular reactions on their part, or will they perhaps be neutral? Will they be able to have an indirect impact on the progress of the project with their views?
- How can we respond to the position of this stakeholder, and what type of reaction might be expected from the stakeholder in regard to our response – in the light of their position? Is it likely that it is possible to reach an agreement with the stakeholder? Commonly, it is necessary to assess and determine the needs of key stakeholders regarding information and documentation.

We refer to the book *Project: Strategy* in this series, where stakeholders were discussed, and the power vs. interest grid was presented, as a method to classify stakeholders according to their importance.

With these reflections, it is possible to create a good picture of the stakeholders directly and indirectly associated with a project, their attitudes, and possible reactions. This assessment is a good foundation for the formal analysis of stakeholders. We propose a five-step process for this purpose, as explained in Figure 3.9.

The process is simple and easy to apply. In step 1, it is important to identify the stakeholders with representative names, so that there is no doubt who they are. A brief description should be given of the reason why they are considered to be stakeholders. It can refer to what input they have towards the project, e.g. do they give a review about the project, take part in decisions, or shape the opinions of those making decisions? Also, write down how you would classify the stakeholder in the PESTLE tool, and whether they are a part of the inner or outer environment. It is possible to create a single group of similar interests from a collection of individuals or groups, although sometimes when you look more closely, the interests of this larger group may not fully align, and it is then necessary to separate them. It may be beneficial to separate internal stakeholders from external stakeholders.

In step 2, the significance of a stakeholder is assessed by applying the power vs. interest grid. Those stakeholders who are critical for the project are usually found in category A (high power and high interest), but stakeholders in categories B and C are also of importance. Further analysis depends on this classification, and it is not necessary to go further with the analysis of stakeholders that fall into category D.

In step 3, the analysis continues for stakeholders in categories A, B, and C. A brief description of stakeholder expectations in regard to the project is given here and, for this, it is necessary to put oneself in the shoes of the stakeholder

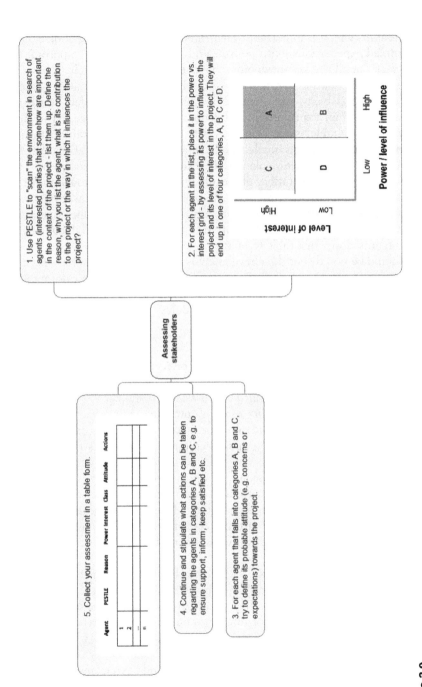

1. Use PESTLE to "scan" the environment in search of agents (interested parties) that somehow are important in the context of the project - list them up. Define the reason, why you list the agent, what is its contribution to the project or the way in which it influences the project?

2. For each agent in the list, place it in the power vs. interest grid – by assessing its power to influence the project and its level of interest in the project. They will end up in one of four categories, A, B, C or D.

Level of Interest

High

Low

C

A

D

B

Low

High

Power / level of influence

Assessing stakeholders

5. Collect your assessment in a table form.

Agent	PESTLE	Reason	Power	Interest	Class	Attitude	Actions
1							
2							
...							
n							

4. Continue and stipulate what actions can be taken regarding the agents in categories A, B and C, e.g. to ensure support, inform, keep satisfied etc.

3. For each agent that falls into categories A, B and C, try to define its probable attitude (e.g. concerns or expectations) towards the project.

Figure 3.9

A process for the analysis of project stakeholders.

and see the project from their perspective. This can outline whether it is felt that they will benefit from its progress and product, or whether it could be detrimental. Here, it is important to remember that the same stakeholder can have mixed expectations, both positive and negative, and it is important to try to map out all the key viewpoints that the stakeholder is likely to have.

In step 4, the analysis continues by using the information at hand to determine if it is advisable to take any action regarding the stakeholders by way of responding to their expectations and, if so, what action is suggested in this regard. As an example, it may be necessary to develop and maintain a strategy on how to engage, inform, involve, and commit the different stakeholders in the project. A communication plan can be a key tool for this purpose, as well as the management of expectations of the different stakeholders through the project life cycle. In some cases, it may be advisable to establish formal or informal networks or alliances with stakeholders as a part of the stakeholder strategy.

Step 5 is to collect all the information from the analysis and document it in an organised way in a table format.

It should be noted that the above analysis of the stakeholders reveals who are active participants in the project, including those who are information providers and who participate in decision-making. This information is crucial in making management plans and time schedules.

Uncertainty

An important part of the environment of a project is the uncertainties that surround it, both in the form of opportunities and risks. Often it is possible, based on experience, to do a quantitative assessment and list these uncertainties and calculate the probability of each outcome, while sometimes this is not possible, and they may come from unexpected angles with unanticipated consequences. In other cases, a more qualitative approach is taken in the risk assessment.

Risks implying negative consequences are more common for most projects, although there can also be opportunities that appear but also disappear if not reacted to in time. For example, a project may be eligible for grant assistance only if an application is made within a certain window of time. It is worth pointing out a few examples of uncertainty in different project types, and these are outlined in Table 3.3.

In some cases, uncertainty can be estimated by probability calculations. For example, in many areas, seismic studies are essential to assess the earthquake risks for structures in an area. The seismic assessment in these cases may conclude that either the area of interest is outside active earthquake zones and the chances of a dangerous earthquake are consequently low, or that it is inside an active earthquake zone and chances are high. Other uncertainties can be difficult to analyse through statistical methods. An example of this is the recent spike and general volatility in commodity markets such as oil and metals, which has a material influence on the profitability of projects.

Table 3.3 Example of uncertainty factors in projects; they can involve various opportunities (+) or risks (−)

Type of project	Uncertainty factors	Explanation
Construction project	Natural disaster (−)	During the execution period, a natural disaster happens which puts the project at risk
	Lowering of the price of concrete (+)	Lowering due to new competition leads to lowering of the total cost of the project
Software project	Changed needs (−)	In the middle of the execution period, new needs arise with the project buyer which call for a re-designing of the software
	30% faster production (+)	The programming proves simpler than was expected, and the progress of the project is faster than had been expected
Event project	Another event at the same time (−)	Another big event takes place at the same time, and competition in regard to attracting viewers is created
	Exchange rate changes (+)	Due to the exchange rate shifts, the performance fees for a foreign artist were less than expected
Product development project	The cost is 50% more than expected (−)	The cost in regard to the product development turns out to be more than was expected, due to an oversight and underestimation in the initial analysis
	Leads to development of new products (+)	In the product development project, ideas come up for new products that it would be possible to develop alongside the original product

What matters most in regard to the evaluation of uncertainty in a project is how information about potential risks or opportunities can lead to contingency planning and the execution of responsive action in the event of their occurrence. Let us first look at risk. How is it possible to respond to a risk in advance? To answer this question, it is necessary to examine how risk is assessed. When a risk associated with a specific event is studied, at least two factors must be analysed. One factor is the likelihood of the event occurring, and the other factor is the consequence of it to the project. The total risk consists of the interplay between these two factors. This interplay can be displayed in a graph, as shown in Figure 3.10.

In fact, other factors might also be taken into account, such as detectability and even controllability of the risk. But we will focus our attention here on likelihood and consequence.

Figure 3.10

Outline of consequences and likelihood in the evaluation of risk.

The focus here is directed on negative uncertainty – that is, risk factors or problems that can arise in the project. With regard to the graph, it is normal for those events that fall under the area "low risk" not to require specific actions. Events that fall under the area "high risk," and even under the area "average risk," do, however, require some form of risk control measures and monitoring. These control measures can include reducing the likelihood of events taking place and, by doing so, moving plots downward on the graph, or reducing their consequences and, hence, moving plots to the left of the graph.

We propose a four-step process for assessing project risk, as explained in Figure 3.11.

The process in Figure 3.11 can be seen as a risk management framework to ensure that risks are managed consistently and systematically, not only in the beginning stages of a project. The circumstances change, and the risk must be monitored and reassessed throughout the project life cycle. Such a risk management framework should be based on the risk management policy of the organisation, and possible industrial, national, or international standards.

In step 1, it is important to define the different occurrences or events with specific and descriptive titles. A database of risks for the organisation based on lessons learned, as described in Chapter 7, may be of help here. Also, write down how you would classify the occurrences in the PESTLE tool and whether they occur in the internal environment of the project or in the external environment.

In step 2, a risk matrix is used to assess the two independent variables for each event. The impact or consequences of the event for the progress and

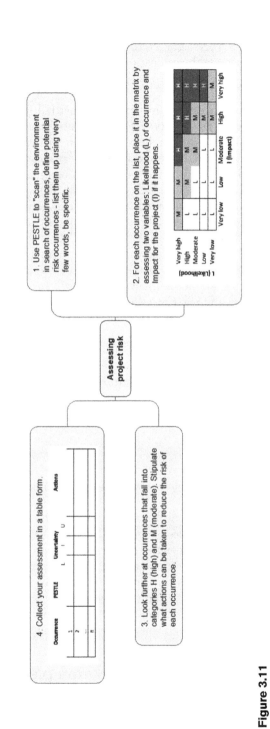

Figure 3.11

A process for the analysis of project risk.

results of the project are assessed, as well as the likelihood that the particular event will occur during the project. Both variables are assessed on a five-step scale, from "very low" to "very high." Note that, even though relevant statistics may be available to guide the evaluation of likelihood, it can be a largely subjective decision, and it is recommended that it be made by more than one experienced assessor.

Step 3 involves deeper investigation into events that fall into the categories H and M, according to the matrix. For these events, there is a reason to plan for action to be taken. A risk can be reduced by reducing the likelihood or mitigating the consequences. More specifically, the risk can be avoided or the likelihood reduced by planning the project in a certain way such that the source of the risk can be removed, the risk can be shared with another party, a contingency plan can be prepared, or the risk can simply be accepted. Whatever kind of action is planned, a brief description of this action should be given here.

Step 4 is to collect all the information from the risk analysis and document it in an organised way in a table format.

It should be noted that the above analysis of risk will reveal what events can threaten the project and what measures can be taken to address them. This information is crucial for any subsequent planning, including the making of a time schedule and a management plan.

Potential opportunities also need to be planned for so that one is in a position to harness them. This will also involve some predetermined course of action. In principle, the same process can be applied to analysing project opportunities.

Uncertainty management will be discussed in more detail in Chapter 7.

Reflection points

- Would you agree that creative thinking is more important in the early stages of a project than in its later stages? Why? If you don't agree, what are your arguments?
- Think of a project you know well and mirror it in the chart shown in Figure 3.5. Try to find examples of aspects that relate to the project – in all quadrants of the chart; inner and outer environment.
- Can you think of a project – either ongoing or concluded – where it was important to define outcomes that are not supposed to be a part of the project? Explain the case briefly and your arguments.
- What can be the downside of framing one's thinking of uncertainty around what can go wrong? Can you explain this, using a real example?

Combined environment analysis – example

A number of different approaches to environment analysis have been discussed in this chapter so far. Based on all the information gained from the

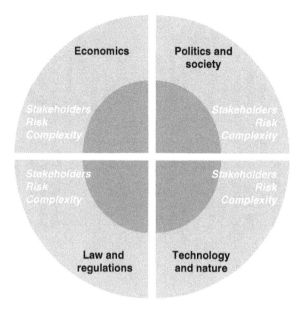

Figure 3.12

A visualisation of a combined analysis of the project environment.

Table 3.4 Analysis of project outcomes (scope) for aluminium dross recycling project. The analysis is based on the process shown in Figure 3.6 (I is Importance, U is Uncertainty, X, Y, and Z are classes of outcomes)

Outcome	Assessment			Observations regarding PM
	I	U	Class	
An operating plant with capacity to process dross from both smelters	High	Low	Y	Emphasis on this in the contract negotiations with the Austrian supplier
Closed process, no waste-product to landfill	High	High	X	The solution of this outstanding issue is a core activity for the project management
Good relationship with the local municipality	High	Low	Y	Be proactive in regular communication with the municipality
All official requirements fulfilled completely and on time	High	High	X	Core emphasis on getting overview of all requirements and setting up a plan to meet them
Full support from the investors throughout the project	Low	High	Z	Inform them regularly on the progress of the project

Table 3.5 Stakeholder analysis for aluminium dross recycling project. The analysis is based on the process shown in Figure 3.9

Agent	PESTLE	Reason	Power	Interest	Class	Attitude	Actions
Austrian vendor of equipment	Technology & nature (outer)	Provider of all machines and installation	H	L	B	Positive, want to deliver as promised	Thorough review of contract, regular status meetings
Environment agency	Technology & nature (outer)	Issues the operation permit	H	L	B	Neutral, want the company to follow law	Make sure that all regulations are followed
Owner of the building	Technology & nature (inner)	Leases building, prepares the building according to specs	H	H	A	Positive but also concerned about the operation	Close co-operation, regular status meetings
Founders of the company	Politics & society (inner)	The entrepreneurs of the company, with their vision	H	H	A	Positive – eager to see their vision materialise	Make sure that the original vision is maintained
New investors	Economics (inner)	Bring in new equity	–	L	D		
Bank	Economics (outer)	Lender of funds to finance the project	H	L	B	Want reassurance of project viability	Prepare a solid business plan according to the bank's requests
The local municipality government	Politics & society (outer)	Own the harbour and the industrial park	H	H	A	Eager to facilitate development of new industry	Keep informed with regular status meetings
The local health control agency	Law & regulations (outer)	Supervises industrial activities, receives complaints	L	H	C	Concerned about new industry	Meet with them to explain the project
Other companies in the industrial park	Politics & society (outer)	Can be opposed to the build-up of new industry in the park	L	H	C	Concerned about new industry	Meet with them to explain the project

Stakeholder	Category	Role / Description				Attitude	Action
People living in the neighbourhood	Politics & society (outer)	Can be opposed to the development of new industry in the park	L	H	C	Concerned about new industry	Meet with them to explain the project
Nature conservation association	Politics & society (outer)	Are very active and visible in public discussion	H	H	A	Generally opposed to the build-up of new industry	Meet with them to explain the project
Administration of occupational safety and health	Law & regulations (outer)	Issues internal operating permit	H	L	B	Neutral, want the company to follow law	Make sure that all regulations are followed
Main technical consultant and project manager	Technology & nature (outer)	Project management and technical supervision on behalf of the company	H	H	A	Takes professional pride in the project, wants to get paid	Give him necessary authority, provide active sponsorship
The CEO of the company	Economics (inner)	Financial responsibility for the project	H	H	A	Is somewhat concerned about closing the project financially	Prepare a solid business plan and a cash flow plan

Table 3.6 Uncertainty analysis for aluminium dross recycling project. The analysis is based on the process shown in Figure 3.11

Occurrence	PESTLE	Uncertainty			Actions
		L	I	U	
Damage of equipment during transport to factory location	Technology & nature (inner)	Mod	High	M	Get insurance quotes and take the most favourable offer asap
Problems in the set-up and the start-up of the factory	Technology & nature (inner)	Mod	V high	H	Remove any doubt in regard to the responsibility of the supplier in the contract
Negative currency fluctuation	Economics (outer)	High	High	H	Get a business bank to evaluate the benefits of securing the exchange rate
The set-up time is overscheduled – the factory may be ready earlier than planned (opportunity)	Technology & nature (inner)	Low	Mod	L	
Delay in the service of loans	Economics (outer)	Mod	High	H	Frequent purposeful communications with loan providers
Problems due to finalisation of operation permit	Law & regulations (inner)	Mod	V high	H	Purposeful communication with Environmental Institute and the premise's owners
Sellers of equipment and technology want to show other potential buyers the new factory (opportunity)	Technology & nature (inner)	Mod	Mod	M	Opportunity for co-operation and new business connections, react positively

project analysis, it is now possible to choose a project management approach and a general project execution architecture that have the highest probability of success.

For a more overall view, we can combine these elements with the PESTLE chart introduced in Figure 3.5, and an outline of this is shown in Figure 3.12. Here we show stakeholder, risk, and complexity elements in the different quadrants previously described, and this highlights where there are overlaps. A numbered list can be made, listing those factors, events, stakeholders, and sources of complexity that are important in the environment of the project,

Table 3.7 Complexity analysis for aluminium dross recycling project. The analysis is based on the process shown in Figure 3.7

Source	PESTLE	Account	Category	Assessment Level	Assessment Class	Actions
Many small investors	Economics (inner)	For a small company, the number of (small) investors is rather high	Organisational	Medium	B	More emphasis on providing regular project status (quarterly) and also well-prepared annual meetings.
Language barrier	Politics and society (inner)	Three languages, English, Icelandic, and German	Organisational	Medium	B	Define English as the official project language, all communication in English
Unresolved process steps	Technology and nature (inner)	The final process step is not yet finalised	Technical	High	A	This must be defined as a special phase in the project life cycle, engaging technical consultants and the equipment contractor.
Financial scope	Economics (inner)	This project is a financial "do or die" for the company	Resource	High	A	Prepare a detailed budget and a cash flow plan and control the budget carefully through the life cycle.
Many official agencies	Law and regulations (inner)	Official permits are issued by at least three agencies	Organisational	Medium	B	Regular meetings with all agencies and internal coordination, supervised by specifically appointed team member.

and each of these items can be reflected as a small number in the figure and explained very briefly to the side of it.

We can use Figure 3.12 as a reference for a more detailed analysis of elements in the project environment.

A real-life example of environment analysis that was carried out in project planning is shown in Table 3.4 (project outcomes), Table 3.5 (stakeholder analysis), Table 3.6 (uncertainty analysis), and Table 3.7 (complexity analysis). The background to this is that one of the present authors is a co-founder of a recycling company that was set up to process aluminium dross from two large aluminium producers in Iceland (Ingason & Sigfusson, 2010, 2014). In 2002, supply contracts were completed with these companies, while funding was finalised in early 2003. An order for machinery from an Austrian engineering company followed shortly afterwards, as well as the signing of a lease agreement for the new business premises. There was an agreed objective that the start of operation of the plant was to take place in November 2003, and Tables 3.4–3.7 show a part of the analysis that was conducted for the project in the spring of 2003 when the project plan was being prepared.

In this case, a combined analysis of the stakeholders, uncertainty, and complexity for the aluminium dross recycling project can be given as shown in Figure 3.13.

In Figure 3.13, and in general, most uncertainty factors fall into the economics, technology, and nature segments, while the stakeholders fall into all segments. Complexity is mostly linked with the inner environment of the project.

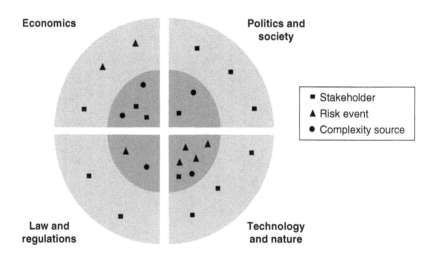

Figure 3.13

Combined analysis of project environment for aluminium dross recycling project. Boxes denote stakeholders, circles denote complexity, and triangles denote uncertainty.

Reflection points

- Look at all the analysis for the aluminium dross recycling project and write a list of the most important observations in terms of managing this project.
- How would the observations from above translate into the project plans?
- Look at the combined analysis in Figure 3.13. Does this representation tell you something new about the project?

Bibliography

Fangel, M. (2013). *Proactive Project Management – How to Make Common Sense Common Practice.* Hillerød, Denmark: Fangel Consulting.

Ingason, H.T., & Sigfusson, T.I. (2010). Maximizing industrial infrastructure efficiency in Iceland. *JOM, 62*(8), 43–49.

Ingason, H.T., & Sigfusson, T.I. (2014). Processing of aluminum dross: The birth of a closed industrial process. *JOM, 66*(11), 2235–2242.

Kerzner, H. (2017). *Project Management: A Systems Approach to Planning, Scheduling, and Controlling.* Hoboken: John Wiley & Sons.

Meredith, J.R., Shafer, S.M., Mantel Jr, S.J., & Sutton, M.M. (2016). *Project Management in Practice.* New York: Wiley Global Education.

Mikkelsen, H., & Riis, J.O. (2017). *Project Management: A Multi-Perspective Leadership Framework.* Bingley: Emerald Publishing Limited.

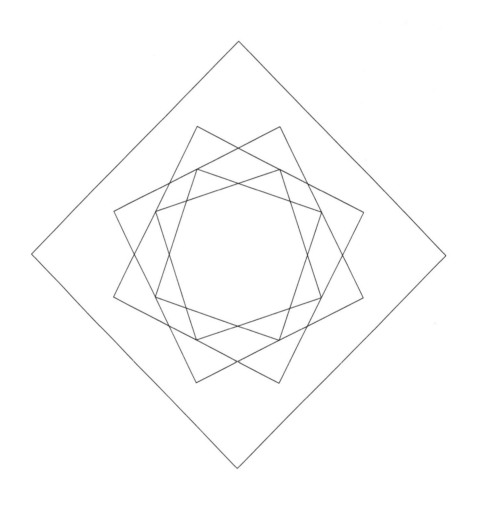

4 Planning: objectives, time, and the critical path

Objectives and their measurements

Goal setting is a prerequisite for success, and this simple truth is something which everyone can recognise when they think about it. The problem is, however, that many people do not think about it, and there are many people whose job it is to give lectures and workshops for the public to remind them that the premise for getting somewhere is to know where one is heading. One of these speakers is Brian Tracy (Brian Tracy International, n.d.). He teaches long and short courses where the emphasis is to point out to people the importance of documenting where they want to head in their personal and work life. Tracy says that the general public does not realise the importance of goal setting, i.e. does not understand that the premise of success is to define for oneself what wishes and expectations one has towards life. He also says that few know how to set goals – it is important that this is done in the correct manner – and believes that systematic goal setting will double the probability of success, but the goals must be measurable and preferably in writing. Tracy also observes that many people are afraid of criticism from their peers and are afraid to fail. He documents many cases in everyday life where people have controlled their fears and managed to achieve goals such as multiplying their yearly income within a few years. Goal setting can, however, be about many things other than physical objectives.

These general truths from everyday life also apply to projects. The same values apply when leaders of a project stand at square one and look ahead. The better idea that people have about what they want the project to yield, the greater the likelihood that this will be the result. Systematic goal setting is a key factor for the project to return what is expected of it. If you start without a goal, there is no way of knowing what the end result will be, nor the path that will be taken to achieve it. Goal setting is key to success in projects, as well as in everyday life.

It is useful to keep the term *value* in mind in this context. We define this term very generally as follows:

Value = Fulfilling of needs / Use of resources

The owners of the project will be aiming to maximise their value, and this can be done by fulfilling as many needs as possible while using the least amount of resources.

Traditional presentation of goals and success measurement

Objective or goal setting in a project involves defining characteristics of the outcome that is expected from a project. When looked at in detail, the potential benefits of a project can be numerous and diverse. Alongside this, there can be a significant variation in how clear an image people have at the start – of the actual results that the project should deliver, and this can depend on the type of project being conceived.

For example, a construction project such as the building of a cabin may begin with considering it to be a nice idea and a hazy notion of what can be afforded and how soon it could be completed. Once early planning work has been undertaken, including site surveying, and the design of the cabin and its utilities are described with drawings, then the outcome can be much better defined. A project plan can be developed that outlines the cost of work, details of work, and the sequencing of tasks to ensure maximum resource utilisation. In doing this, it is possible to define with some precision what funds are needed and when the cabin should be ready for use. These will then, most commonly, become the two main objectives in the project, i.e. to build this cabin within a budget of X and by the date Y. Other objectives can, of course, be added, such as only using locally derived materials or ensuring that the cabin has a certain high energy efficiency rating, etc.

If, on the other hand, the project is the development of a new drug, it is initially not known what its outcome will be. In fact, the starting point may only be that a need in the market has been identified, and that a successful breakthrough may have a certain ballpark value. Project definition and the setting of goals can, therefore, be unclear at the outset, and early concept work can have many dead ends. Even after successful initial concept development work, a prototype drug will have to undergo a series of controlled clinical trials with uncertain outcomes. Despite all the uncertainty, it is still necessary to set goals based on the knowledge that is present at a particular time in a project. In the case of drug development, this usually involves setting criteria for the statistical measurement of success and quite possibly having a series of milestones which demand that certain minimum requirements are to be met before proceeding with the next stage.

In all projects, it is important to go as far as possible in defining the characteristics of the outcome in the early stages. In this work, it can be beneficial to have a reference framework that acts as a guide in the setting of objectives. This will often begin with the desires of the project buyer or user needs and the resources available. This can help to provide detail for aspects of the overall framework, especially in regard to describing the nature and quality of the project products and the financing and timing requirements. It can often be that the setting of measurable objectives in this regard is a gradual, iterative process as various aspects of a project and their implications for the final outcome are considered in turn. There can be an element of snakes and ladders in this process as setbacks are encountered. For example, in the case of the summer cabin project described above, an early design may not be approved due to local planning restrictions.

The reference framework will also include aspects such as management structure, environment, health, and safety, and a series of objectives can be set for these areas, together with planned actions, in order that these objectives are met. The execution of a particular project can often be expected to increase knowledge levels in a company or organisation in a particular field, although this may not be included as a recognised product of a project. This outcome could be defined in advance and, if this is done correctly, it may greatly increase the chances of achieving objectives, not just in the particular project in question, but in future ones also.

The traditional representation of goals in projects is based on dividing them into three main categories:

- Performance of the project – including scope, specifications, and quality.
- Cost of the project.
- Time frame of the project.

In project management, these categories are often represented as corners of the so-called *Iron Triangle*, as shown in Figure 4.1. This representation was put forward by Dr Martin Barnes (Lock, 2017) and it emphasises that there is interplay and consequent balancing between these categories of objectives. In a particular project it might, for example, be the most important thing to complete it with minimal cost, but this focus could result in a reduced emphasis on the time objectives. In this case, the project could potentially be delayed

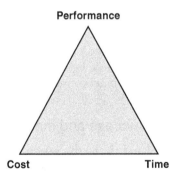

Performance

Cost   **Time**

Figure 4.1

Iron Triangle showing categories of objectives in projects.

if it is not time-prioritised, as people may work on it intermittently between carrying out other tasks.

The performance of a project has been referred to previously and can vary widely depending on the project type. It is normal in professional projects for there to be a list of specifications and quality standards for a product of a project, and fulfilling these is an important objective, as well as meeting time and cost demands. Project planning should take into account how the quality requirements and quality standards applicable to the project and its deliverables are to be fulfilled. The project quality management describes how this is planned, but also controlled and managed through continuous review during the project. Quality audits can play an important part here – they are important in the context of quality assurance and they determine the performance of the project quality management.

A greater emphasis on project cost might mean that the demands for functionality and quality of the solution might be reduced. This approach is formalised in areas such as value engineering and planned obsolescence and will depend on the judgement of the project manager, after listening to expert advice if considered necessary. A common issue in this regard for construction projects can be to decide what materials to use in structures, as they will have different properties (e.g. strength, corrosion, resistance, etc.), as well as different costs, with higher durability normally associated with higher costs. In areas such as aircraft or ship construction, one will find a high degree of specifications in what is allowed in terms of construction materials and methods, regardless of the costs, and regulations are strictly enforced.

> An example of a project (or programme) where time was the main driving factor was in the preventative fixes that were implemented worldwide in computer systems in anticipation of the potential so-called Y2K problem. This originated from the use of two (rather than four) digits to convey a year in earlier programming in order to save on memory requirements and had been identified by some computer programmers long before it became more widely recognised in the middle of the 1990s. There was a high level of uncertainty as the year 2000 approached, and many large companies ended up paying large amounts of money (hundreds of billions of US dollars globally) in order to hire computer programming experts and meet the strict time deadline. If we look at this overall episode as one giant project, we could portray it as shown in Figure 4.2, where time is clearly the dominant consideration in the setting of objectives.

Project management success and measurement scale

An important concept related to the discussion of goals or objectives is the measurement of the success of a project and its management. This will involve the establishment of success criteria by which progress is measured and should be done alongside the setting of goals and objectives in early project planning. Success criteria can be formal – addressing the stated project objectives – and

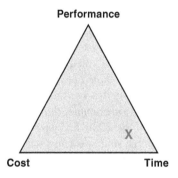

Performance

Cost   X   **Time**

Figure 4.2

Project management view of the Y2K phenomenon as a giant project.

informal, and they are used by the stakeholders to rate and judge the success of the project.

Success measurement scales should be determined at the outset of a new project and be able to provide an accurate assessment of performance. It is important that they are defined clearly and unambiguously and that they are tailored to the needs of each project. As a simple example, if it is defined as a goal in a particular project that the product of the project will be complete in 12 months, then the measure of success will be how close to this target date the product was completed in the end. Was the project perhaps completed in 11 months instead of 12? Or was it completed in 13 months? In a similar manner, the success measurement scale can be defined in relation to other objectives defined in the project, such as being completed under budget or exceeding quality specifications. It is important to bear in mind that "project success" and "project management success" are two separate things. This distinction is evident in projects where the project management went according to plan, but the technical objectives of the project were not achieved. Likewise, one may think of a project in which management was erratic and poorly executed, but the project, nevertheless, ultimately gave the outcomes expected. In all of this, there may be reasonable explanations, and luck can also play its part.

In otherwise lengthy projects and/or those that involve several identifiable phases, it can be useful to have measurable milestones which point the way towards successful completion of the overall project. These can be important elements, as project-related payment schedules can often be linked to achieving milestone requirements. Other payment-related factors such as bonus or penalty clauses in contracts require that success is well defined and measured. The concept of goal setting in projects encourages the defining of goals in a measurable manner, as long as this is possible. The reality is that in very many cases, it is possible to quantify goals, and this should be done if at all possible. Numerical targets are, in general, more decisive than goals in the form of text.

A simple illustration of this would be if advocates of a project set themselves a goal of "finishing the project as soon as possible" or "completing the project within six months." The flaws in relation to this representation are obvious. What does "as soon as possible" mean? What date do they have in mind when they say that the project should be completed within six months? In this example, it would be very easy to set out measurable objectives in a clear and decisive manner by saying, for example, that the project should be completed no later than the first of June 2021. Likewise, a major focus is often on the financial aspects of projects, and advocates will agree on the goal of delivering the project "with the lowest cost possible." Again, we are looking at a poor representation of goals, as there is no way to measure success against this statement as it does not provide a clear guide. Cost is a very measurable dimension and, if it matters in the project, there is a need for it to be framed clearly in the project plan that is to be followed. The advocates of a particular project could therefore say that the total cost of the project should be aimed at 1 million GBP. That presentation is simple and decisive.

When an objective is defined at the beginning of a project in a numerical way, then it is also possible to define the expectations that people have regarding the final outcome, from the lowest expectations to the highest expectations. This concept is shown graphically in Figure 4.3, where the meter relates to a specific objective, and actual success is measured using the scale shown from the lowest expectations to the highest. A full project assessment might consist of a large number of these meters and could be considered to be analogous to a pilot looking at his flight instruments during the flying of an aeroplane.

It is good to clearly understand underlying concepts when discussing success measurement scales. Lim and Mohamed (1999) emphasised the differences between the terms "criteria" and "factors" in goal setting in projects. Criteria are defined as a set of standards upon which a judgement or decision can be based. Factors, on the other hand, are defined as situations or influences that are relevant to outcomes. "Critical factors" are then those factors that are most important, but they should not be confused with standards. In the text below, however, the term is used for criteria and vice versa.

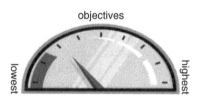

Figure 4.3

Measurement of success relating to a particular objective.

More modern presentation of objectives and success measurement scale

Many have criticised the traditional presentation of the objectives in projects, which are presented in Figure 4.1, and there is a large body of literature covering this aspect. Turner et al. (1996) argue that although the key factors for the criteria of success in projects are normally "on time, within budget allocations and according to the original technical definition," this viewpoint applies, first and foremost, to the viewpoint of contractors, and there is also a need for other viewpoints to be taken into account. Wateridge (1998) concludes that six measurement scales of success in projects can be defined.

- The project delivers profit to the owner and contractors.
- The project achieves the business purpose that was defined.
- The project reaches its set objectives.
- The project is delivered within the technical criteria frame in regard to the function of the solution.
- The project is delivered according to definition, within the financial frame, and on schedule.
- All concerned are happy during the project and about what comes out of the project. This refers to the users, the managers who are behind the project – its backers – and the project group.

Lim and Mohamed (1999) point out that when a project is finished, the usage stage of the product, which involves the ultimate test for the original purpose of the project, takes over. They point out that users will emphasise that the results match the results that were aimed for, or even better, and that this matters more to them than the criteria about finishing the project on time and within budget. There are examples where users are willing to forgive and forget large deviations in regard to this if they are sufficiently satisfied with the result. An example of this is the Opera House in Sydney previously described. Related to this idea, Fangel (2013) has made a distinction between the goals that relate to the project itself and the impacts that the product of the project is to achieve, and Shenhar et al. (2001) describe performance in projects in four main categories over four different time scales, as shown in Figure 4.4.

The above presentation shows that success measurement scales operate on a number of different levels, and it cannot be estimated whether full success has been obtained until a project is finished, even though a project has been delivered satisfactorily according to traditional criteria. Over time, project success measurement will become more and more apparent as the product is put to use, and one can see how this is viewed by users and affects the future status of the project owner. These criteria are most often not measurable until after a substantial passage of time and are therefore hardly usable as criteria for the performance of projects. They can, however, have a major bearing on longer-term considerations such as reputation. It should be recognised also

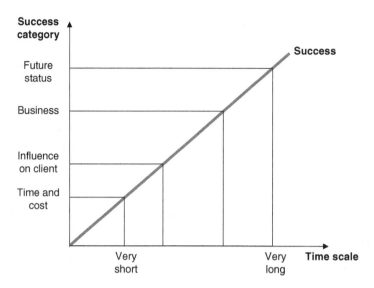

Figure 4.4

Success of projects and time frame.

that greater emphasis is now given to the importance of the participants in the project – those who prepare the project and execute it – who have a direct interest in the success of the project. The interests of the participants and the project advocates should coincide in this respect and, to ensure this, the intertwining of these interests should be jointly considered when the project objectives are being defined. By doing this, increased commitment of the participants to the project can be fostered, and their motivational levels to carry out tasks greatly improved.

In the light of these discussions, it is possible to broaden the concept behind the triangle in Figure 4.1 so that it better covers the modern representation of objectives and success measurement scales of projects. To do this, the desired outcomes of a project can be defined initially in terms of the following three different viewpoints: (1) in terms of specified objectives and the desired outcome of the project itself, (2) its impact or business objectives, and (3) the objectives of the participants. In all of these dimensions, the three basic categories of objectives shown in Figure 4.1 (i.e. time, cost, and performance) can be considered. This is shown graphically in Figure 4.5.

In all projects, it is necessary to define the outcome from as many angles as possible. This can be done by considering the three dimensions, along with the traditional main categories of objectives. The focus on the three dimensions can of course be very varied between projects. By far, the most common dimension of interest relates to the outcome and the different objectives that have been set in this regard. In a normal construction project, another dimension will reflect the interests of the contractor who has made a contract about

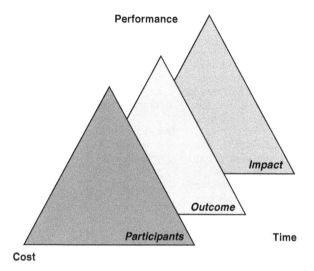

Figure 4.5

Main categories of objective in three dimensions.

the specific execution and needs to deliver a project on time that complies with quality measures and is within the cost frame that was negotiated. The project buyer will have the same interests as the developer in this respect but will also be very interested in the last dimension – the impact of the outcome of the project. The dimension that involves the participants in the project reflects a new way of thinking that has developed in recent times and is widely considered to be a good indicator of success in projects. The idea is, as previously stated, that in order to succeed in a particular project, the needs and interests of the individuals linked with the project need to be considered as part of the project objectives. This can energise and unite the workforce as they carry out their tasks, and a good system of communication and feedback is a key element of this approach. Further explanations and examples of objectives that belong to each dimension are outlined in Table 4.1.

In the late 1990s, ferro-silicon manufacturer Icelandic Alloys Ltd. (now Elkem Iceland, a part of China National Bluestar) decided to increase their production capacity at their factory in Grundartangi, north of Reykjavik, by 60%. This overall objective included a number of individual objectives, e.g. the addition of a third large furnace, a new storage space and transport systems, and strengthening the management and operational structure of the company. The first phase of the project was a definition phase; gathering information about the needs, equipment, manufacturers, and contractors so that decisions could be made about the next steps. Icelandic Alloys hired Tryggvi Sigurbjarnarson, a consulting engineer, to be the project manager in the first phase of this project. Sigurbjarnarson had to assemble a project team and approached

Table 4.1 Examples of objectives relating to the three project dimensions

Objective	Participants	Outcome	Impact
Financial objectives	Financial criteria of the participants that are related to their work in the project	Cost of the project, financial frame which has been set for the project	Yield that is obtained from the operation of the project's outcome
Time objectives	Use of the participants' time, e.g. avoiding too much stress, flexible work time, loss of business due to overruns, etc.	Milestones in the project and final delivery at a particular time	When should the effect of the outcome's use become noticeable?
Performance	Ability, knowledge and experience of participants, new and improved business connections, standing in their professional field including reputation	Characteristics of the project's product, description of the product – can also refer to safety matters and potential patent(s)	Description of what the outcome should return – can also refer to the company's or institute's image, knowledge within it and business connections

Dr. Helgi Thor Ingason (co-author of this book), who was his former student at the University of Iceland and worked in the research and development department of Icelandic Alloys at that time. Tryggvi requested that Helgi should become the assistant project manager and said to him: "You might not necessarily gain anything in particular at the end, but this project is very large, and you have the opportunity to gain both knowledge and experience in project management – a subject that I know you are very interested in. When this ends, it is quite possible that a new and exciting career may open for you." The expansion project was completed in the autumn of 1999, and some of the objectives of Iceland Alloys were met. The project, however, represented a turning point for Helgi, as project management became his field of practice and research.

Method for defining objectives

During the planning stages of projects, when objectives are in the process of becoming defined, it is possible to use Figure 4.6 as a structural guide to define and develop the project goal hierarchy. This is based on the dimensions that we have discussed.

The starting point is, of course, the information at hand; for example, the basic project idea from the project charter and information from the project analysis. Primarily, the setting of objectives should be in alignment with the scope definition, which reflected the prioritisation of needs.

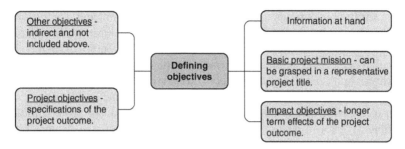

Figure 4.6

Structural guide to define a project goal hierarchy. Start with the information at hand (top right) and end with other objectives (top left).

The project mission or a project mission statement should be defined. This can already be grasped in a representative project title, but if not, it is worth some effort to think of a short and concise representation of the basic project mission.

Impact objectives reflect the longer-term effects that the project outcome will lead to. These might also be called organisational goals, and they reflect how the underlying needs of the stakeholders will be met. Some general examples of such impact objectives might be market share, profit, unemployment rate, CO_2 emissions, client satisfaction, or literacy rate. A table format (see Table 4.2) should be used to capture the impact objectives in a structured way.

Each impact objective gets one row in the table. For each objective, the row in the table is filled out as follows:

Column 1 is for defining and describing the objective briefly in words. It is necessary to be specific and, if possible, define the objective in such a way that it can be represented numerically. The appropriate unit of measurement for the objective is shown in Column 2. Column 3 outlines the maximum expectations for the objective – this is the best potential performance that is possible to achieve for this specific objective. Column 4 outlines the minimum expectations for objectives – these are the minimum performance or levels that are required to avoid negative reviews.

Project objectives or project goals are the specifications of the outcome of the project. These could be seen as a description of what is to be the tangible

Table 4.2 Capturing impact objectives in a table format

Definition of impact objectives	Further description (if necessary)	Numerical representation (if possible)	Maximum expectation	Minimum expectation
1				
2				
...				
n				

or intangible outcome of the project when it is completed. Project objectives could be the project budget or the project duration, but also the technical specifications of the project outcome. Examples of such technical specifications could be flexibility, efficiency, performance, capacity, throughput, size, volume, or safety. The same table format as before is used to capture the project objectives in a structured way.

Other objectives are consequential benefits, side effects of the project, indirect objectives, and items not included as either impact or project objectives. These are positive effects of the project, and by defining them and including them formally as objectives, they will potentially be achieved. Examples of other objectives could be the image of the organisation, knowledge level within the organisation, project management competence of the project team, and, last but not least, objectives that have to do with personal interests of the project team members. The same table format as before is used to capture the project objectives in a structured way.

The Icelandic men's football team participated in the World Cup in Russia in the summer of 2018, and the team's participation in the competition could be viewed as a project with defined objectives made in the planning stages. To explain this, a hypothetical description of their starting objectives is given in the following example.

Basic project mission: To reach the Round of 16 in the FIFA World Cup in Russia in 2018 (see Tables 4.3, 4.4, and 4.5).

In this example, the difference between impact objectives and project objectives should be noted. The success of the team could have a significant impact on the development of the sport in Iceland by increasing the number of participants and watchers and by making it easier for the team to receive funds in the future. Here, we are talking about impact objectives, and it will not be clear if these objectives will be reached until sometime after the tournament ends. Project objectives, on the other hand, are limited to the actual contest,

Table 4.3 Hypothetical impact objectives for Iceland in FIFA World Cup in Russia in 2018

Definition of impact objectives	Unit of measurement	Maximum expectation	Minimum expectation
Number of football players in Iceland	Increase in a year in %	25%	5%
Increased attendance at football games in Iceland	Increase in a year in %	40%	10%
Increased level of sponsorship of the national football team	Increase in a year in %	100%	30%
Financial support of local football clubs in Iceland	Increase in a year in %	20%	5%

Table 4.4 Hypothetical project objectives for Iceland in FIFA World Cup in Russia in 2018

Definition of project objectives	Numerical representation (if possible)	Maximum expectation	Minimum expectation
Success of the team	Place	Quarter finals	16th place
Fund-raising due to participation	Obtaining of grants	All costs	50% of costs
Injury amongst the team players	Injured players upon home return	0	0
Icelandic players chosen for team of tournament	Number of players	2	0
Prize money	USD million	22	8

and it was immediately clear at the end of it whether they had been achieved. Participants in the project are defined as those who are directly linked with the team, and constitute a wider group that would include, amongst others, the people working for the Icelandic National Broadcasting Service – RUV – who broadcasted the games directly from Russia. The success of the overall project is in part dependent on how well RUV conducts their broadcast to garner the support of the nation for the team. RUV also has a vested interest in getting as many viewers as possible for their own business objectives, including advertising revenue.

Reflection points

- Do you relate to the statement regarding personal goal setting? Think about your own goal setting in view of this text.
- With reference to the *Iron Triangle*, think of a project where cost was the dominant consideration in the setting of an objective. Then think

Table 4.5 Hypothetical other objectives for Iceland in FIFA World Cup in Russia in 2018

Definition of other objectives	Numerical representation (if possible)	Maximum expectation	Minimum expectation
Players and trainers offered professional contracts	Number of players that receive new offers	6	2
Average viewing of live broadcasts	% of the nation	75%	25%
Image of Icelandic supporters	Number of negative news about Icelandic supporters in Russia	0	0

of another project where performance was the dominant consideration. How was this apparent?

- Review the case of the Sydney Opera House from Chapter 2 in view of the three dimensions of objectives in Figure 4.5 and Table 4.1.
- Look at the hypothetical objectives for Iceland in the FIFA World Cup in Russia. Can you reflect on the actual outcome in the light of these objectives? Can you think of any other hypothetical objectives and place them in the different categories: impact objectives, project objectives, or other objectives?

Master plan and work breakdown structure

Once the characteristics of the expected outcomes of a project have been defined and the environment of the project has been analysed, we then reach the core of planning, which is how to realise the objectives that have been set. In this regard, timing is a fundamental aspect of projects, and this is reflected in its position as one of the three corners in the *Iron Triangle*. It is closely related to cost, as time overruns in project completion are invariably associated with higher costs, and it is taken as a given that project buyers are looking to complete projects in as short a time as possible, although not at the expense of defined quality standards. In order to achieve this, it is necessary to review the full scope of work that needs to be carried out at the early planning stages of a project. The overall work required can then be divided into a series of distinct work units that together combine to give the desired result. Such project structure is commonly called work breakdown structure (WBS), which includes an overall division followed by sub-divisions, and the WBS defines the work required to produce the project deliverables (IPMA, 2015; APM, 2012). The WBS is one of the most important elements in project management. Through this, the relationship between different work units, their estimated time for completion, and the need for sequencing can be analysed, and the most effective time pathways for project completion can be identified.

The division of overall work requirements in a project can become complex, depending on its scope, and can often involve several sub-divisions into work units. This book will use the terms "work parts," "tasks," and "work packages" in this context. We will talk about a specific project being initially divided into phases (if required), then into main tasks or tasks, and, finally, each of these can be sub-divided into work packages. The term "master plan" is useful as a framework for the breakdown of the project. The master plan of a project includes the following:

- The presentation of the project life cycle and its main milestones from beginning to end.
- The systematic breakdown of the project into distinct work units.

- Decisions on the nature of individual pathways in the project, including related work packages and tasks and their internal logical connection.
- Graphical presentation of the time schedule of the project, which is based on the above elements.

From this list, it can be seen that the creation of the master plan involves gaining a good overall understanding of the project, its main phases, its work breakdown structure, and the connections between its largest work units. Outlining the master plan involves mapping the big steps in the project. Another related term – detailed plan – is used for the mapping of smaller steps in the project. When working on the outline of the master plan, it is necessary to consider some important points:

- In most cases, certain critical timings will have been defined, for example, when the project is to be completed. The outline of the master plan takes these time scales into consideration.
- In a small project, the objectives can be simple and clear. In larger projects, products are delivered, and decisions are made continuously throughout the whole lifetime of the project. It is good to document clearly the products to be delivered and which decisions are made at each stage of the project.
- Keep in mind the scope definition – this needs to be aligned with the master plan because structuring the project scope entails a systematic division of the project content into work units.
- It always needs to be kept in mind that there may be circumstances where it is desirable to make fundamental changes to the project, delay it, or even to stop it.
- There can often be many people involved in decision-making in projects. It is then common at critical moments in the project for there to be a need to ensure the approval of multiple stakeholders before it is possible to continue. While developing the master plan, it is important to consider that it can take time to produce results and make interim decisions in projects. This time is often longer than expected.
- What happens if a dispute among those who commit to the project occurs, or with important stakeholders in the project environment? This can affect the whole progress of the project, and during the making of the master plan it is prudent to anticipate responses to this. How to react to conflicts will be further discussed later in the book.

Now we will look at the principal aspects of the master plan.

Phases and milestones

We have already discussed the concept of a project life cycle. In all plan making, it is important that each part of a project can be placed in the overall context of the project. The first step in determining the master plan of a project is therefore to consider a suitable phase division and to outline where these divisions are within the project's life cycle. In this way, you can get a good feeling for the main work segments of the project. This makes what comes after – a more detailed work breakdown and the development of a holistic time schedule – easier. As has been mentioned before, there is no single correct representation of the phases and lifetime of a project – this presentation must be based on the nature of each project. For example, two experienced project managers can present two different master plans for a single project and both can be usable and correct. The difference between them is that people who have different experiences and knowledge create them. The transitions between different phases within projects can be described as milestones, and in many cases major decisions that can affect the entire project are taken upon reaching milestones.

For each project, the appropriate stage approach should be chosen, for example, the life cycle model and number of phases. A traditional linear approach or waterfall approach may be proper in some projects while an iterative or spiral approach may be proper in other projects. Reference is made to a discussion on the project life cycle in Chapter 2. A common set of project phases is as follows:

- Definition
- Planning
- Execution
- Handover – product delivery

These phases together delineate the life cycle of projects. For example, we can look at a construction project which involves the building of a new company headquarters. The life cycle of this project could be as shown in Figure 4.7. The definition phase is rather short – the company has a simple management structure and can be quick to make a decision. The black triangle at the

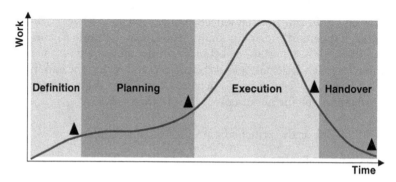

Figure 4.7

Project life cycle and phases for the construction of an office building.

end of the definition phase reflects the first *milestone* – the phase ends with the decision to proceed with the project. Then, planning, design, and needs analysis are undertaken, and tender documents are produced. The phase ends by reaching an agreement with a contractor on the basis of an offer made, and the resultant contract is the second milestone in the project. This is represented by the second black triangle. The actual execution is completed when the developer and the buyer agree that the former has returned the building according to the contract, and that the building is ready for use (third triangle). The final stage of the project involves the handover of the work and the start of operations. It also includes the settling of the project finances and is completed when the full use of the building has begun (fourth triangle).

A well-known musician giving a concert is an example of an event project. In such a project, the life cycle can look somewhat different, as shown in Figure 4.8, even though it contains the same main phases as described for the previous example. The definition phase involves, amongst other things, the reaching of an agreement with the musician or his agents about the timing of the concert, fees, and facilities that the musician needs to have in association with the event. The planning phase may take a long time and requires the concert organiser to make agreements on, for example, stage facilities and security arrangements that they have to provide according to the contract with the musicians. This will also be the stage when most of the ticket sales are likely to occur, and there may commonly be a milestone included whereby a certain number of tickets need to be sold before a final decision is made to host the event. The actual execution phase happens over a very short time compared with the planning phase and includes aspects such as the construction of the stage and erection of the sound system, as well as the staging of the actual concert. The execution phase is completed when the musician has sung their last song and the audience have left the venue. The final product delivery involves the clean-up phase and the settling of payments.

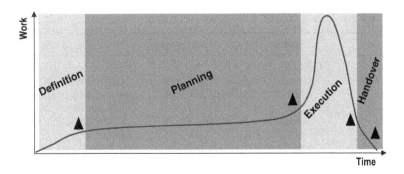

Figure 4.8

Project life cycle and phases for a concert.

In the earliest stages of planning, it is a very useful exercise to outline the life cycle of a project and to define its main phases within the context of time estimates and dates. In most cases, important deadlines have been determined for when the product of the project is to be in full use. Having defined timing makes the pictorial presentation of the project's life cycle more focused and gives a better overview of the project to facilitate further planning. It is good to also construct a table that provides an overview of the phases and the milestones related to them, including the results or deliverables from each phase. This can include the criteria for decision-making between the different phases, and an exemplary template is shown in Table 4.6.

Main tasks, tasks, and work packages

The next level (or levels) of division in a project, after separation into phases, involves recognising distinct work units. These units are within each of the phases and they are called main tasks. Moving on, we separate the main tasks into tasks (or activities), and the final work unit is the so-called work package. An example of a main task in the master plan for a motorway construction project would be the road grading prior to the placing of the bitumen surface, whereas another main task in the same project would be the installation of noise barriers. It can be seen that the former is part of a necessary overall logical sequence within the project, with later tasks depending upon its completion, whereas the latter can be considered a stand-alone project that only needs to be completed within the overall project time.

One of the basic elements of planning in projects is to define the scope of the project, which includes defining the different work that needs to be completed in order to deliver the desired project outcome. It is important to carry out this breakdown as part of the detailed planning of the execution phase, as it will shed light on the feasibility of the desired project timeline and the requirements for project organisation, including the formation of work teams and the allocation of budgets and resources. In more complex projects, it is

Table 4.6 Overview of phases in a project

Phases	Phase results or deliverables	Decisions
Definition	Overview of the results that are produced in this phase of the project; of what type are they?	Overview of decisions which need to be made at the end of this phase
Planning	Overview of the results that are produced in this phase	Decisions which need to be made at the end of this phase
Execution	Overview of the results that are produced in this phase	Decisions which need to be made at the end of this phase
Product delivery	Overview of the results that are produced in this phase	Decisions which need to be made at the end of this phase

also an essential step in recognising the necessary sequencing of work that needs to be carried out.

As previously described, in construction projects (and other types) it is common that the buyer hires a contractor to carry out the necessary work. As part of this process, the project buyer needs to define what they want from the contractor, and this information is set out in the tender documents that include drawings, quantity lists, procedures, and work descriptions. This defines the scope of the project and, if it is not properly done, there is a risk that the project expands and becomes more time-consuming and more resource demanding and costly than was originally intended. Unforeseen circumstances can occur in projects that incur extra costs and can cause disputes between project buyers and contractors over who has responsibility for this. The contractor might consider a particular work package he is asked to carry out in conjunction with the project to be additional, or outside of the contract, and that it would need to be paid for separately. The project buyer might look at this differently – in his opinion, the work package was within the contract and therefore there should be no additional payment. It is, therefore, important that there is a clear understanding of what the scope of the project is, including all the work packages and contingency planning. This should be defined in writing as thoroughly as the complexity level and the size of the project warrant. For example, a contractor on the motorway construction project may encounter poor ground conditions that require lengthy and costly stabilisation works. If not covered by the contract, such a situation can quickly descend into a pitched legal battle between the contractor and the project buyer.

The division of the overall work required to complete the project into tasks or work packages can be analogous to the design of a building, as shown in Figure 4.9. Here, we see the gradual design emerging with simple line drawings at the outset, followed by a series of intermediate stages of increasing detail, and then the final image showing a complete design. In defining a project, we create an image of the final desired product that may be clear or fuzzy, and then need to work back and determine how we can achieve this. This involves a systematic analysis of all the required tasks, as well as their structuring.

In Figure 4.9, rough outlines of the house are drawn up at the beginning that show the overall perspective and delineate the main structure by showing where the different individual elements lie in relation to each other. In the next layers, detail is added to the picture, step-by-step, in a way that shows the correct perspective. In doing this, the drafter never loses the overview of the project. If, from the outset, the drafter was to focus on drawing a particular window of the building in great detail, it is then likely that this will lead to an imbalance of forms in the final drawing, and it will be a poor representation as a result (or a failure in terms of project success).

The same basic rules apply to the activity breakdown of a project, where the most important thing is not to lose the overview. The breakdown of a project defines what is required to create the products of the project. Projects

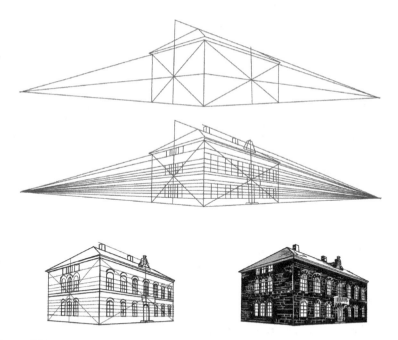

Figure 4.9

Work breakdown analogy – progression of building design from initial perspective drawing to final detail.

are broken down in a process involving layers, just as the drawings of the building are created in a layered process. Meredith et al. (2016) suggest that in each layer, an item should be broken into no less than 2, and no more than 20, work parts. First, a project should be broken down into at least two main parts: project management and project work. Such a breakdown is particularly useful to illustrate the separation of management work and substantive work in the project. Figure 4.10 shows a traditional example of a simple breakdown

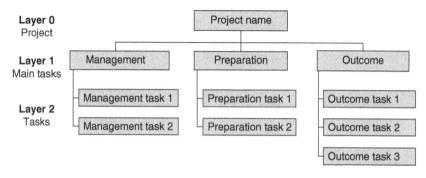

Figure 4.10

Breakdown of a project – traditional presentation.

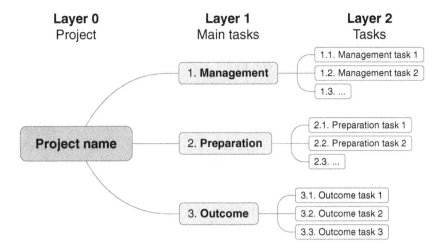

Layer 0
Project

Layer 1
Main tasks

Layer 2
Tasks

1. **Management**
- 1.1. Management task 1
- 1.2. Management task 2
- 1.3. ...

Project name

2. **Preparation**
- 2.1. Preparation task 1
- 2.2. Preparation task 2
- 2.3. ...

3. **Outcome**
- 3.1. Outcome task 1
- 3.2. Outcome task 2
- 3.3. Outcome task 3

Figure 4.11

Breakdown of a project into two layers.

structure. In this case, there are three main tasks: management, preparation, and the outcome itself. These main sections are then divided further into tasks.

It may be useful to use mind maps to present information related to planning in projects, and Figure 4.11 shows the same information from the previous figure rearranged in the form of a mind map. Attention is drawn to the numbering system for work items, as shown in the picture. Such numbering can be very useful in further planning, for example, when it comes to assessing the need for resources and compiling the costs of individual parts and of the project as a whole.

The presentation shown above can also be reduced to one layer, as shown in Figure 4.12. This should be sufficient for simple projects, such as the one shown where there are seven main factors.

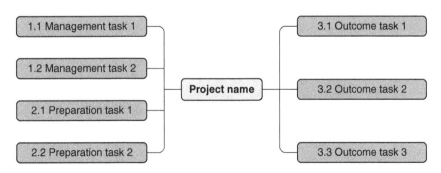

- 1.1 Management task 1
- 1.2 Management task 2
- 2.1 Preparation task 1
- 2.2 Preparation task 2

Project name

- 3.1 Outcome task 1
- 3.2 Outcome task 2
- 3.3 Outcome task 3

Figure 4.12

Breakdown of a project into one layer.

In this case, there is no need for further breakdown, and each of the seven tasks becomes a separate work package. In terms of the range of work elements that are likely to be encountered while performing the breakdown of a project, these can have several forms. For one, we can look at the management of a project as a distinct main task or process parallel to the execution works throughout the life cycle of a project. This management process may, in turn, be broken down into a series of sub-components covering different work areas. The act itself of making a project plan falls under the category of management and is a defined main task. Monitoring of execution is another main task, as is updating the project plan in response to changing circumstances. From a management perspective, the important aspect in this is that the administration units are sufficiently large and well-resourced to deal with the main tasks that they have to oversee, and that each project will have different features in this regard. The range of main tasks will usually be split into different areas of required expertise, with specialists performing the works on a contractual basis. The final work packages need to be sufficiently small for it to be possible to estimate the required time and resources for their completion with satisfactory accuracy. Some illustrative examples are discussed.

The environmental analysis carried out at the beginning of the planning process should yield results that can be used directly in the breakdown of the project. The tables for analysis of stakeholders, uncertainty, complexity, and major products that we have already described include a column for actions, and these tasks will become important elements of the master plan of the project. It is a good rule, therefore, to review the analysis of the environment when projects are being broken down. Figure 4.13 reflects this context.

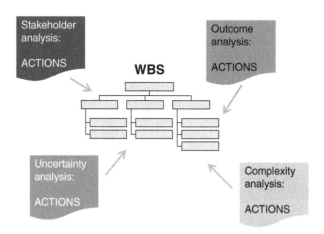

Figure 4.13

Analysis of the environment and related actions as important factors in the breakdown of a project.

As an example of the breakdown of a simple project, we can refer to the building of a cabin which was previously mentioned. In Figure 4.14, a simple presentation of the breakdown of such a project is shown. Here the project is broken down into five main tasks, which represent the necessary categories of the overall project work. These are then each broken down further into tasks in the second layer, as indicated. As an example, the project management is broken down into planning, making of contracts, and finally supervision and monitoring, while the groundwork is divided into road laying, brick work (for front lawn), and finally soil improvements. And so it continues for all the different main tasks, and more can be added, or else they can be further divided into a third layer and so on.

There are a number of ways to go about breaking down a project. One way is to look at the project breakdown in the context of time through phases, sub-phases, and milestones, similar to Figure 4.14. Another way is to look at the breakdown from the divisions or departments which are involved in the project (see Figure 4.15). If the project involves, e.g. setting up a new information system in the marketing department of a company, then it could be broken down into the financial department, the technical department, and the marketing department – in the first management layer. Then it would be continued in the second management layer with actions, e.g. by breaking the financial department into needs analysis, financial estimation, and documentation.

Another way to break down projects would be to look at the final products that come out of them. For example, it is not uncommon for a PhD project to be written up in the form of several published papers that cover different aspects of the total work carried out, and these can be planned in advance and the time and resources allocated in this manner. Overall, the approach to project breakdown chosen depends on the nature of each project and the working style of the project manager. In all cases, it has to be ensured that the breakdown is done in sufficient detail, but not taken further than that. If it is possible to get by with a breakdown into 20 tasks or work packages – which represent the most suitable administrative units – it is not necessary to go further and break it down into 40 or 200 work packages. This can only serve to increase the levels of complexity for the management, which is most likely to lead to increased costs and may even affect the quality of the product.

Scheduling

For each task or activity, the effort and duration necessary to realise the task must be determined. The allocation and distribution of resources are closely linked with scheduling; what resources are needed for each task and in what quantity. In preparing the schedule, it is good to keep in mind that it is, by nature, a control tool to achieve a specified performance, usually in terms of

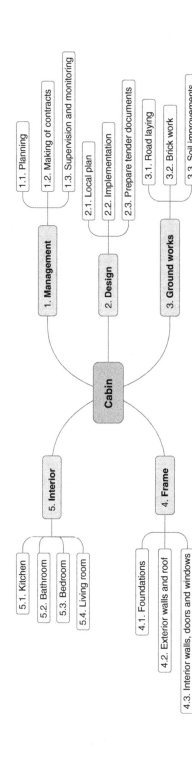

Figure 4.14

Breakdown of the work parts in building a cabin.

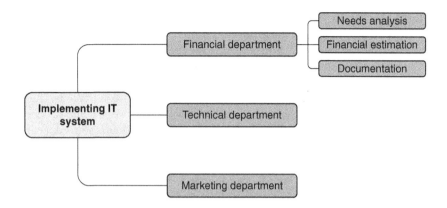

Figure 4.15

Breakdown according to departments.

time and cost. A time schedule serves three main purposes, with reference to the life cycle of projects:

- At the beginning of a project, it creates an overview of time and resources, thus also costs.
- During a project, it is useful for monitoring the status and progress and as a basis for control and management decisions about changes that may need to be taken in the project. Changes in the availability or quality of resources and changes in the schedule typically affect each other.
- At the end of a project, it is useful as evidence of settlement and in the resolution of disputes, if any occur.

For this reason, it is necessary to build up a time schedule with the aim of utilising it for all of the above items. The making of a good schedule has two main inputs: (1) the experience and knowledge of those charged with its preparation and (2) the tools and methods that are used to compile and present the required information. The setting up of detailed schedules can be a very complicated task in large complex projects, and this area has benefitted greatly from computerisation, with a wide range of practical software applications now available to assist in their preparation and management.

Outline of project master plan

Once the project has been broken down into phases and further sub-divisions, the sequencing of tasks then needs to be considered. If the dependencies between the tasks are known, as well as their durations, the time schedule or activity flow can be defined, and light shed on the critical path. The initial purpose of making a time schedule is to create an overview of the project and how long it should take to complete. People will either want to know when the project is expected to be completed, depending on whether it starts at a certain time, or when it needs to be started, so that the product is ready for some specified deadline. In the former case, the time schedule for each task is aimed so that the project is finished *As Soon As Possible* – ASAP, but in the latter case this is reversed, and scheduling of the tasks aims to have the project finished *As Late As Possible* – ALAP. The reason for creating this overview is so that the inner context of the work phases is determined. There is, then, a need to determine whether it is possible to work on two specific tasks in parallel, or whether one needs to be finished before the other is started, i.e. to decide if they are inter-dependent. If a certain task called B is dependent on A, it is said that A is a prerequisite for B. Decisions in this matter will vary from one project to another, and each decision made will have a specific set of consequences that need to be taken into account. The decision to process two main tasks in parallel, instead of completing one before the other begins may, for example, lead to increased costs for the project. That additional cost may potentially be justified by the fact that the project will take less time.

A classic example of phases or main tasks that can sometimes overlap is design and execution in a construction project. Logically, the design of a structure should be completed before construction begins. This arrangement means that the structural requirements are fully defined before practical execution begins, and that it is possible to agree on fixed contracts for the execution after cost estimation (assuming the costs are predictable). The reality, however, is that design and execution often overlap substantially, with the technical design not completed before the practical execution begins. It goes without saying that it is then difficult to make decisions concerning the execution on the basis of the design, and this would normally lead to higher costs. The justification for having it this way is that it often may save time, i.e. it will be possible to use the structures earlier and therefore start to create value for the owners earlier. The difference between these methods is shown in Figure 4.16.

It should be pointed out that even though this comparison is quite decisive in a simple diagram, the reality is often more complex. Significant risks may be taken by planning a project in such a way that the phases overlap. If it is managed poorly, then a costly execution may be initiated without the existence of a satisfactory plan covering what is to be done, how it should be done, and who should do it. If the aim is to save time by allowing phases to overlap, it is necessary to carry out a detailed uncertainty analysis and to ensure that the interactions and communications between the participants in the project run smoothly, as there is really no room for mistakes.

The connection relationship between two adjacent tasks in a project can vary, but most commonly four categories are mentioned. These categories are explained in Figures 4.17–4.20. For this purpose, we use the term work part instead of main task or task.

The most common connection is, as described in Figure 4.17, *finish to start*, or FS. If we are discussing work parts A and B that are connected in this manner, then B cannot begin until A is finished. An example of such a

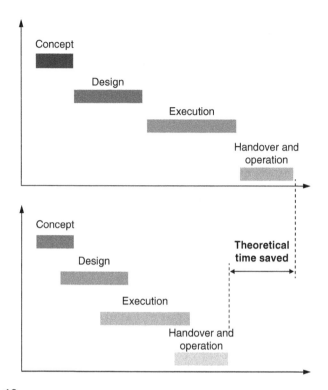

Figure 4.16

Possible time saving in regard to working on main tasks or phases in parallel.

connection could be a specific construction project where a decision is made that the design needs to be finished before the actual execution can begin. This will be the case for some projects that have a formal tendering process.

It is also common that phases or work packages are connected through parallel starts or SS (*start to start*) – this connection is shown in Figure 4.18. In this instance, work for part B cannot begin until part A has begun. An example of this could be a construction project where the supervision over the execution cannot begin until the actual execution itself has commenced.

The third type of connection is parallel finish or FF (*finish to finish*) – see Figure 4.19. In this case, work part B cannot finish until work part A is finished. An example of such a connection in a construction project is the

Figure 4.17

Logical connection of work parts – finish/start (FS).

Figure 4.18

Logical connection of work parts – start/start (SS).

conclusion phase and final delivery of the product to the work buyer. This cannot be completed until after the execution phase is finished.

The fourth and last type of connection is *start to finish* or SF, and this is shown in Figure 4.20. Here, work part B cannot finish until work part A has started. This is a rare connection type and can be confused with an FS type connection. It could be viewed as work part B being embedded within work part A, hence the need for A to have started before B can be finished. An example would be the final inspection of a construction project – part of the inspection might involve how the operation is going and therefore the inspection cannot go ahead until the operation has started.

In the context of the above, there are three kinds of dependencies between adjacent work parts and these are: (1) logical (e.g. it is impossible to proofread a book until it is written); (2) resource constraints (e.g. if only one person is executing a project then it is not possible to pour concrete and paint a wall at the same time); and (3) discretionary (e.g. a garden renovation project will start with the back garden rather than the front – even though it could be done the other way round).

Graphical presentation of time schedule

A *Gantt chart* is a graphical representation of the time schedule of a project. It is associated with the American industrial engineer Henry Gantt, who originally presented it in 1903 in a published article on the subject of management methods for production companies. The method was primarily intended as an aid in production management, and has been very widely used since then, with early examples of use, for example, being in large complex projects like building a ship. Figure 4.21 illustrates how a Gantt chart can be used in production management in an industrial company that has multiple tasks running in different departments.

Figure 4.19

Logical connection of work parts – finish/finish (FF).

Figure 4.20

Logical connection of work parts – start/finish (SF).

The widespread usage of Gantt charts really began in the 1960s and is associated with increased computerisation which facilitated graphical presentation. Today they are used as a tool in project management in all sectors, and they are the standard form of visual presentation of time schedules for projects (Wilson, 2003). The reason for the popularity of graphical charts is undoubtedly that, by using them, it is possible to give an easily understandable overview of the major work parts of a project, including their context.

The earlier example of the cabin construction project outlined in Figure 4.14 is shown in Figure 4.22 as a Gantt chart. Here, the timeline can be clearly viewed as well as the context of the work breakdown. The work divisions are categorised in rows on the left side of the picture, and the graphical chart can be seen on the right. The first layer of work division is shown in black. The arrows between the different bars on the graph signify the dependency relationship, and the project milestones are shown as diamonds.

Time schedules can also be reflected in projects graphically as a network diagram. Two types of network diagrams are used: (1) box grid (e.g. *Activity on Node* – AON) and (2) arrow grid (e.g. *Activity on Arc* – AOA). In Figure 4.23, the letters A, B, and C symbolise work parts.

A box grid is characterised by having work parts as nodes on a grid. The knot nodes are those nodes in the grid where two or more arrows meet up.

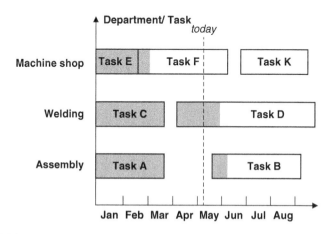

Figure 4.21

Gantt chart to manage the production in a factory.

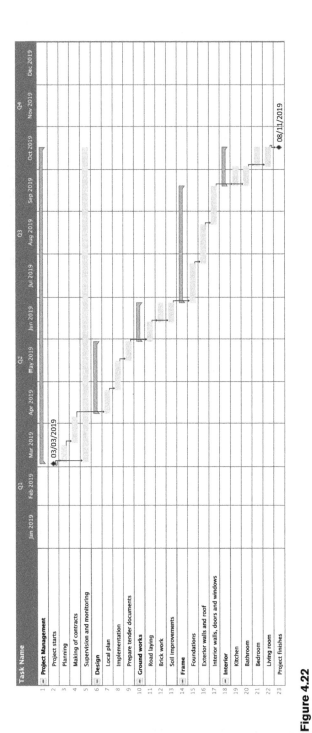

Figure 4.22

Gantt chart of the same cabin building project as shown in Figure 4.14.

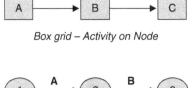

Box grid – Activity on Node

Arrow grid – Activity on Arc

Figure 4.23

The two main types of network diagrams.

In arrow grids, the work parts are on a line which connects the nodes. It is best to explain this with simple figures (see Figure 4.24).

Figure 4.25 shows a box grid (AON) for a simple project with the tasks A, B, C, and D. The two first mentioned can start at the same time, and their beginning is independent from other work phases. On the other hand, task D cannot start until A and B are finished. Task C can begin when task A is finished. The Start and Finish milestones are symbolised with diamonds. They take no time but are an important part of the whole picture, as the grid has to start in one node and end in another.

The information shown in Figure 4.24 is reorganised into an arrow grid in Figure 4.25 and again shows the tasks A, B, C, and D. They are connected together with two nodes between the Start and Finish milestones. The tasks A and B mark the start of the project and are independent from other work phases. C can start when A is finished. D can start when A and B are finished. The conditionality of task D in regard to A is reflected in the dotted line between nodes 2 and 1. This fictional task has no time length and only serves the purpose of highlighting that work phase D cannot start until task A is finished.

The box grid and arrow grid methods each have pros and cons. The main pro about the box grid is that it is simple and easily explained to others. Various other pros can be mentioned in regard to the arrow grid, e.g. that it is possible to have the arrows at different lengths in proportion to different time lengths of tasks.

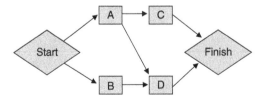

Figure 4.24

Example of a box grid (AON).

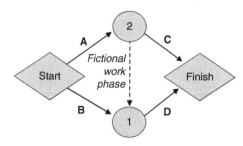

Figure 4.25

Example of an arrow grid (AOA).

The critical path

If the breakdown of a project is laid down together with the start time, and the logical context of all the tasks has been decided, it is possible to determine one or more ways through the project that determine the timing of the finishing of the project. The tasks that line up to enable the shortest possible route to project completion are said to outline the "critical path" of the project. The cumulative work time for these tasks adds up to the total time taken for the project as a whole. The project ends when the last task in the critical path is finished. If the tasks on the critical path take longer than expected, it means that the project takes longer accordingly. The tasks that are not on the critical path have, on the other hand, a certain flexibility in terms of start and finish, or duration. This is commonly referred to as slack. This means that although a task that is not on the critical path is delayed, or takes longer than expected, it will not affect the project as a whole, as long as the change is not greater than the slack.

The *critical path method* (CPM) focuses on identifying these dominant ways in the projects and evaluates the slack in those tasks that are not on the critical path. This is valuable information for those who manage a project. They need to take special care that there will be no delay on those tasks that belong to the critical path. The slack of other tasks indicates the flexibility to shift them in time – depending on circumstances – without them affecting the duration of the project.

Let us look at a simple example of the calculation of the critical path. The example is based on the same project as shown in Figures 4.24 and 4.25. The information can be seen in Table 4.7 where, in the last column, the time length for each task has been estimated in weeks.

Table 4.7 Information in an example for calculations of the critical path

Task	Prerequisites	Time [weeks]
A	None	2
B	None	1
C	A	3
D	A & B	1

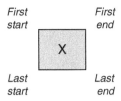

First start		First end
	X	
Last start		Last end

Figure 4.26

Information that needs to be documented for the calculations of a critical path.

The calculation of the critical path is based on the logic of the box grid in Figure 4.24 as well as the information about timing related to each task, as shown in Table 4.7. The information shown in Figure 4.26 is calculated for each node as the next phase in this process.

The determination of the critical path first involves calculating from the start to the finish of the project the first start and first end for each task, as shown in the box grid in Figure 4.27. When this information is available, it is calculated back from the end of the project to the start, the last end to the last beginning of each task. When this is finished, it will be revealed that for some tasks the first start and the last start are one and the same thing. Such tasks are said to lie on the critical path. When these numbers are not comparable, then those tasks are not on the critical path, and the difference is called a *slack* of the associated task. Such a slack can be seen as a time buffer for that task. If the slack of the task is two weeks, then that means that its start can be delayed by two weeks without that delay affecting the overall time of the project.

In Figure 4.27, the first start in task D is two (weeks), not one, as A is the limiting precursor, not B. It is clear from this grid that the project takes five weeks and not three, and that the dominant task for determining the finishing of the project is C and not D. Now it is possible to calculate back over the project from its finish to the start. Then a new picture can be seen, as shown in Figure 4.28.

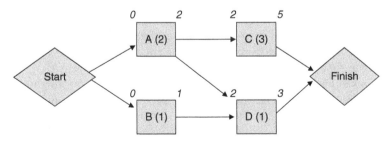

Figure 4.27

Example of the critical path – calculations from start to finish.

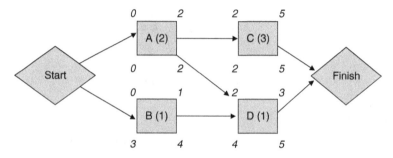

Figure 4.28

Example of the critical path – calculations from the finish to the start.

The last finish of the tasks C and D is five weeks. Therefore, the last start is determined by this duration. When the last finish for the task A is evaluated, then it must be determined by the task C and not D. The last finish of B is determined, on the other hand, by the last start of D. Now it is clear that tasks B and D have a slack, and that the slack for B is three weeks while the slack for D is two weeks. A and C have no slack and they form the critical path of the project, which in total will take five weeks.

From this it is clear that if a delay happens with task A or C, then the project as a whole will be delayed. The same does not apply to tasks B and D as long as the delay is within the slack that has been calculated. In the managing of this project, particular care, therefore, needs to be taken so that there will not be a delay in tasks A and C.

Reflection points

- Think of a large construction project you know, where the execution was in the hands of one or more contractors. Add a new phase, a development phase, where suppliers and contractors are brought into the project. Redraw Figure 4.7 to demonstrate this situation, add new milestones as appropriate – what do they represent?
- What can happen in the development of the work breakdown structure if an item is broken into 200 work parts, on a layer – instead of the maximum of 20? Explain the possible consequences.
- Look at the two different WBS for the same project, as shown in Figures 4.11 and 4.12. Which WBS do you like more? Why?
- Look at Figure 4.16 again. If a strategic decision is made to work on project phases in parallel, elaborate on the possible managerial consequences of such a decision.
- Look back at the case in Figure 4.27. Assume that the duration of task D is three weeks instead of one week. Redo the calculations. What is the critical path now?

Bibliography

APM. (2012). *APM Body of Knowledge* (6th ed.). Princes Risborough: Association of Project Management.

Brian Tracy International. (n.d.). Retrieved from www.briantracy.com.

Fangel, M. (2013). *Proactive Project Management – How to Make Common Sense Common Practice*. Hillerød, Denmark: Fangel Consulting as.

IPMA. (2015). *Individual Competence Baseline for Project, Programme & Portfolio Management*, version 4. Zurich: IPMA.

Lim, C.S., & Mohamed, M.Z. (1999). Criteria of project success: An exploratory re-examination. *International Journal of Project Management, 17*(4), 243–248.

Lock, D. (2017). *Project Management*. London: Routledge.

Meredith, J.R., Shafer, S.M., Mantel Jr, S.J., & Sutton, M.M. (2016). *Project Management in Practice*. New York: Wiley Global Education.

Shenhar, A.J., Dvir, D., Levy, O., & Maltz, A.C. (2001). Project success: A multidimensional strategic concept. *Long Range Planning, 34*(6), 699–725.

Turner, J.R., Grude, K.V., & Thurloway, L. (Eds.) (1996). *The Project Manager as Change Agent: Leadership, Influence and Negotiation*. London: McGraw-Hill.

Wateridge, J. (1998). How can IS/IT projects be measured for success? *International Journal of Project Management, 16*(1), 59–63.

Wilson, J.M. (2003). Gantt charts: A centenary appreciation. *European Journal of Operational Research, 149*(2), 430–437.

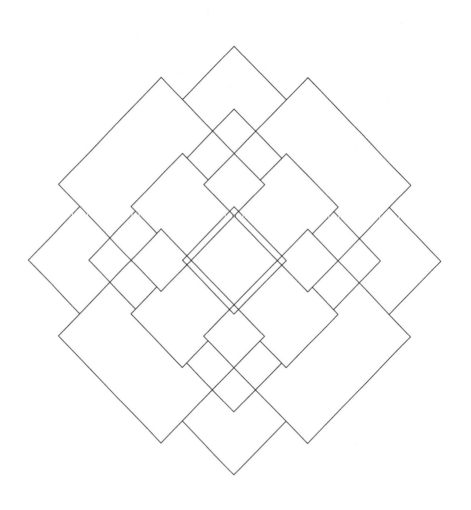

5 Planning: resources, management structure, and role/task division

••

Resources and cost plan

In Chapter 2, we discussed the measurement scale of success and the main categories and dimensions of objectives. Traditionally, objectives in projects are said to revolve around time, performance, and cost, together with other factors, although, in reality, projects are often evaluated on whether they are successfully delivered according to the budget. It is, therefore, extremely important to adopt effective practices for creating budget schedules and following them through. In this context, it is worth bearing in mind that the schedule is built up from the beginning with the intention that it should be used as an instrument in the pursuit of the project. Its key purpose is to record faithfully all the criteria that form the basis for decisions, sources of information, and more. A decision that is considered wrong at one time may have been considered correct at the time it was taken. The criteria are, therefore, not any less important than the decision itself.

The foundation of cost estimation is assessing which resources are needed in order to deliver the expected outcome, and this is based on the breakdown of the project into work parts. In this respect, we start below by outlining the main reasons for deviations from the cost estimates in projects:

- Those who estimated the cost misunderstood the nature of the project. The cost estimate is therefore tailored to something different from the project in hand.
- The schedule was ill-defined, the breakdown of it inaccurate, and it was missing important items.
- Uncertainty was not taken into account in the schedule making, e.g. inflation, interest, and exchange rates.
- The financial requirements during the construction period were not considered, and there was, therefore, a lack of finance for the execution of the project.
- The design phase was in its early stages when construction began.

- Midway through, decisions with regard to changing the scope were made, which led to the final product of the project becoming different from what was originally intended.
- The costs of managing the project were not considered.
- The indirect costs in the project were not considered.
- A conscious decision was made at the outset not to look at the end costs.

In the discussion that follows, the above issues will be addressed in a direct and indirect manner, and we demonstrate how it is possible to avoid these negative outcomes.

The cost of a project – the cost during the life cycle of a product

Depending on the nature of a project and the viewpoint of the entities that execute it, a project can be seen to end once a product is delivered or, alternatively, it may be seen to end when the product itself reaches the end of its useful life. In the latter case, the cost of a project tends to be viewed in terms of the overall project life cycle. The period of interest for the so-called "life cycle cost" covers the entire project, including the building and operation of the product, as well as the demolition or recycling of it once it reaches the end of its useful life. This is shown in Figure 5.1.

This particularly relates to construction projects; for example, a factory that takes three years to build and has a useful life of 50 years. In this case, after the operation period ends, decisions must be made about whether to demolish the structures, reconstruct them, or arrange them in another way. The whole period, from start to finish, is called the life cycle of a product, and the life cycle cost covers all costs during this period, i.e. not only the construction costs at the beginning, but also the operating costs and the costs of finishing after use. If people consider the costs in a product's total life cycle, it can be expected that decisions at the start will be different than if only the initial costs are considered. In a construction project, it can thus be advantageous to choose a more expensive design, more expensive materials, and more expensive labour in terms of looking at the operation of the structure over a long period, even though the initial cost will be higher than otherwise. In other cases, where the product of a project is handed over to a third party, there is most likely a wish to keep costs to a minimum while ensuring a certain threshold of customer quality satisfaction.

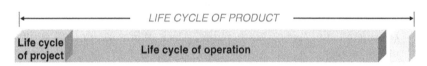

Figure 5.1

Life cycle of a product – the costs during the life cycle.

Resources

Upon completion of the breakdown of the project into work parts – and when the duration of these work parts has been evaluated – the basis for the scheduling has then been laid down. By breaking down the project and dividing it into an appropriate number of work parts so that a good overview can be obtained over each one, it is possible, amongst other things, to assess all of the resources necessary to carry out all of the work parts in terms of quality and quantity. The right providers of resources must be identified; the resources can be sourced within the organisation (internal resources) or provided by an external supplier (external resources). A decision must be made on which resources or services are to be procured and whether project partners will be acquired for some aspects of the project. The classical "make or buy" strategy must be defined – perhaps there is a shortage of internal resources or a conscious strategy to acquire resources externally. The work resources we are referring to are what is needed in terms of labour, equipment, materials, infrastructure, tools, services, and facilities that are necessary to complete particular work parts and/or the project as a whole. The outcome of this assessment is a strategic resource plan, and it should also stipulate who is responsible for which part of the definition, acquiring, allocation, development, distribution, and freeing of the different resources.

An important part of the preparation may include a comparison of the necessary resources and available resources. If these do not match, then measures need to be taken to either improve the use of the resources, acquire new resources, or limit the scope. Typically, projects are competing for limited resources, and there are conflicting resource needs between projects, and between a project and the organisation. In each project, there is a need to ensure that the right resources are available at the right time. Systematic planning identifies the criteria for obtaining this objective. After a project is broken down and the planning of resources for each project phase is underway, it may, perhaps, be revealed that there is a need for a large number of employees for a short period during the execution phase. It may be more economical, then, to extend the execution period somewhat if it leads to an important reduction in the manpower needed during that short period. This is called levelling or balancing the resources. When levelling the resources, the critical path of the project may or may not be influenced. It may, for example, be possible to move some of the tasks that are not on the critical path and thus level the use of resources, still concluding the project on the same date.

As outlined above, resources can be of various types. Labour is of crucial importance but needs to be further broken down in terms of more specific requirements. Projects will most often need a variety of people including those with management experience, technical specialists, craftsmen, general labourers, and the right balance needs to be found in this. They will also need different proportions of labour types during different phases of a project. In a construction project, for example, technical consultant and management man-hours are likely to dominate in the planning stages, whereas craftsmen and general labour man-hours will dominate in the execution phase.

Another category of resources is raw materials, and this category will, of course, vary widely depending on the nature of the project. An obvious example of this is a project that involves building a cabin out of timber, where it is clear that timber will be a determining factor in the resources. In a project that, for example, involves the implementation of a new organisational chart within a public institute, there are few actual raw materials required and little or no procurement needed. In this example, the resources required are likely to be an existing workforce that is flexible and can embrace a shift in responsibility and workload, as well as, potentially/possibly, new staff, if required.

When an overview of all the resources needed to do a project is available in the form of estimated quantities, the unit price of these resources can then be checked in order to be able to assess the costs associated with them.

Several types of cost factors related to resources in a project are highlighted below. Some of them are direct costs, others are indirect.

- Time-dependent costs – These include all salaries that are related to a project, regardless of the type of workforce. An example might be the salaries of labourers, craftsmen, and technicians. Non-labour costs can also be time-dependent, such as perishable goods or equipment rental.
- Equipment needs – This refers to equipment that is purchased and is used for the project, and needs to be operated, maintained, and depreciated. Examples could be machinery and tools where charging a specific amount per unit time for each device is a common approach. Such costs, therefore, are also time-dependent.
- Raw materials – This refers to all the materials used in the project to create the final outcome, e.g. steel and concrete in a building foundation. Raw material costs are not generally time-dependent, although an exception to this is the case where they may have been purchased and degrade or become obsolete over time.
- Other direct costs can be, e.g. travel expenses, training costs, and ongoing operating costs.
- Indirect costs – This refers to various indirect factors, such as transport, insurance, administration, overhead fees, or licences.
- Management and control – This includes, for example, the project office, legal and financial services, and other management infrastructure.

All the cost factors listed above can be assessed by analysing the resource needs. To estimate the amount of resources, two methods are primarily used that have been referred to by a number of other authors (e.g. Meredith et al., 2016). These can be briefly summarised as top-down and bottom-up methods and are discussed in more detail below.

The first method (top-down) is diagnostic and analytical evaluation primarily based on experience. As an illustration, we can think of a company that has opened branches in four countries. If information about the cost of these projects is collected, the company has good criteria by which to evaluate the necessary resources for opening the next branch without much effort. The executive director will then create a cost framework and a general description of the characteristics and location of the new branch. Those responsible for the preparation and execution of the project receive this information and carry out the work accordingly. They try to maximise the value for the company and ensure that the expectations of the project are delivered within a given cost frame. Such assessment (or analysis evaluation) is a cheap and quick way to assess the resources and costs. In an analysis evaluation, sufficient experience of similar completed projects is needed, and this is then combined with the particulars of the project being assessed. This experience may come from external experts who are hired to advise on the project. Care needs to be taken that the parameters within different projects are, in fact, comparable in this regard.

The second method (bottom-up) involves building up an overall cost model of a project by analysing the cost of individual work elements and then adding them together to arrive at a total estimated cost figure. The breakdown of a project is thus the foundation of this and is required in order to be able to estimate the costs associated with each different work package. The criteria of the calculations are that sufficiently accurate planning has taken place, and that the product of the project has been defined in enough detail so that the information about what is to be done, and how it is to be done, is available with reasonable accuracy. It can be argued that the evaluation of the resources and the construction of the cost plan for a project, carried out in a bottom-up fashion, is an exercise in accuracy, and not particularly complicated. It requires careful consideration not to overlook any important work elements and details, and to cost the individual work packages accurately. There is a danger that, if this is not done efficiently, it can lead to negative outcomes, such as encountering cash flow difficulties during the execution stage of a project. To ensure disciplined work procedures, and to reduce the likelihood of something being forgotten, it is prudent to establish a systematic method in regard to evaluating resource needs. The method can include putting together a checklist or questionnaire that is used to record the types of resources, their availability and cost, who the providers of the resources are, when they are needed, and other necessary information. An example of this type of form is shown in Table 5.1.

The form in Table 5.1 is filled in for the whole project – in case of a small project – or for each work package in the project breakdown, as shown in Chapter 4. This can be executed straightforwardly by using individual Excel tables to organise the information within a form and by using different Excel worksheets for each different form. In this way, the breakdown of the project is linked to the evaluation of the resources (see Figure 5.2).

Another approach that can be taken is to build the resources plan on one Excel worksheet. In this case, work factors are put into the rows of the table and the types of resources into columns. Further development of a cost estimate by adding the cost information to the resources plan will be discussed

Table 5.1 An example of a simple form to gather information about required resources

Project: _____
Date: _____

Resources	Source Who can provide the resource?	Quantity Units and quantity	When When is this needed in the project?	Comments E.g. unit price – if known – and whether it is available
Workforce 1				
Workforce 2				
Material 1				
Material 2				
Tool 1				
Tool 2				
Other				

later. If we are looking at a small project, having things on one sheet will give a good overview of the project at a glance, but in large projects with many work factors, the table will be too big, and the overview is lost.

Budgets and accuracy

Budgets are as varied as they are numerous, and they can serve multiple purposes. Rough estimates at the earliest stages of project planning give an indication of the scale in terms of the cost of a project. That clue may be sufficient to make important decisions, such as whether it is wise to continue working on the project or if it should be put on ice or rethought in some other form. It may be cheap to do a rough estimate such as described above, and this can save a lot of money if it identifies shortcomings in a project at this early stage before a significant investment is made. In this case, perhaps an analysis evaluation that is based on the experience of the project's organisers or participants of other similar projects is enough. In other cases, it may be necessary to make a bottom-up type of cost estimate by breaking down the project and calculating the costs as previously described.

It is important to realise the accuracy demands of the budget that is being worked towards. At the same time, it is also important to keep in mind that the accuracy of a budget will change depending on where the project is in its life cycle. To simplify, budgets can be divided into four main categories that have an increasing accuracy range as shown in Table 5.2. This table is loosely based on similar presentations by Kerzner (2017), Lock (2017), and The Association of Cost Engineers (n.d.).

The first category is an indication of the cost, which can be based on a simple analytical evaluation that may potentially be created in a very short time, but the accuracy of such an evaluation can never be great. It can be expected that the final cost could range from as much as 50% higher to 35% lower than the estimate. The second category is feasibility. In this case, further steps are

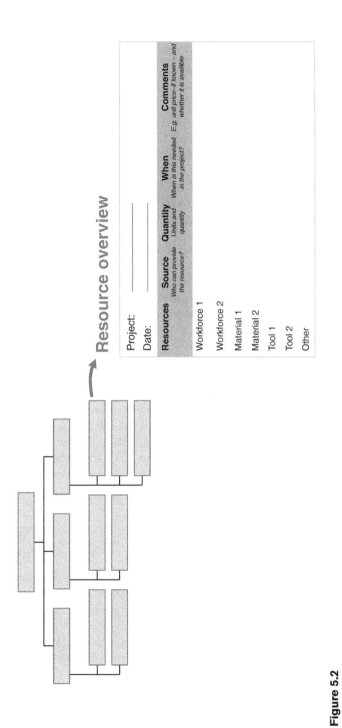

Figure 5.2

Evaluation of resources and links to the project breakdown.

Table 5.2 Types of budgets

Type of budgets	Method used to evaluate resources	Uncertainty	Work
Indication of scale	Analysis evaluation	+50%, −35%	Days
Feasibility	Analysis evaluation	+35%, −20%	Days − weeks
Formed/moulded idea	Calculations	+25%, −15%	Weeks
Fully formed product	Calculations	+15%, −5%	Months

taken, and quite a bit more work is put into evaluating individual cost items, for example, by engaging with suppliers (e.g. receiving preliminary quotes) and external consultants, albeit still at the analytical evaluation level. If the aim is to have a more accurate cost plan, it is necessary to build it on the breakdown of the project, where there will be more detailed definition of its scope and related bottom-up calculations. In the third category, one is now making a budget for a formed idea about the product of the project, and the work associated with this can take many weeks, but the uncertainty can be reduced. The fourth and final category is a budget for a fully formed product and, as the table shows, it can take months to create this, and it is dependent on the scope of the project being accurately defined. If we are looking at the structure of this budget, then it includes a finished design and an accurate breakdown of all the work parts, as well as information about the cost of all resources that are typically based on bids (fully designed structures). The accuracy of such planning is considerable, but some uncertainty can still be anticipated, and it can be expected that the final outcome will be in the range of +15% to −5%. The reason for this is that the project environment can change, and various unforeseen factors are always present in all projects. It is possible to insure oneself to a certain extent with binding agreements and other mechanisms, but some risk to the owner of the project will, however, always be unavoidable.

Whoever makes a budget needs to be aware that its recipient will potentially make momentous and consequential decisions based on it. A recipient has, therefore, a right to be informed about the accuracy of the plan and the references behind the numbers presented.

Cost estimation

When an evaluation of the project's resource needs has been carried out, it is then necessary to obtain information about costs in regard to these resources. In order to do this, the required resources are normally standardised as units, and the unit costs for each are investigated. For example, in a short project, labour resources will be categorised into, e.g. specialists, workers and craftsmen, the requirement of each labour type measured in units such as man-hours, and an agreed-upon representative cost per hour. For longer projects, the labour unit may refer to weeks and months and use average salaries as a reference. Raw materials are evaluated in appropriate units, with examples being iron and steel in kilos, concrete in cubic metres, and timber in cross section and length.

Machines and tools can be evaluated as a whole, e.g. if a computer or a specialised piece of equipment needs to be bought for the project. It is also common to evaluate tools and equipment in terms of time periods, e.g. if a crane truck needs to be rented for the project, then it is necessary to estimate for how many hours or days it is required. This also applies to equipment and materials that are bought and are required to be depreciated over time.

When resources are evaluated in such a manner, information about the unit prices then needs to be obtained. It can be tricky to evaluate them with accuracy – these prices can change depending on a number of factors, and suppliers may be reluctant to divulge information by providing cost estimations for projects that are speculative. Companies that are active in the tender market in construction projects have established price databases that rely on parameter input (e.g. number of kilos of raw materials and number of general labour man-hours, etc.) and keep them updated.

Evaluating the cost of resources simply involves multiplying together the number of units and unit prices. For example, if 500 cubic metres of concrete is needed for a structure and the cost per cubic metre is 120 GBP when in the mould, then the cost in relation to the concrete is 60,000 GBP in total. This parameter-based method is used regardless of whether analysis evaluation or calculations have been used to evaluate the resources. If the breakdown and the calculations are laid down as a basis, it is possible to calculate the total cost for each work package by multiplying together each type of resource and the appropriate unit price. The results of such calculations can be seen in Figure 5.3 where the calculations of cost for single tasks have been placed

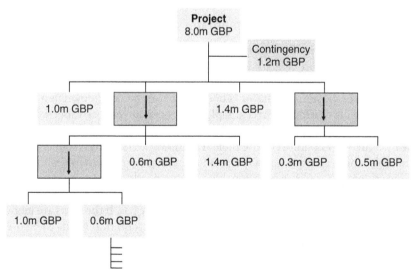

Figure 5.3

The calculation of the cost, based on the breakdown.

into a pictorial framework of a project. Following on from this, it is possible to add together the costs of all work factors to give a total estimated cost, in this case 8 million GBP.

Attention is drawn to the item contingency which has been added before the total cost was calculated. This is needed, as experience suggests that various things can be overlooked in the development of a cost plan, even though it is carefully prepared. Various changes may also occur in the environment of the project that can lead to increased costs. Contingency estimates can be evaluated by statistical methods, but it is most common, however, for them to be evaluated from experience while keeping in mind the nature of the cost plan.

Contingency expenses can be used as needed by the project manager during the execution of the project. If nothing unforeseen occurs during the project, then there is no need to make use of this expense, and the total cost of the project will then be reduced accordingly. This can be compared to sick leave, where employees are entitled to leave – a certain number of days in a month – but this is only to be used when and if they are ill. It is preferable for the employee never to have to use their sick leave, and the same goes for the contingency category in the cost estimates of a project.

It should be noted that in the discussions in this book it is assumed that the cost is measured at constant exchange rates. Looking at the development of the economy in Iceland over recent decades, it can be seen that sometimes there are periods where inflation is significant. At such times, it is necessary to take the effects of inflation into account, particularly if the project spans a long period.

Construction of the cost estimate

The breaking down of the project into tasks is convenient in order to divide it into units that can be defined, assessed, and managed. The breakdown also provides criteria for analysing the resource requirements, as has been mentioned before. In simple tasks, it is possible to use the breakdown as a foundation for the cost estimate. An example of this can be seen in Table 5.3, which relates to a simple six-month project. In the first column of the table are the tasks. The other columns of the table represent the required resources. In this example, there are four participants in the project, which involves ten tasks. This project is simple enough for the resource needs and cost calculations to be presented in a single table.

Table 5.3 can give a good overview if the tasks are few. If the tasks are many – and the resources are varied – then a different presentation needs to be used. In that case, a *Cost Breakdown Structure* (CBS) can be used. The cost of the project is then divided into two main sections: direct costs and indirect costs. An example of such a presentation is shown in Figure 5.4.

Direct costs are debited directly from the project in proportion to time, volume, and contracts. The project will have employees on a monthly or

Table 5.3 An example of a cost estimate for a simple project

Breakdown	John [hours]	Jane [hours]	Peter [hours]	Anne [hours]	Total [hours]	Materials [GBP]	Other cost [GBP]	Total cost [GBP]
Task 1	19	45	15	5	84	2,000	1,475	7,350
Task 2	12			30	42			2,400
Task 3	23				23		920	2,070
Task 4		35		10	45	11,400	400	13,800
Task 5			45	15	60		475	3,850
Task 6			20	21	41		940	3,300
Task 7	20	65			85		1,350	4,950
Task 8	20	2			22			1,080
Task 9				10	10	4,600		5,200
Task 10	10	55	10		75			3,250
Total hours	104	202	90	91	487			
Unit price [GBP per hour]	50	40	55	60				
Total	5,200	8,080	4,950	5,460		18,000	5,560	47,250

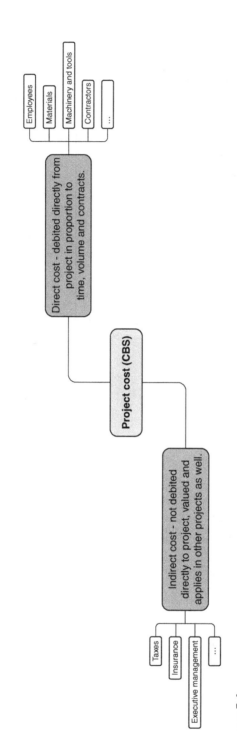

Figure 5.4

A breakdown of a project according to cost factors (CBS).

hourly salary, while the raw materials are bought according to a framework agreement. Machinery and tools may be bought or rented and debited accordingly, and so on with all the other items. It is a different matter in regard to indirect costs, as these are not debited straight from the project, but instead are valued and applied in proportion to the project. For example, we can think of a company that, at any one time, undertakes ten equally large, parallel projects as part of its daily operations. The executive management of the company split their time between these projects, and the costs allocated to a particular project within this group are therefore considered as indirect costs. Indirect costs also cover aspects such as insurance that has been bought as part of a project. This includes both mandatory insurances, e.g. third-party cover, as well as unique insurances, where the buyer decides to insure against threats to their interests.

A detailed cost breakdown structure can be built up from the building blocks introduced here but will need to be tailored for individual projects. An example of a cost breakdown for a simple construction project from the perspective of the project buyer is shown in Figure 5.5.

In Figure 5.5, the project buyer will oversee the cost estimates and agree upon the financial terms of the project. They will then hire one or more contractors to carry out the project after the design work that the buyer has paid for is finished. The project buyer also funds the executive monitoring, as well as a project manager who is responsible for the daily management and coordination. The buyer may also have purchased special insurances for damages that the project may cause to a third party, and also takes into account finance costs, which include interest costs before the product of the project begins to generate revenue. Finally, the project buyer is aware that there is some uncertainty in the estimates and, therefore, they have a contingency fund that the project manager has a right to use in the interests of the project, if necessary.

Cash outflow

When the direct and indirect costs of projects have been estimated, there is then a need to consider when the funding is needed to ensure the availability of financial resources at the right time. The largest part of the cost is probably needed during the execution phase of the project, and the buyer needs to realise the capital requirements to ensure that he has the necessary cash resources when needed. This may be subject to an approval process by investors, financial institutions, or simply the organisational approval process. This is called cash flow management, and an advantage of assessing the outflow of cash in a project is that it is then possible to calculate the capital cost during the construction time with some accuracy. The financing cost during the construction period is a cost factor that is often forgotten, but it can be significant.

As an illustrative example, we can consider an international communications and information technology company that is upgrading its technical systems and implementing a quality system according to the ISO 9001 standard. The company estimates that the project will take one year, and the total cost

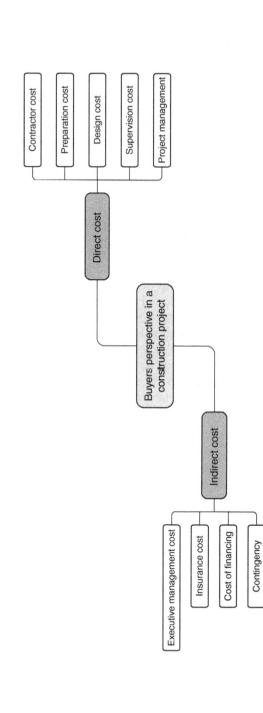

Figure 5.5

Construction of a cost estimate from the perspective of the buyer.

is estimated at 2 million GBP. The finance costs for the execution period are first estimated in a simple way by giving a linear cash outflow, which assumes that there is an equal funding requirement over the whole of the lifetime of the project. In this case, zero pounds are paid at the start of the project, and the total amount is paid by the end. It is also assumed that the interest rate is 15%. Given these premises, the cost of capital during construction is calculated using a simple model, as these assumptions correspond to the fact that half the amount has 15% interest for one year, or that the full amount has a 15% interest rate over six months, as shown below:

Cost of capital = capital cost / 2 × 15% interest per annum

2,000,000 GBP / 2 × 15% = 150,000 GBP

∴ The real total cost of the project is 2,150,000 GBP

The calculations described above can be useful to get a quick idea of the capital cost. The uncertainty, however, is considerable, because it is unknown whether a linear cash outflow over the project lifetime is a valid assumption. If budgets are tight, and liquidity a major factor in projects, detailed information about the cash outflow is required, and more work is needed. It is not complicated to do this, but it requires that the cost of each task is distributed over the lifetime of the project according to the best information available. This is outlined in Table 5.4, which is based on the same simple project example presented in Table 5.3.

In Table 5.4, each cost factor – in this instance the cost per task – has been taken and distributed over the six-month lifetime of the project. It is non-linear as, in some months, we are looking at contracts for the purchase of equipment, and it is also the case that the wages are spread unevenly over the lifetime of the project. Once this compilation is done, then the cash outflow for each month can be calculated together with the cumulative outflow, as shown in the bottom two lines of the table. This outlines the cash requirements of the project and can be plotted on a simple graph, as shown in Figure 5.6. This is a useful way to visualise the cash requirements for each month, as well as the cumulative cash outflow. The magnitude variations of the parameters (incremental cost and cumulative cost) can be shown with separate scales on the y-axis, and this is a simple operation in Excel. The bars in the figure then correspond to the incremental costs and relate to the scale on the left, while the line represents cumulative costs and relates to the scale on the right.

Once the cash requirements for each month are established, then it is possible to begin to calculate the cost of funding. More criteria are actually needed for this, however, including the interest rate to be charged and further details related to timing. If these criteria are given, then it is possible to calculate the total real capital costs, including financing costs, and to prepare a loan

Table 5.4 The cost estimate: evaluation of cash outflow and calculations of accumulated outflow

Breakdown	Total cost [GBP]	M 1	M 2	M 3	M 4	M 5	M 6
Task 1	7,350		1,000	2,500	1,750	1,000	1,100
Task 2	2,400	400	400	400	400	400	400
Task 3	2,070			1,000	300	300	470
Task 4	13,800	500	11,000	600	900	800	
Task 5	3,850	1,000	400	1,000	450	1,000	
Task 6	3,300	600	600	400	400	350	950
Task 7	4,950			1,200	1,200	1,200	1,350
Task 8	1,080	1,080					
Task 9	5,200		5,000	200			
Task 10	3,250	500	500	500	500	500	750
Total	47,250						
Cash flow per month		4,080	18,900	7,800	5,900	5,550	5,020
Accumulated cash flow		4,080	22,980	30,780	36,680	42,230	47,250

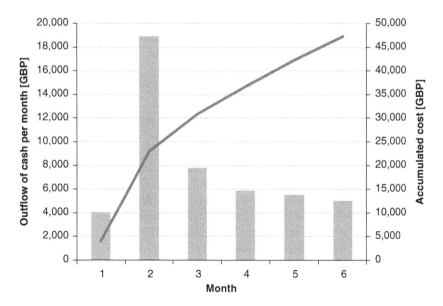

Figure 5.6

Graphical presentation of monthly outflow of cash and cumulative cost for a six-month project.

schedule if the project includes debt finance. The longer the life cycle of a project is, the more crucial the cost of capital and cash flow management will be.

Reflection points

- Think of a project about which you have some insight that went off the rails in terms of cost. Mirror this project in the list of reasons for deviations from cost estimates in projects from the beginning of this chapter. Can you find one or more likely explanations from the list?
- What are the pros and cons of the top-down and bottom-up methods to estimate the amount of resources needed for a project? Can both methods work together? Explain by using an example.
- Table 5.2 states that the range of uncertainty is higher on the plus side, i.e. that it is more likely that a project will be over budget than below it. What is your experience? What might be the explanation for this?
- How is the item "contingency" associated with the uncertainty we talk about in the reflection point above? Explain.

Management structure and role/task division

In Chapter 2, we have discussed the management structure of an organisation, but in this section, we focus on the management structure of a project – a temporary organisation. This relates to answering the following: Who does what? Who is responsible for each work part? Who is available to assist and provide expertise? How is it possible to ensure that everyone is informed about what is expected of them? These questions are classic problems in project management. It is crucial in the preparation and follow-up of each project to answer them and to ensure that there is a full understanding of what this entails. If this understanding is there, then the project can be successful, even though various other things in the preparation are lacking. If, however, a management structure and clear division of roles have not been created, it can be almost impossible to realise the objectives of a project.

It is, therefore, very important to carefully consider all eventualities when a management structure is being designed and implemented. Different influences from the organisation are important; contextual characteristics, such as its strategy, structures and processes, power and interest, culture and values. This furthermore requires looking at the people involved in the project from a broad perspective, including, e.g. their experience, technical abilities, political/communication skills, awareness, and motivation. Many people can be linked to a project, directly and/or indirectly, and careful analysis of the environment – in particular stakeholders – defines these participants. Some participants are active and are involved in the project directly, while others are passive, receiving information about progress made, but are not otherwise involved in the operations.

In small and straightforward projects, the organisational structure should be simple. At a basic level, this can solely involve the executive manager of a company talking to one of their employees and defining a project that the employee will manage and execute, being responsible for communicating the progress to the key stakeholders, and producing a final summary report. In larger and more complex projects, there is a need for a more extensive organisational structure which needs to be designed with the project requirements and the company's traditions and characteristics in mind.

Management structure in projects

Management structuring during project planning determines who does what, how responsibility and authority are arranged, and includes, among other things, the definition of how decisions are made. In this context, it is worth pointing out the following important points:

- Responsibility in a project must be seen in the context of authority. It is not sufficient to give a person great responsibility in theory, unless it also comes with the authority to make decisions. Responsibility without authority is, at best, inefficient, and leads to that person's time being poorly used, as the person will constantly have to approach their boss if decisions need to be taken in the project. The boss in question may have many irons in the fire, or be otherwise disengaged, with the result that there may be a delay in regard to decisions being taken and/or the decisions may be poorly considered.

- Inconsistency between responsibility and authority includes contradictory messages, and it is likely to lead to misunderstanding, which in turn can lead to mistakes. At worst, this leads to confusion and a lack of organisation, and this can undo a project. It is also a possibility that the affected persons will become so unhappy that they will leave the company.
- Project management organisation needs to be adapted to the needs of each project. The projects are as diverse as they are numerous. The general rule is that in every project there is a need to consider a suitable management structure, choose suitable people for the work, and for the correct individuals to have authority. In this context, it must also be kept in mind that the management structure must be monitored, and it may change over the lifetime of the project. A specific management structure and division of labour can work well in one phase but, when the next phase begins, the emphasis and priorities can significantly change, and a modified or new management structure may be required.
- The management structure needs to be related to the interests of the project. Those who are chosen to manage a project need to do it in agreement with the criteria of the project itself and the project's objectives as a guiding light. These objectives must coincide with the interests of the parent company or institute in a larger context. This is not necessarily the case in a narrower context, however, for example, if the project is controversial for some reason. Some projects are inherently political such as one that involves changing the internal organisation within a company. In this case, it is not certain that all of the department managers within the company will see the project in the same manner, and it is, therefore, necessary to choose a project manager who can be independent and make a decision regardless of the interests of certain departments or department managers.

Project management model

Each project has its own characteristics, and the management system needs to be designed to meet the needs of each project. It is possible to set up a simple model that provides a summary of the typical roles and management structures in projects, and a general model in this regard is shown in Figure 5.7.

In Figure 5.7, the work buyer is placed at the top of the organisational chart. The work buyer designates a sponsor or steering committee to oversee their interests and to ensure that their policies or direction will be followed in the project. A typical part of the accountability of a project sponsor or steering committee is to secure financing for the project. The work buyer and their representatives have individuals and groups on their side who they consult in connection with the project, e.g. lawyers and technical advisers. These individuals and groups are collectively referred to as the support group of the work buyer.

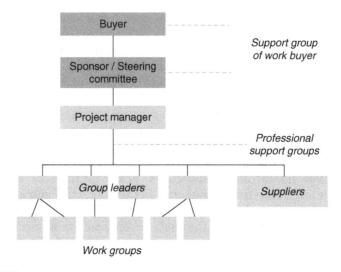

Figure 5.7

Management model for a project which shows the main roles and their connections.

A project manager is appointed by the representatives of the work buyer or by the work buyer him- or herself, who conducts the project on their behalf. The project manager hires employees to work on the project and organises their work, both individually and as work groups. If there is a work group involved, then the project manager chooses a group leader to keep track of the work of the group and they stay informed of progress within the group. The project manager also seeks advice and assistance from the professional support groups, such as the technical advisers. The project analysis should have shed light on users, partners, and suppliers, as stakeholders, and in most cases, it is a vital part of the project management activities to engage with them and make sure that information has been acquired on needs and requirements – also during the period of implementation or start-up of the project outcome. The project manager and his team deal with service and resource suppliers and coordinate the follow-up of contracts that have been made, for instance, in regard to purchases of equipment and its installation. The roles that have been discussed here will be looked at in more detail later.

It is possible to look at the management model in another way whilst also considering its larger context (Mikkelsen & Riis, 2017). This is done in Figure 5.8, which shows that the work buyer, project sponsor(s), and project manager make up the decisions part of the model. The support groups of the work buyer and the sponsor form the influence part. The project manager and the group leaders – sometimes called the project management team – form the project management part of the model, while the group leaders, along with the work groups themselves, form the work part of the model. Finally, the sellers of resources and services, e.g. technical advisors of the project, fall under the resources part of the model.

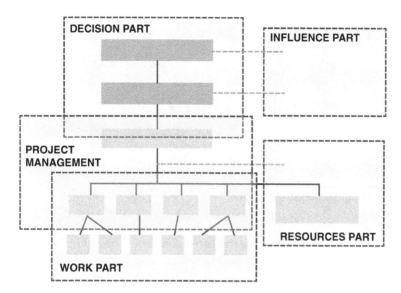

Figure 5.8

Influencing factors in management organisation of a project.

Organisation chart

A project's organisation chart is a graphical representation of its management structure. The organisation chart takes into account the characteristics and the environment of each project and is therefore unique to each project. As a result, there is no actual organisational chart template that one can apply widely, but examples like that shown in Figure 5.7 can be modified to create different structures for new projects. In designing a project organisational chart, it is worth pointing out some general rules, which are as follows:

- Power is dependent on location. The higher the participants are located in the organisational chart – the more responsibility they carry.
- An unbroken line from superiors to subordinates reflects powers of authorisation.
- An organisational chart must be decisive in terms of authority and responsibility with, for example, a subordinate only having one superior.
- Organisational charts can show more than just the relationship between superiors and subordinates – it can also show various parties that are linked to the project indirectly, e.g. consultants or information providers. The flow of information between these parties and participants in the project can be shown as a broken line.

An example of an organisational chart for a common type of project is shown in Figure 5.9. In this case, a software company undertakes to develop and set

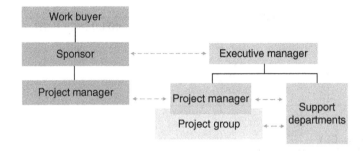

Figure 5.9

Example of a project organisation chart.

up accounting systems for a large industrial company. The industrial company (the work buyer) entrusts a particular group of its employees to carry out the daily communication and follow-ups of the project on its behalf, on the basis of an executive manager in the industrial company signing an agreement with an executive manager of the software company. The executive manager in the software company decides to entrust a particular employee with the role of managing the project, and together they choose a work group made up of a selection of employees who will be directly involved in the project and subordinate to the project manager. In addition, the project group will also be able to seek out a particular service from the support department of the software company. Much emphasis is placed on the notion that the management organisation does not restrict the flow of information between participants in the project. As shown in Figure 5.9, the executive director of the industrial company is the project sponsor, acting on behalf of the work buyer, and ensures that the company's interests are looked after.

Division of labour

It is necessary to clearly define the division of labour in a project so that all parties know what their role is and what is expected of them in this role. The breakdown of a project into its constituent works parts, together with the presentation of an organisation chart, provides a basis for defining the division of labour. A common approach to this is to create a so-called "responsibility assignment matrix" (RAM) or "RACI matrix" that reflects precisely the relationship between these variables. In addition, there is a need to define basic types of participation: that is, what participants contribute to a project and the manner in which they participate. Some basic types in regard to participation are listed below.

- Responsibility (R) – Some participants in projects have the role of carrying the responsibility and making decisions, when appropriate. Only one participant is responsible for each work part.

- Execution (E) – Other participants contribute by executing a work part. Those who execute can be more than one.
- Acceptance (A) – Some work parts are such that one or more participants must give their consent.
- Information (I) – There is often a reason for informing participants about progress in a certain work part or work parts – without these participants necessarily being active in the project.

It is common in projects that all of these basic participant types will be present, but it is also possible to think of simple tasks where there is no need for all of the above types. The responsibility assignment matrix is often presented as a matrix where the rows are work factors and the columns are the participants. A general representation of a responsibility assignment matrix is shown in Figure 5.10.

In Figure 5.10, each box represents a relationship between a work part and a participant, and an X indicates that the participant is involved in that specific work part. If there is no X, then the participant is not involved in that work part. If participation is occurring, then there is a need to select an appropriate letter, e.g. R, E, A, or I (or other letters), which it has been decided to use to indicate the nature of participation. This is demonstrated in Figure 5.11.

Figure 5.11 shows a version of a responsibility assignment matrix in a simple project with ten work parts. In the project, there are four active participants, including one project manager. In addition, also linked to the project are a sponsor and the chief financial officer (CFO) of the company, who need to be informed about progress in certain key areas. The responsibility assignment matrix is a simple but effective tool for reflecting who does what and where the

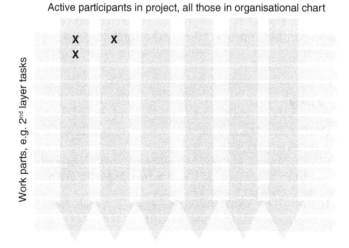

Figure 5.10

Responsibility assignment matrix in a project – general representation.

Breakdown	John Project manager	Jane Participants	Peter Participants	Anne Participants	Harry Sponsor	Sophie CFO
Task 1	R	E		E	A	I
Task 2				E		
Task 3	R / E		E		A	
Task 4		E	I			
Task 5	I		R / E			
Task 6	R		E	E	I	I
Task 7	R	E	I	E		
Task 8	R	E			I	I
Task 9	I			R / E		
Task 10	R	E			A	I

Figure 5.11

Responsibility assignment matrix – example of representation in a simple project.

responsibility lies. The matrix can easily be adapted so that it serves a bigger purpose in more complex projects and is more useful as a management tool. This will be discussed in more detail later in the book.

Reflection points

- It is stated that responsibility in a project must be seen in the context of authority. Do you know this from your own project experience? What happened when you, or a person you know, was given high responsibility but no real authority to make decisions?
- What are some of the reasons why the project management organisation needs to be adapted to the needs of a project, and how does this happen in practice? Do you know examples?
- Look back at the responsibility assignment matrix. What can happen in a project if the letter R is assigned to more than one active participant for the same task? Can you use a real or imaginary example to explain your point?

Bibliography

Kerzner, H. (2017). *Project Management: A Systems Approach to Planning, Scheduling, and Controlling*. Hoboken: John Wiley & Sons.

Lock, D. (2017). *The Essentials of Project Management*. London: Routledge.

Meredith, J.R., Shafer, S.M., Mantel Jr, S.J., & Sutton, M.M. (2016). *Project Management in Practice*. New York: Wiley Global Education.

Mikkelsen, H., & Riis, J.O. (2017). *Project Management: A Multi-Perspective Leadership Framework*. Bingley: Emerald Publishing Limited.

The Association of Cost Engineers. (n.d.). Glossary of common project control terms. Retrieved from www.acoste.org.uk/uploads/terminology.pdf.

6 Project start-up, co-operation, and information

••

Project start-up

Start-up is a period during the lifetime of a project that begins when it has been decided to initiate a project, or a particular phase of a project, and ends when the necessary conditions for effective co-operation between those who will take part in the execution phase are available – or when the project ends. This period is usually characterised by as yet unclarified expectations, lack of information, great uncertainty, and time pressure. The scope of a project start-up depends on the scope of the project. In large projects, start-up can take days, weeks, or months, while, in smaller projects, start-up may involve one meeting or a start-up workshop, taking just part of a day. Start-up is often associated with the beginning of a project (i.e. prior to execution) and can be viewed in the context of planning, which has been discussed in the preceding chapters. We prefer, however, to look at start-up as a management method that can be applied, not only at the beginning, but also during the project, for example, at the beginning of a new phase.

To explain the concept of a start-up, it is possible to look at a simple analogy. A driver does not make special arrangements when they want to start a journey. They get into the car, turn the key, put the car in gear, and drive off. It is different for a pilot, however, who is preparing for take-off. They need to go through an extensive process before setting off. Among other things, they need to go over a detailed checklist to ensure that all the equipment is working properly. They need to make a flight plan that takes into account the plane loadings and weather conditions when they are in the air, with defined alternative plans in case of incidents such as a forced diversion. They must also ensure that all the passengers have boarded the plane and that their baggage is on board. When this and many other things have been ensured, they can then get take-off authorisation from the control tower. The preparation of the flight journey is therefore an extensive process that requires information gathering, processing of information, and the following of formal procedures. This is how a start-up can be viewed (see Figure 6.1).

A well-organised start-up, with good participation from the major stakeholders, provides the basis for the smooth running of the project, or the next

Figure 6.1

Project start-up.

project phase. The specific objectives for the next phase are defined, necessary organisational changes are made, and the project management plan is reviewed, updated, reconfirmed, and published. The project gets good support from the outset, and its importance is made clear to all the participants. At the project start-up, discussion and debates may be conducted about the components of the project, the objectives and methods, conflicts and opportunities. In this process, misconceptions are corrected, and a shared vision is created, with the emphasis on the various key components. A well-organised start-up is therefore invaluable for encapsulating the group, promoting its work spirit and creating empathy.

In a project start-up, it is possible to create an overview of the project quickly by reviewing the main aspects of project management, re-evaluating the environment, analysing uncertainty and/or stakeholders, viewing the status of the project against its objectives, and evaluating the usefulness and the activity of the management organisation. This is why it can be relevant when starting a new phase in a project and when new participants join a project. A related concept is the project kick-off meeting, which is more like a platform to disseminate information about the plans, demands, and goals of the project or a project phase to the project team.

Partnerships and agreements

In Chapter 2, the context of individual companies and departments within them was discussed. Projects often have multiple contacts with the environment outside of the companies, however, including the buying of equipment, materials, and services. Co-operation with other companies or organisations must be defined in terms of goals, expectations, and role division. Such factors

---

are taken into consideration and actions coordinated in the planning, as has been discussed.

Procurement and contracts

Aspects that come under the category of procurement and contracts should be particularly mentioned in this context. The goal in procurement and contracts from a universal viewpoint is to provide a situation where the exchange of goods and services is favourable to both sides, or a so-called win-win situation. Naturally, within this, each side of a transaction will be concerned with their own interests, and agreements between the parties need to account for the risk involved in the project environment and who is responsible when the costs, timing, or quality expectations of a project are not met. The start-up can require, therefore, significant legal and technical oversight, as the signing of a bad contract in a project can be very damaging to individual parties in certain circumstances.

Tendering and selection of contractors and suppliers

Traditionally, the client would coordinate the tendering process and the selection of contractors and suppliers in projects. They have consultants or employees on their side who prepare the tender by creating technical specifications and compiling the tender documentation, as well as going over the bids submitted by potential contractors and choosing what seems most advantageous. The client manages the communications with the (potential) contractors, both during the bidding process and also once those who are to execute the project and take care of the operation period have been selected. The client also takes care of the funding of the project, including dealing with financing institutes, individual investors, investment funds, or others who possess capital and with whom the client is interested in working. Finally, the client prepares for the operation phase of the product of the project by preparing the right management structure and hiring and training people for their new roles, if necessary. The characteristics of this method include the fact that there is no direct link between consultants, contractors, those who finance, and those who are to take over the operation of the product, but instead the client has control of the coordination and sharing of information between these parties.

The tendering itself, its preparation, execution, and follow-up is a formal process that needs to be carried out according to established rules. There are various laws and regulations which apply when the tender is used to establish a trade between two or more parties for works, products, or services, and these need to be applied according to the requirements of the jurisdiction one is operating in. In this regard, there are two main types of tenders:

- General tendering, where an offer is made by advertisement and an unspecified number are given an option to make a bid. Then, the buyer may accept any bid or reject all of them.

- Closed tendering, where certain parties are given the option of making a bid. Then, the buyer is only allowed to accept the most favourable bid or reject all of them.

For example, in the European Union (EU), one would need to have knowledge of the EU Directive on the Co-ordination of Procurement Procedures (The European Parliament and the Council of the European Union, 2014, p. 65) if involved in the public tendering process. In addition to the laws and regulations for public tendering, contract parties in various fields have set up rules about co-operation and trade among themselves. Such rules are called general contract terms and are often the result of years of development and collaboration within sectors. They cover rules, norms, and traditions that have been shaped by experience, and reflect good practice and harmony for those participating. Due to the wide range of origins of these elements, a project manager will need to research which of them is most relevant to their undertaking.

In addition, we can mention contract terms that have been drawn up by the United Nations. When machinery is bought from foreign suppliers, for example, UNECE 188 can be applied and, if the installation of the equipment is included in the purchase, then UNECE 188a can be applied. By referring to such international contract terms, it is possible to save a lot of work and ensure mutual understanding of important principles such as delivery times and payment arrangements. Another example of international contract terms are the FIDIC terms, which are written by the International Federation of Consulting Engineers. The FIDIC terms are often used in the execution of projects that include construction execution and delivery, and installation of mechanical and electrical equipment.

The selection process can include various steps. One step could be the request for information (RFI), another step could be the request for proposal (RFP), and yet another step could be the request for quotation (RFQ). When a supplier or a partner has been selected, there may be a negotiation process in order to reach agreement on contractual terms and conditions.

Safeguarding the quality of the selection of partners and suppliers, participating in the negotiation process, reaching an agreement on contractual terms, and supervising the execution of contracts are core project management responsibilities. Disputes and disagreements between the contract parties during the course of a project are difficult to avoid, and if there are deviations from a contract, e.g. regarding delivery time, it is crucial to take action to address the issue, solve it if possible, or escalate it within the organisation. Different techniques can be applied, from soft notices to renegotiations. A contract partner may remain in default even after such techniques are applied, and further actions may include penalty claims or even legal consultation, followed by legal actions.

Conflicts may arise, and an important aspect of conflict management in projects is to have performed good risk analysis and scenario planning prior to entering negotiations with other parties. This provides a firm platform for defining co-operation and doing business. Invariably, a written agreement should be made, general contract terms agreed upon, and it should be determined from the outset what provisions are to be applied or not applied in the project. Among other things, it is important to determine how disputes are to be solved. This will reduce the risk of a potential conflict causing delays in the project. This is an important factor in many of the contract terms that were mentioned above. If changes are made after the contracts have been made successfully, then the contract parties need to ensure that they take care of their own interests. A good project plan and its follow-up, along with a clear contract, make it easier to enforce an outcome in such cases.

Other ways of arranging project executions

While the method described in the last section is the traditional and common method, other methods of arranging executions have become established in recent years, particularly in the context of public projects. To illustrate, a very brief overview of a few other methods is given below:

- BOT or "Build – Operate – Transfer" is a version where a private sector entity makes a contract with a public sector entity in regard to financing, designing, building, and operating – e.g. a school – for a particular period, sometimes 20 or 30 years. When the period ends, ownership is transferred to the public sector entity.
- PPP or "Public-Private Partnership" is an arrangement whereby a private sector entity provides facilities and services that are normally provided by public authorities. It is often said that financing by the private sector needs to be part of an arrangement, but this is not always the case, and ratios of private to public financing can differ widely between projects.
- PFI or "Private Finance Initiative" is a name for a method that was originally developed by the British Government to provide funding for PPP projects. The projects are wide-ranging and involve providing the public institutes with a variety of facilities and taking care of their operations. The private sector receives a payment for this that is dependent on how certain performance objectives are met.

Joint ventures

Companies often form partnerships with others to put together joint bids in the tender process.

An example could be for two or more small engineering firms to come together as a group when a tender is put out for a big design or monitoring project. To enhance their competitiveness, therefore, the firms have opted to work together. The joint venture arrangements can have many different forms. Sometimes a separate company is created around the partnership, while other times a contract is drawn up between the partnering entities, which states

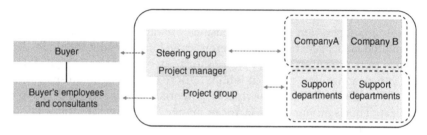

Figure 6.2

Joint venture – an example of a simple organisation.

their responsibilities and duties during the project. In some cases, where the co-operation is based on mutual trust that has been built up over a long time, a written contract is not made.

There are many different methods by which companies can work together on projects. Figure 6.2 shows a simple example of a joint venture reflected in the organisational chart.

In this example, two companies, A and B, have decided to jointly undertake a project for a particular client. The companies have signed a contract that defines the manner in which they intend to work together on the project. They have then formed a steering group which consists of representatives from both companies. The steering group holds regular meetings, and the representatives of companies A and B ensure that important information about the project is shared. The steering group has hired a project manager and a project group. The members of this group will, in most cases, come from the support departments of the individual companies, although they are, nevertheless, employees of the project while it exists. The project group can also seek assistance from the support departments of the companies, e.g. in regard to a solution of a technical issue. A frame contract between the project group and the companies exists for defining and accounting for such work.

It is important that great care is taken, and due process adhered to, in all business dealings between the parties that are involved in such projects. Creating the contract includes defining the business criteria at the start, as well as the rights and duties of the different parties, and the documenting of mutual understandings in a formal manner.

Reflection points

- Explain the difference between an initial project start-up workshop and a project kick-off meeting using as an example a small- or medium-sized project you know well, or an imaginary project.
- Do you know a PFI (private finance imitative) project? What is special about this type of project – and what can its impact be on the product life cycle, as compared to a more conventional contractor – client arrangement?

- Elaborate on the joint venture arrangement in context with lessons learned and management of knowledge. Use examples you know, if you can.

Information management

Communication and control

After the initial planning, proper project control must be in place during the project to monitor the use of resources, measure progress, report and communicate, and take necessary remedial action and decisions in order to meet the project objectives. Control is based on the project objectives, the plans, and the contracts, and project control includes measuring the actual progress and performance, comparing against the project baseline, and taking any necessary actions. This calls for control systems, such as time-writing systems, status or progress meetings, and evaluation of resources, as well as methods such as earned value analysis, to measure realised progress against baseline and make adjustments to the project plan if necessary.

The project manager takes a deep interest in maximising the likelihood of the project being successful and ensuring that it satisfies the conditions in relation to costs, time, and quality of the solution, as well as that all the participants are satisfied. Regular evaluation of the quality and availability of assigned resources is a vital part of this. One of the most important things to do in relation to this is to have an efficient communication system so that relevant information is shared between key stakeholders in a fast and secure way. An obvious benefit of this is that it is then possible to gain from the knowledge and experience of all the participants in a timely manner, and that potential problems can be recognised early and different scenarios planned for. A part of this is necessary and proper documentation of information, such as budget specifications, plans, and status reports. A mutual understanding between all those involved in the project needs to be ensured in terms of definitions, objectives, and role divisions. However, there can be too much information. There is a need to make a distinction between formal and informal communication and to be clear about the level of formal documentation required. Overwhelming the interested parties with too much information should be avoided, and redundant information should be limited or prevented. The right people should get the right information and assessing and defining this is an important project management duty.

The reality for a project manager is, more often than not, that they do not have direct authority over the people who work with them in a project. They, therefore, need to apply other methods to get their way and to ensure that project objectives will be attained. They need to appeal to people differently and create an atmosphere in the working group that ensures good progression; an atmosphere that encourages participants to contribute and to be able to work on their own initiative within acceptable boundaries for the project. Various approaches can be used to create such an atmosphere in the work group, but these need to be built up systematically. First and foremost, the project manager needs to lead by good example, and they also need to realise that the group is composed of individuals who are different, with pros and cons, strengths and weaknesses. They need to be sensitive towards different viewpoints, attitudes, and interests and apply active listening. These topics are discussed in detail in our books *Project: Leadership* and *Project: Communication* – in this series.

A prerequisite for generating a successful atmosphere is having a purposeful and efficient flow of information between those involved. Everyone needs to be informed about what is expected of them at all times. They need to be able to carry out their work without constant intervention, and they need to periodically receive information about how they are performing. It is also essential that they have the potential to improve the situation if something has gone a different way than intended. The type of information that is associated with different projects will vary widely.

An information system is a framework for the way in which information created during the project will be stored, as well as how external data and information is received and transmitted. In the spirit of modern management etiquette, it is essential that traceability is ensured and that a record of information is kept, particularly associated with decisions and their criteria. A decision needs to be made in relation to where this type of information is to be stored. A general description of what will be saved, where it will be saved, and who is responsible for saving it also needs to be established. This may refer to technical systems of various kinds as well as procedures for how they are to be used.

Figure 6.3 reflects a simple project where a particular company has undertaken to execute a project for a client. The communication channels in this

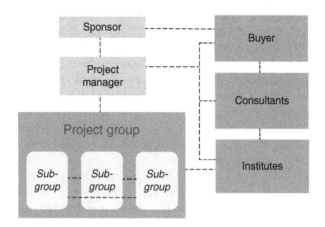

Figure 6.3

One example of many communication channels in a project.

---

small project are, however, numerous. The company has appointed a sponsor who is responsible for ensuring that the project objectives are met, as well as communicating with the representatives of the client. The sponsor has chosen a project manager who steers the project group. That group consists of a number of employees who work on the project as individuals, but there are also three work sub-groups in the project. Others that are linked to this project are consultants acting for the client who work on various technical aspects requiring specialist knowledge. In addition, there are various institutes that need to be consulted in order to get approval for a project, e.g. the Environmental Institute in a construction project of a particular type or the Data Protection Office in an IT project where the aim is to collect data regarding individuals. Communications channels between parties are represented with broken lines in the figure. Even with the simple structure for this exemplary project, there are still many interconnected channels, and it must be ensured that the communication between the different project groups does not break down. If this is not done, and there are barriers in the flow of information between parties, this can cause anything from delays in a project to its premature cessation.

In a project like this, it is necessary to have a formal infrastructure and processes for dialogue between groups and individuals. This can be in the form of an arranged meeting system whereby the dialogue is scheduled, and individual participants can contribute, update reports, and discuss real or potential problems. A communication system like this is formulated during the initial stages of a project and then updated during the lifetime of the project, as required. The communication system describes what individuals and groups in the project will formally talk about in regard to issues relating to the project, how often meetings need to occur, and how the preparation, execution, and follow-up of such meetings shall be arranged. An example of such a system can be seen in Table 6.1. The table shows different types of meetings (first column) that are held during the project. These meetings are irregularly held during the project, and the duration of each meeting varies. The latter columns show which individuals participate in what type of meeting, and different shading is used, so that a quick glance at the table by individual participants will give them a clear understanding of their obligations.

An important part of communication system design is the format for recording the minutes of each meeting in the project. In this regard, templates can be very useful as a simple and effective tool to ensure that the correct information is collected for the minimum amount of effort. An example of a template for recording minutes can be seen in Figure 6.4.

Project handbook

It is common in larger projects to document the outline and structural organisation of a project, including the formal communication system previously discussed, in what is referred to as a "project handbook." As the name suggests, it is a comprehensive database or information system for the project and an

Table 6.1 An example of a formal meeting system in relation to a simple project

Type of meeting	Time	Format	Sponsor	Project	Work group 1	Work group 2	Work group 3	Client	Client	Environment Institute
Start-up meeting	*At the beginning of each phase*	*1/2 a day each time*	▤	▤	▤	▤	▤			
Needs analysis meeting	*At the beginning of the project*	*2 days*		■	■	■	■	■	■	
Status meetings	*Every 2 weeks*	*1/2 hour each time*	▨	▨						
Work meetings	*Every 2 weeks*	*2 hours each time*		▦			▦			
Consultation meetings	*At the beginning and end of a project*	*2 hours each time*		▧				▧	▧	▧
Co-ordination meetings	*Every week*	*2 hours each time*		▦	▦	▦	▦			

invaluable reference for participants of a project, including project managers, steering group members, and other stakeholders. The simplest form of a handbook is the project's document folder that is in the keeping of the project manager and is accessible by the main participants. It holds plans related to the project, including information on time and cost estimates. It also contains a list of the main participants and stakeholders related to the project in one way or another and their contact information. Modern handbooks are most commonly stored and updated on the project website, and access to them is controlled as deemed appropriate.

In its first version, the handbook is not very different from the original project plan, along with the formal communication that took place in the early stages of the project. As the project progresses, information that is collected in a handbook includes minutes, formal documents, instructions, deviation

	Meeting occasion			Page
Minutes of meeting				1

Date		Time	Place / Secretary	

Attendees & copies

Agenda:	2. Issues to be discussed
1. Progress since last meeting	3. Plan next meeting

Nr.	Description				
1					
2					
3					
	Next meeting:				

Issues in process

/ Issue description	Responsibility	Est. del.

Figure 6.4

An example of a template form for recording minutes of a status meeting.

reports, and other reports. They are placed in this handbook according to established procedures, and access to them is directed so that those in need can access the data when needed. A project handbook is a living management tool and is an invaluable information source which can be consulted when criteria for decisions, material results from processing, important work documents, and prepared documents need to be found. It is important to design the structure of the handbook in a rational manner right from the start. One way to achieve this is to use the structure of the project plan as a guide. Another way is to arrange the classification of information in a handbook on the basis of the breakdown of the project, for example, into phases and work parts, as well as the organisational chart.

There are a number of different options regarding how one goes about compiling a project handbook, and there are many technical solutions available to assist in this process. In all cases, however, it is essential to go the whole way, i.e. it is not enough to buy the technological solution, but its use needs to be ensured by designing processes around its use and training people in the project team to use the system. This will be further discussed later.

Formal and informal communication

An essential ingredient in the success of a project group in working together, making good decisions, and attaining objectives is good communication. Communication can take place in various ways, such as verbal or written, and

Figure 6.5

Documentation gone over the limit.

it can be formal or informal and direct or indirect. The means of communication can be meetings, conversations, messages and letters, phone calls, email and text messages. Another essential ingredient regarding the effectiveness of project groups is trust between their members. The concept of trust can be interpreted in different ways, but here we prefer to define it as follows: "Belief by another person or a group that the person in question will meet expectations in the future." Trust between members of the project group enhances creativity and critical thinking and creates a positive environment in which participants are willing to put in more effort and look at challenges in the project as opportunities.

For simplicity, it is possible to divide communications in projects into two groups – informal communication and formal communication. In the modern business environment, there is an increasing tendency to use formal communication, as it serves, amongst other things, the purposes of reducing the risk of a misunderstanding and clarifying responsibility and authority, as well as ensuring traceability. Examples of formal communication in projects include formal letters, emails, reports, and communications on the project's progress in documents or on the internet. In these cases, the communication is documented, with outlines of who wrote it, who sent it, and descriptions of the content and purpose. Formal relations are important in the event of disputes and can be of benefit in settling disputes and bringing matters to a conclusion.

Examples of informal communication in projects are phone calls and chats between people in informal situations, even conversations at work. More often than not, important conversations occur in informal situations, and there can be an opportunity to resolve difficult issues that are more difficult to deal with at the meeting table. In such cases, it can be preferable to document the results in some way (e.g. in a follow-up email) to formalise it and ensure that it is fully understood by all and traceable.

Reports are one example of formal data that emerge in projects. Commonly, a variety of reports are created when working on projects. For example, progress reports are compiled for each milestone (end of phase) in projects. These reports cover how successfully a certain phase was completed according to a schedule and also look at whether the overall project is on schedule. If that is not the case, then there is a discussion about what actions should be taken so that the project can be brought back on schedule. Another example is incident reports that are compiled when events occur that affect the progress of the project. This type of report outlines the event, the cause(s), and what response there was to ensure the least impact on the project. Further examples are status reports on the status of the project work, cost, time, resources, risk – in the current and previous phases, and reports forecasting the development of the project in the coming phases. In addition, there are reports due to changes in projects where there is a significant deviation from the original approved plan and final reports and future plans.

It is the job of the project manager to oversee the main reports in a project, making sure that they are informative, accurate, concise, and delivered to the right people – e.g. team members, sponsors, project boards, or organisation management – in a timely manner. For this reason, it is advisable to use templates where possible and to work on the document on an ongoing basis so that it is already substantially complete when project deadlines are approaching. In some cases – if the project manager or his team are very experienced – it may be sufficient and acceptable to the stakeholders to report only by exception, i.e. to issue a report only when there is something significant that needs to be reported.

IT

Management of information and information technology (IT) are two sides of the same coin in a modern organisation, and one of the main challenges for a project manager is to maintain an overview of all the possibilities offered by modern IT to facilitate effective communication. The internet has opened up new opportunities for communication and collaboration in projects. The term *virtual project* is used for projects that are carried out over the internet by people who rarely or never meet during the project but nevertheless work together to achieve shared project objectives. This is possible by utilising information systems and creating a web-based work zone. Multiple individuals based in different parts of the world can work on project documents simultaneously, and online meetings can be held with multiple participants. Information can be downloaded and uploaded, providing a valuable communication channel to inform stakeholders and others about the progress in projects. Globalisation and the development of computer technology have meant that larger companies often use workforce expertise from around the world in the form of distributed work groups (Ingason et al., 2010). With widely dispersed work groups, new problems are created for managers when members meet infrequently and primarily communicate through electronic media, across different time zones, cultures, and locations. Building trust can be difficult under such circumstances, and there can be concerns about the security of data in cyberspace. On the plus side, substantial savings can be made in projects in terms of time and travel costs if electronic communication is widely utilised. Figure 6.6 shows a number of options that the internet opens up, along with examples of available solutions.

Utilisation of the internet can involve some challenges. For example, in regard to group bonding, it can be a challenge to build up a good atmosphere in a group of people who do not meet face to face, or do so only on rare occasions. It is important to provide the proper tools and establish processes. Rules need to be in place to control usage, and the people involved need to be properly trained and follow established procedures. Sensitive information contained in files needs to be carefully handled at all times and security features used, including encryption.

Meetings as a management tool

One of the most important tools in project management is meetings. They are, however, management tools that are often abused. An enormous amount of time is wasted by having poorly organised meetings, meetings where progress is not guaranteed, and no follow-up occurs. It can, therefore, be said that meetings are a double-edged sword – an important weapon when it is applied with skill, but also blunt and, at worst, harmful if it leads to reducing the participants' confidence in the abilities of the manager. Different types of meetings commonly found in projects are as follows:

- Start-up meetings – These have been discussed earlier in the book.
- Decision meetings – These are held to make certain important decisions. For example, a meeting of a project manager with a steering group to make formal decisions on tender arrangements, the selection of contractors, or responses to emerging problems due to changes in the environment of the project.
- Brainstorming meetings – These are used to gather information and ideas and process them to arrive at solutions. The philosophy behind them is that two or more heads are better than one.
- Coordination meetings – These are held between groups and individuals who work separately on specific aspects of a project but need to meet to

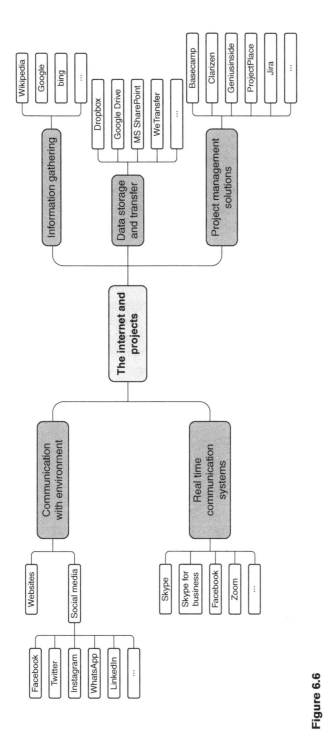

Figure 6.6

Example of internet usage areas and solutions in projects.

ensure continuity. This applies to, e.g. design and engineering teams who need to make sure that their work is compatible.

- Status or progress meetings – These are held to monitor the work to date in a project and how it corresponds to the schedule. The client and/or their representatives meet with the people executing the project, including contractors. At a progress meeting, the agenda is simple – the status of the project is evaluated, including progress made since the last meeting and the proposed progress by the next meeting.
- Crisis meetings – These are meetings that are arranged at short notice when difficult issues arise that require immediate action (see Figure 6.7).

A couple of simple key points should be kept in mind regarding meetings as a management tool in projects. A key trick of the trade behind the use of this tool involves making a distinction between preparation, execution, and follow-up.

- Preparation involves deciding objectives and finding out who is required to participate in meetings, writing up an agenda, agreeing on a location, and sending each participant the arrangement details with reasonable notice, as well as information about any data they need to prepare.
- The execution of a meeting involves creating an atmosphere of progress, following the presented agenda, documenting results, facilitating the meeting, ensuring a balance between the contributions from the participants of the meeting, and achieving the goals defined at the start.

Figure 6.7

Project meeting.

- The follow-up involves writing the minutes, distributing them to the parties concerned, and seeking approval, if needed. Sometimes the writing of the minutes is done during the meeting (as opposed to just taking notes for later editing) and they are signed off at the end of the meeting.

Change and quality control

A project's environment is constantly changing. As Charles Darwin once said, "It is not the strongest of the species, nor the most intelligent, but the one most adaptable to change." This notion can certainly be applied to projects. Plans are made, but unforeseen circumstances can intervene and make it necessary to deviate from the original plans. Dvir and Lechler (2004) wrote a paper with a title that captured this in a somewhat provocative way: "Plans are nothing, changing plans is everything." Once the project plan has been approved, and the project has been officially launched, formal changes need to be dealt with in a formal manner. This process is covered by the term "change control." It involves the setting up of protocols to enable change to occur in projects in a way that is compatible with the interests of all stakeholders and that follows the regulatory environment of a particular project. It also involves ensuring that best practice is followed throughout the change process, from initial acceptance to completion.

In this context, it is in order to shed light on the importance of a quality approach for the project, including appropriate quality control. The output of the project must be fit for purpose, and it is necessary to review the project – and its deliverables – regularly throughout the project to ensure that quality goals are achieved, communicated, understood, accepted, and followed. It is important to verify that established quality requirements, objectives, and standards have been met; this can be ongoing over the project life cycle, but it is typically linked to the end of each of the project phases. If problems are discovered in good time, there can be sufficient time to discover the causes of the problems and any defects, and to plan and execute corrective and preventive actions. Quality audits can be a part of the project reporting progress and are performed by members of the project team, by the organisation, or by external parties such as the client.

Changes can be of various types, and typically they are necessary because of unanticipated situations or occurrences. Sometimes it is necessary to change contract terms or project specifications with customers or suppliers. The largest changes are often those that are requested by the client in regard to changing the scope of the project or specifications of the deliverable. Assuming that the requested changes do not affect safety, reliability, or otherwise affect results in a negative manner, such changes are generally agreed by those undertaking the work, provided that the buyer has agreed to bear any costs involved. Requests for change can increase the risk of delays in projects, whether it be in staffing, contract terms and conditions, or otherwise. It is not uncommon for a change in technical approach to occur during the execution stage in projects when original plans proved unviable. A common example may be unexpectedly poor soil conditions being encountered during a construction project, requiring a major rethink of the structure design.

In all cases, changes must be monitored against the original project objectives and the project plans. If the project manager or stakeholders feel there is a need to deviate from the plans that have been approved, the request for such a change/changes is examined and analysed by the appropriate parties within the project. This may be the project manager or the project manager working alongside a sponsor or steering group. This can also be a consultative body which the stakeholders have agreed upon, e.g. a group comprised of representatives of the contractor and the client.

It is possible that, when a change proposal is evaluated, there is no need to deviate from the plan. If, however, it is deemed necessary to make changes, then there is a need to keep track of them and to look at these changes and their implications in context. Changing plans can have a variety of consequences for projects. It can affect the costs, timing, and characteristics of the result, and it can affect the communication of those involved in the project and, hence, the work spirit and atmosphere. In other words, changes can affect one or more of the foundation objectives set at the beginning of a project. It is, therefore, necessary to view them from this perspective well before decisions are made.

It may be possible to execute changes in more than one way, and a range of options should be looked at to find out which one is the most favourable, with the needs of the project in mind. Once this has been analysed, then it should be clearer what effects the changes will have and what their consequences are likely to be. At this point, the appropriate party needs to make a decision in regard to the proposed changes. If they lead to higher costs than initially agreed upon in the contract between the client and the contractor, the client will have to make the decision about the changes and confirm that they will handle the extra cost. The objective of change control is, therefore, not to prevent changes, but to make sure that they have the least negative impact on the project, and that solutions are chosen that are the most appropriate whilst keeping the interest of the project in mind. At the start of a project, a process for change control should be adopted and agreed with all relevant stakeholders. The change control process could include such topics as the identification, description, classification, and assessment of a change, and even rejection or approval – followed by implementation and verification of the change. Figure 6.8 shows a much simpler example of a process for change control in a project.

Hof Cultural and Conference Center in Akureyri, Iceland (see Figure 6.9), is an example of a major project where systematic change control was applied from the beginning to the end. Change suggestions underwent professional analysis, and decisions that led to increased costs were made by the project buyers, i.e. the town's representatives. The original idea was that the building would be 3,500 sq. m. in size and, when these ideas were presented in 2003, it was estimated that it would cost the equivalent of 1.2 billion ISK, which corresponds to 2.1 billion ISK in inflation-adjusted prices in the year

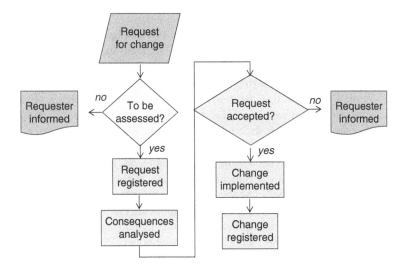

Figure 6.8

An example of a simple process for change control.

2011 (or approximately 11 million GBP). A design competition was held, and 33 proposals were received, with Arkþing's proposal being selected. When construction was about to begin in the middle of 2005, it was decided to expand the building to 4,700 sq. m. in order to accommodate users such as the Akureyri Music School. In September 2005, the building plans were expanded again, reaching 5,400 sq. m., and later that year it was decided to

Figure 6.9

The House of Culture at Hof in Akureyri, Iceland (Menningarfélag Akureyrar, n.d. – photograph by Audunn Nielsson).

include a basement, bringing the total floor size to 7,400 sq. m. The reason for the basement was technical in nature, as it had been found that the house would sink under its own weight, and the basement was part of the efforts to stem that risk.

It is clear, then, that significant changes occurred to the building plans from the initial ideas through the design and initial execution periods. The main changes are that it was decided to place the Akureyri tourist office there, as well as the Akureyri Music School and the Akureyri Theatre Society. Changes were also made regarding the utility rooms, and the kitchen was expanded. The projected budget in November 2009 estimated that the final cost would be 3.4 billion ISK (this also includes the effect of the intervening devaluation of the Icelandic Krona). The largest expense factors were design, supervision, and management (over 9%); concreting and cladding (29%); finishing of the interior (35%); and stage equipment (11%) (Menningarfélag Akureyrar, n.d.).

Economic difficulties that began in the autumn of 2008 affected this project. Unemployment was a growing feature during this time, and the local authorities made a conscious decision to extend the project time for as long as possible to lessen the rate of unemployment and to provide work for people during the trough in economic activity. As it was a big project, this provided some local relief from the financial crisis.

Change control was handled in this large project by having established protocols between the different stakeholders. When the project owners (Akureyri Properties) came up with new ideas, or experienced construction-related issues, they submitted requests to change the project plan, which were then evaluated by the local council in Akureyri. The council, therefore, had the final say in these matters.

Earned value

"Earned value management," or EVM, is a simple but powerful method of monitoring performance during projects. This involves comparing information from the most recent project plan and current capital expenditure at particular times during a project to evaluate the progress of a project and draw conclusions in regard to the status of the project relative to time and cost objectives. It requires detailed plans to be in place, disciplined work methods, and the proper analysis of up-to-date information during the execution of a project regarding, e.g. actual costs, liabilities, expenses bound by purchase orders but not yet paid, expected costs, and cash flows. More specifically, there needs to be a financial management and reporting system in place linked to the cost structure and time schedule so that an overview of the financial status of the project is always at hand. Before looking at earned value management in more detail, it is necessary to look at the budget presentation and cost estimates and review the discussion about the evaluation of cash flow. It is wise to build a cost estimate from the outset with a view to how it can best be used. Thus, it may not only be used to assess the cost of the project but also as a management tool during the execution of the project. Table 6.2 shows such a configuration for the same simple project as was introduced in Chapter 5. The total cost of each work part has been estimated, and that number is shown in the second column of the table. In the other columns, we take note of the percentage of work estimated as complete, actual costs that are paid out, and the differences between the latter and the original estimates. This is done without reference to contingency funds (included in the overall project budget), as these are not intended to be included in the cost estimate of the follow-up of the project, but instead as a form of insurance fund that the project manager can use if it is deemed absolutely necessary.

The goal of financial controlling is to spot deviations from plans early enough so that appropriate measures can be taken, and this method is based on the premise that it is possible to evaluate the financial status of a project at a specific time. The column entitled "Completed" shows the project manager's evaluation of how much has been executed within each work part – regardless of how much has been paid. This is done by the project manager first estimating the amount of work completed as a percentage of the total (e.g. 50%), and then multiplying this by the original cost estimate in the second column to give a monetary value. The column entitled "Paid out" contains information on how much has been paid at that time for each work part – and for the project as a whole. The column entitled "Difference" is then the difference between the total estimated costs and what has been paid to date. The column entitled "Comments" is – as the name implies – to record information and clarification, if necessary. This arrangement, as described, is a practical method for establishing earned value on an ongoing basis in a project. The main parameters used in the calculation of earned value are as follows:

- *Planned value (PV)* (also called Budgeted Cost of Work Scheduled or BCWS) – This refers to the approved cost for completing a work part (or total including all work parts) within a specified period.
- *Actual cost (AC)* (also called Actual Cost of Work Performed or ACWP) – This refers to all costs, direct and indirect, that have been incurred in the project – or in a certain work part – at a given time. This information should be available from the accounting system of the company. The corresponding column in Table 6.2 is the column entitled "Paid." It should be noted, however, that "Paid" does not always reflect accrued expenses and does not, therefore, necessarily reflect AC. In some cases, a payment is agreed upon in advance, but the contractor may potentially need to use more time and resources than was agreed upon. In the calculation of the earned value, accrued expenses will have to be used.
- *Budget at completion* (BAC) – This is the total budget allocated to a project or work part within a project.
- *Earned value (EV)* (also called Budgeted Cost of Work Performed or BCWP) – This parameter reflects the proportion of the work that has been completed and is obtained using pre-defined metrics for calculation. The

Table 6.2 Cost estimate: an example of a presentation which can also be used in the follow-up of the project

Breakdown	Estimated cost [GBP]	Completed [GBP]	Paid out [GBP]	Difference [GBP]	Comments
Task 1	7,350				
Task 2	2,400				
Task 3	2,070				
Task 4	13,800				
Task 5	3,850				
Task 6	3,300				
Task 7	4,950				
Task 8	1,080				
Task 9	5,200				
Task 10	3,250				
Total	47,250				

corresponding column in Table 6.2 is the column entitled "Completed." Earned value can be estimated directly, e.g. by the project manager estimating what percentage of a particular work part – or the project as a whole – is completed. This approach is called "Percentage Complete" (PC). Simple rules can be used in association with this, e.g. the progress of the work part is 0% until it is completed, when it is then 100%. An alternative arrangement is that progress is 0% until the initial project phase, 50% after it is started, and 100% when it is fully completed. Other ratios may be used, such as 25% once started and 100% upon completion. These ratios are then projected into cost figures by multiplying the ratio by the project's BAC, which represents the initial cost estimation of the project, or a particular project part in question. This is reflected by the formula EV = PC x BAC.

- *Estimate at completion (EAC)* – This is the revised estimated total cost at the end of the project.

The variables PV, AC, and EV are used to assess whether a project or individual work parts are on schedule or not. There are simple formulae that are used in this assessment:

- *Cost variance (CV)* = EV – AC
- *Cost performance index (CPI)* = EV/AC
- *Schedule variance (SV)* = EV – PV
- *Schedule performance index (SPI)* = EV/PV
- The revised total cost at the end of the project can be calculated using the formula EAC = AC/EV x BAC

Figure 6.10 shows the relationship of these key variables in the method of earned value. The figure shows a particular project where the status is taken on day X.

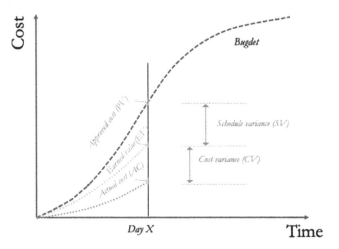

Figure 6.10

Pictorial representation of the main variables in the calculation of earned value.

Comparing the difference between EV and, individually, PV and AC, gives two values, i.e. CV and SV. CV indicates whether the cost is below the estimated budget (when CV is a positive number) or above the estimated budget (when CV is a negative number). SV indicates whether the project is ahead of (when SV is a positive number) or behind (when SV is a negative number) the schedule. This approach can be the framework for a performance management system, as it allows the project manager to assess the current situation and forecast this into the future. In this way, problems can be foreseen, and necessary mitigation planning – followed by appropriate actions – can be taken to avoid negative outcomes in a project.

> *To give a simple example, we can talk about a hypothetical project that involves investigating the knowledge and experience base of project managers in Iceland and Denmark. The intention is that the project will take 10 months and that 100 people will be interviewed each month. It is expected that each interview will cost €300, and the total budgeted cost of the project is therefore €300,000.*
>
> *By the end of the first month, 75 interviews are taken, and they cost €15,000 (AC). As the intention was to perform 100 interviews per month, the project is already behind schedule. The percentage completed (PC) is therefore 75/1000 or 7.5%. The EV is therefore 7.5% x €300,000, or €22,500. The PV on that day was 100 x €300 or €30,000. On average, each interview has cost €200, so the project is under budget. More specifically, the schedule variance (SV) and the cost variance (CV) of the project can be calculated as follows:*

- CV = EV – AC = €22,500 – €15,000 = €7,500
- SV = EV – PV = €22,500 – €30,000 = – €7,500
- EAC = AC/EV x BAC = €15,000/€22,500 x €300,000 = €200,000

It therefore seems that the project will take longer than planned but will be delivered significantly below the estimated budget.

Reflection points

- In this chapter, we used the term "change control." You may have heard of "change management." What is – in your view – the difference between change control and management of change (change management)? Can you explain this with examples?
- Think about how the extent of formal and informal communication develops through a project life cycle. Explain this with a simple graph.
- What can be the direct and indirect impact on a project team – and the project – if the project manager fails in the preparation, execution, and follow-up of meetings?
- What is required in order to apply the earned value method? What are – in your view – the strengths and weaknesses of this method?

Bibliography

Dvir, D., & Lechler, T. (2004). Plans are nothing, changing plans is everything: The impact of changes on project success. *Research Policy, 33*(1), 1–15.

Ingason, H.T., Haflidason, T., & Jonasson, H.I. (2010). Communication and trust in distributed project teams. *Project Perspectives, 32,* 34–39.

Menningarfélag Akureyrar. (n.d.). Hof cultural center. Retrieved from www.mak.is/en/mak/hof.

The European Parliament and the Council of the European Union. (2014). Directive 2014/24/EU on public procurement. *Official Journal of the European Union, 57*(65), 65.

7 Uncertainty and risk management

••

Types of uncertainty

It is a normal occurrence that project managers receive news or notice signs that some aspect of their project is either not proceeding as planned, or will not proceed as planned, for various reasons. Competent project managers will either have foreseen this, and have an appropriate mitigation plan in place, or be able to react quickly to unforeseen events to limit the amount of damage that might be caused to a project. Steen Lichtenberg is a well-known scholar in the field of project management who has covered a range of topics in this area, including developing strategies for the creation of cost schedules for projects whilst taking uncertainty into account. At the beginning of his book – *Proactive Management of Uncertainty Using the Successive Principle* (Lichtenberg, 2000) – he outlines the realities experienced by project managers, whereby there can be little available information at the planning/ execution stages of a project, and assumptions that have been made can be associated with a range of uncertainties. This, he argues, requires flexibility and adaptability on the part of the project manager and that all options are kept open to find solutions to problems.

Frank Knight has been called the founder of risk management. He distinguished risk from uncertainty by defining risk as measurable uncertainty (Knight, 1921). We will, however, define uncertainty as either risk or opportunity. An opportunity is an event favourable to the project, while a risk is an event harmful to the project.

It can be argued that all project managers use uncertainty management of some sort in the daily management of their tasks/projects. The difference lies in how formal the method is, and often the uncertainty management only involves evaluating from one day to the next what can happen in the project and responding to it. Uncertainty management – as a management method – is a considerably more extensive and formal process, as will be discussed here. Uncertainty management takes place during all phases of the project life cycle, and typically the main purpose is to minimise the negative impact of this uncertainty, i.e. minimise risk.

Uncertainty can be of various types, and its sources can be numerous. Examples include financial or technological uncertainty, uncertainty due to legislation or politics, and uncertainty in relation to the environment and health and safety. It is useful to further define the main types of uncertainty in the execution of projects. Ward and Chapman (2003) describe to what extent uncertainty is greatest at the beginning of projects and discuss the uncertainty categories that they consider most important. These are as follows:

- *Regarding plans* – This refers to the prerequisites of plans, their usefulness in the follow-up, and the value and accuracy of the information upon which they are based. It refers to all types of plans, including time, costs, and other resources. Examples of uncertainties falling into this category are that the necessary resources for the project are not properly scheduled at the beginning, and so projects do not get finished. It can also be a risk in a complex project that it is not broken down sufficiently during schedule planning.
- *Regarding design and transportation* – Uncertainty regarding a design refers, e.g. to changes made to the definition of the product of a project during its whole life cycle. This also includes technical uncertainty, e.g. missing out on new technology that could save time in the project. Uncertainty regarding transportation can be acute in many projects that are based on resources being transferred between locations.
- *Regarding objectives and priorities* – This refers to a wide range of uncertainty in relation to objectives, their definition, their importance, and prioritising, and how far participants in the project are willing to go in regard to compromising on these objectives.
- *Regarding the interaction of stakeholders* – This includes uncertainty regarding definition of responsibilities and authority, differences in understanding amongst people in regard to their roles and the above issues, communication problems, and people's ability and skills, amongst other factors.

Given that Chapman and Ward's list refers to the preparation stage of projects in particular, it is possible to add a further couple of uncertainty categories so that the list covers the entire life cycle of projects and can be used as a checklist for assessing uncertainty factors (BSI, 2010).

- *Regarding laws, regulations, and standards* – This refers to uncertainties that arise in connection with unclear provisions of laws, regulations, and standards, or the risk of failing to take these into account in the project. In particular, the uncertainty associated with changes in laws, regulations, and standards should be pointed out, as well as the risk of not taking into account such changes. We can also mention the uncertainty in relation to intellectual property rights related to a project.

- *Regarding health and safety* – The health of people involved in a project, including those with knowledge and skills that are not easy or impossible to replace, as well as injuries caused by accidents during a project, and health effects from the products of projects.
- *Regarding politics and environmental issues* – This refers to the uncertainty related to politics in the external environment of the project, where opposing political forces can affect the progress of the project, for example, because of their belief that it will affect them and their environment in negative ways.
- *Regarding finance* – For example, regarding changes in foreign exchange rates, unstable interest rates, inflation, and availability of funds.
- *Regarding suppliers* – For example, regarding the performance of contractors and sellers of equipment, whether services and equipment are delivered on time and are of the right quality.
- *Regarding the nature of the results* – Whether things are properly designed and/or properly installed and work as intended and whether the security is adequate.
- *Regarding human factors* – For example, uncertainty regarding the skills and experience of management, the policy of the company, the strategies of the company for selecting employees, and the participation of a sponsor or steering committee in a project.

Two main categories

Risks in projects concern whether expectations will be fulfilled or not, regardless of what type they are. A useful way of viewing the risks that are associated with projects is to divide them into two main categories. These are listed below and shown together with linked responses in Figure 7.1.

- Risks related to project processes, the skills of those involved in the project, e.g. of the project manager and the project team, and the knowledge of these entities and their working methods.
- Risks related to the project environment. This refers to situations and events that occur outside of the project and those associated with the project that one cannot do anything about, except to prepare for their possible occurrence.

As Figure 7.1 shows, there are two main categories of risk, and the responses to risk can be twofold. People can try to reduce the risk probability in advance, and this can be done in various ways, or they can try to mitigate risks by preparing an action plan that alleviates negative outcomes should they occur (see also the discussion about risk analysis in Chapter 3). In the former case, choices can be made regarding many of the elements in a project at the planning stage, including reducing or increasing the scope of a project in order to eliminate a degree of unwanted uncertainty. A simple example of increasing a

RISK-EXPECTATIONS
WILL NOT BE FULLFILLED

RISK RELATED
TO PROJECT PROCESSES

RISK RELATED TO THE
PROJECT ENVIRONMENT

RISK MANAGEMENT
BEFORE: REDUCE PROBILITY
AFTER: PREPARE ACTION PLAN

Figure 7.1

Risk associated with processes and the environment.

project's scope could be testing a range of technologies before committing to further investment in one of them in order to give the best possible chance of the optimum outcome being achieved. In the latter case, a common approach to deal with risk in projects is to create contingency plans that define the responses that should be taken if unexpected adverse events occur. If proper procedures and work methods are in place and there is proper staffing of the task group, it is possible to minimise the risks associated with project processes. Risks related to the environment cannot be controlled, although the exposure of a project to them can be controlled to varying degrees, and contingency plans can also be made.

Process of risk management

It is desirable to look at uncertainty management in a formal way and implement a risk management framework as part of the daily management of the project in a formal manner. A framework helps to ensure that risk is managed throughout the project life cycle and should include methods to identify, categorise, evaluate, assess, and treat risk. The framework should be based on the risk management policy of the organisation and relevant international, national, and industrial standards. One part of such a framework would be a process for uncertainty or risk management. An archetype of such a process is found in different sources (APM, 2004; Chapman & Ward, 2003). Figure 7.2 shows a simple process of risk or uncertainty management in projects.

The figure shows the breakdown of the different stages in the process, and these are repeated continuously over the life cycle of the project. The element termed "Managing the process" is to the right and reflects the fact that this is a specific process that needs to be managed with each step. Information is

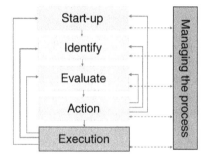

Figure 7.2

Process of risk management in projects.

collected at each stage and is used to make decisions about the next steps. This information can be stored in a database and used for future reference in later projects. A breakdown of the individual steps in the process is given below.

- *Start-up* – This involves customising the general process of risk management in the company to a specific task or project and starting the process formally. This part of the process of uncertainty management relates primarily to the beginning of a project.
- *Identify* – This revolves around analysing uncertainty factors, and various methods can be used to do this. For example, it is very useful to build on past experience by referring to a database of uncertainties that should have been developed.
- *Evaluate* – This deals with understanding what is involved in the uncertainty and valuing it as accurately as is deemed necessary. This assessment can be qualitative or quantitative, depending on the situation. In Chapter 3, we looked at a simple method of evaluating uncertainty by looking at it from the perspective of likelihood and consequences.
- *Action* – This deals with defining actions that can be carried out in response to the uncertainty. If we are looking at a negative uncertainty, i.e. a risk, the actions revolve around minimising the likelihood or minimising the consequences. If we are looking at a positive uncertainty or an opportunity in the project, then this is turned around, and people will want to increase the likelihood or the consequences.
- *Execution* – This simply involves executing those actions that were defined in the previous steps.
- *Managing the process* – This includes follow-up on the risk management process and making sure that it is applied systematically, that information is gathered from applying the process, and that this information is used for continuously improving the process. Even more importantly – that a risk database is maintained in the organisation so that it may learn from experience and apply experience from concluded projects in new projects.

PERT

PERT, which stands for Project (or Programme) Evaluation Review Technique, is a commonly used analytical tool for making work plans. It is often used in conjunction with the critical path method that has previously been discussed in relation to work scheduling. The PERT method is based on simple statistics and utilises information about uncertainty regarding the duration of work phases. For this reason, we discuss PERT here in relation to uncertainty management, but readers are advised to also review Chapter 4 about time scheduling and the critical path method.

In the process of determining the critical path, assumptions are made – often with limited information – about the duration of each task. It is seldom possible, however, to say for certain what these durations will be, as they can change, owing to the variability of the project environment. The PERT method deals with evaluating the uncertainty for each task and, in turn, the uncertainty in relation to the total time of the project. PERT assumes that the time of each task can be described as a beta (probability) distribution. This is illustrated in Figure 7.3, which shows an example of a beta distribution with the horizontal axis representing time and the vertical axis representing probability.

In Figure 7.3, the gap from (a) to (b) reflects the time uncertainty for the completion of a specific task where (a) is the shortest possible time, or the most optimistic forecast, and (b) is the longest possible time, or the most pessimistic forecast, while (m) is the most likely time. When a, b, and m have been evaluated for a specific task, then it is possible to calculate the expected duration (TE *or time expected*) and the variance (σ^2) according to the following formulae:

$$TE = \frac{a + 4 \times m + b}{6}$$

$$\sigma^2 = \left(\frac{b-a}{6} \right)^2$$

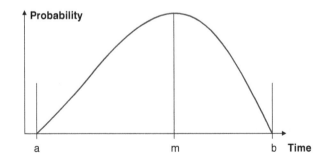

Figure 7.3

Probability distribution for the time length of a task.

As the top formula shows, the expected duration is a kind of average number where the most likely forecast gets a quadruple value within the dividend sum calculation compared to the most optimistic and most pessimistic forecasts. This leads to the divisor being 6 in this case, as 6 values are used in the top line. The bottom formula calculates the variance, and one can calculate the *standard deviation* by taking the square root of this. Calculations of the standard deviation are based on the criterion that the standard deviation of the beta distribution is one-sixth part of its total span.

When the expected duration and variance have been calculated for all tasks, it is then possible to draw conclusions regarding the duration of the project as a whole. For example, it is interesting to know how likely it is that the project will be finished within the specified time. Such calculations are based on statistical rules (e.g. *central limit theorem*) which state that if the tasks are sufficiently many and independent, then their sum is normally distributed. Therefore, it is possible to use a table for normal distribution to draw conclusions concerning the project as a whole if these conditions are met. For this, it is necessary to calculate a so-called Z-value as follows:

$$Z = \frac{T - \sum TE_c}{\sqrt{\sum \sigma_c^2}}$$

In the above equation, T is the total time of the project which is being looked at. $\sum TE_c$ is the total time of the critical path of the project, and $\sum \sigma_c^2$ is the sum of the variance of tasks on the critical path. The Z-value can be put into tables for normal distribution to find the proportion of the normal distribution, which is to the right of the Z-value in the normal distribution. This proportion is called P or *probability*. To explain these calculations in the simplest manner, it is easiest to continue with the example that was the basis of the discussion about the critical path, introduced in Chapter 4. The critical path in that example was as shown in the thick lines in the arrow graph in Figure 7.4.

The most optimistic and pessimistic forecasts about the time length of the individual tasks, along with the most probable forecast, are shown in Table 7.1, along with the calculations of the expected duration (TE) and variance (σ^2), according to the given formulae.

It can be seen that the critical path (A + C) is five days, and that the sum of the variance of the critical path is 0.5 days. It might be of interest, for example, to calculate the probability of the project being finished within six days (T = 6). It is then necessary to calculate the Z-value according to the formula above, and the result is that Z = 1.00 in this case. This corresponds to a probability (P) of 0.8413 for a normal distribution. It can be said, therefore, that the probability that this project will be finished in six days is 84.13%.

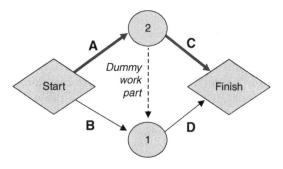

Figure 7.4

Critical path example.

Reflection points

- Review the case of the herring factory in Djupavik from Chapter 2 in the uncertainty categories presented by Ward and Chapman. Can you find examples of uncertainty in this case that are not included in the categories?
- Why is it important to separate risk related to project processes from risk related to project environment? Explain with an example.
- What are some of the advantages and limitations of applying PERT in a project? What does it take to use this method?

Decision-making and risk

Herbert Simon received the Nobel Prize in economics in 1978 for research that looked at decision-making within economic organisations. Simon said that decision-making was the essence of all administrative processes, and companies that had a modern approach to decision-making would have a competitive advantage in a world where the business environment was undergoing rapid development. Few doubt these words, as making decisions is, without a doubt, the most important and difficult thing managers need to do. The same, of course, applies in everyday life for people with responsibilities.

To illustrate this, we can talk about an intermediate manager in a company who, upon discovering a potential problem, is faced with having to make a

Table 7.1 Evaluation of estimated task durations using PERT

Work part	a	b	m	TE	σ^2
A	1	4	2	2.17	0.25
B	1	3	1	1.33	0.11
C	1	4	3	2.83	0.25
D	0.5	3	1	1.25	0.17

choice between three options. The first of these options would be considered as taking an independent line and would have a series of significant knock-on effects, if taken. The second option would be perceived as following conventional wisdom and would have well-anticipated effects. The third option would be to ignore the issue and make no decision.

After assessing these options, the manager has convinced himself that the first option is probably the best for the company in the medium to long term. If he decides then to take the first option, and this turns out to be the outcome, then this is likely to be considered as just part of his work duties, and there is no special award or recognition for this. If he is wrong, and things turn out badly after taking the first option, then there is the risk that he will be punished in some way, even to the point of losing his job if there is enough at stake. If he takes the second option and it turns out badly, then there may be enquiries from senior management, but no further action will be taken, as known procedures were followed. If he takes the third option, it is likely that the problem will emerge in such a way that blame cannot be attributed to him. Either blame will be attributed to others, or the problem will be considered to be an unavoidable consequence of business.

With these potential scenarios in mind, either the second or third options might be tempting for that individual to choose. The third option, in particular, might be the most tempting, as many people can develop a decision-making phobia, and this could well be the option that they take. They consider that there is little chance that the medium- to long-term effects of taking this decision will affect them personally.

If one stands back a bit, however, it can be seen that there is a risk that the damage done to the company by not reacting in time, or reacting in the wrong way, is ultimately serious enough to cause forced redundancies, and the manager could lose their job anyway. Alternatively, an unanticipated in-depth analysis of the problem, once it surfaces, could be traced back to their decision not to apply the correct action, with the same negative consequences for the manager in question.

Some find it easier than others to analyse information in a short time, make a decision, and stick with it. Having said this, it does not mean that the ability to make decisions is exclusively innate. Making a decision is largely based on skills that can be trained, just like skills in sport (Russo et al., 1989). Decision-making requires coordinating different perspectives, analysing the available information, weighing and evaluating, selecting and rejecting, compromising if that is deemed appropriate, and finally choosing the solution that, on the whole, is considered the most favourable. The importance of correct decisions is largely dependent on the environment. A poor decision can have few serious consequences when the economy is expanding and demand is high. The same poor decision taken during a deep recession can be the difference between bankruptcy and survival for an enterprise.

In their book, *Decision by Objectives*, Ernest Forman and Mary Ann Selly discuss basic concepts of decision theory, amongst other things (Forman &

Selly, 2001). They believe that decisions in companies are often made at meetings in a rather chaotic way, where there is no certainty that the selected route is the best in regard to the interests of the company. To discover how one can achieve better results in decision-making, it is useful to examine a simple model by Herbert Simon in regard to the decision-making process. He divided the process into three phases:

- *Intelligence.* Here, an attempt is made to identify problems and opportunities, for example, through direction setting and by listening to employees, customers, and competitors.
- *Design.* Here, the ideas or options are examined in more detail, for example, by brainstorming, by discussing the theoretical background and examining relevant empirical evidence, or by undertaking new research and making comparisons.
- *Choice.* Here, the best solution is chosen.

Once it has been decided which projects will be undertaken, good preparation needs to take place. It is important to define the project well, identify the factors in the environment that affect it, and determine phase division, emphasis in project management, organisational structures, and the roles of all those involved. You then need to establish the set of goals for each project and determine the scale that shall be used for performance or efficacy evaluation.

Portfolio management and project selection

We end this chapter on uncertainty and risk management with a brief introduction to portfolio management and project selection, where there is always the risk of making the wrong decision and prioritising the wrong projects. Cooper et al. (1999) define the management of a portfolio as dynamic decision-making, where the business priorities are constantly being reviewed and updated. In this process, new projects are evaluated, selected, and placed in order of priority. Projects in progress have the highest priority, although if they have a poor track record to date, they may be written off or their priorities/priority reduced, and their resources allocated to other, more successful projects that are underway, or to new ventures. This process takes place in an environment where information is uncertain and variable, opportunities appear and disappear, and a variety of objectives and policies and relationships between entities that increase the decision-making complexity must be taken into consideration.

Meredith et al. (2016) put forward a comprehensive process in eight steps to manage portfolios of companies and organisations (i.e. *Project Portfolio Process*) with the main objective of converting the results of direction setting into actual success in the business operation. The process is designed to keep track of both new projects and projects in progress, with the prerequisite that direction setting has taken place. Emphasis is placed on identifying which subjects or tasks are classified as projects and which subjects or tasks are not. Here there is a need for each individual company to have a definition of what constitutes a project, and this may involve financial scope, perceived complexity, and other factors. Projects are prioritised, and special attention directed to those projects that support the policies and goals of the business. These are then closely monitored to ensure that they receive sufficient attention and resources. The aim is to find those projects that will benefit the company or have a positive impact on other tasks. Projects that involve too much risk or are too expensive are excluded. The eight steps are as follows:

- Establishing a project oversight committee responsible for finance, management of resources, and management of projects. On this committee would sit, for example, the main project managers and experts in risk management.
- Setting the classification/categories/parameters of projects and the influence factors that are attributed to these elements as a basis for the selection of projects. Different kinds of classification could be suitable for different projects, depending on their origin. For example, one category may include direction-setting projects, another category would be based on optimising tasks from daily operations, and another category could include research projects that could yield results in the longer term.
- Gathering information and data about each project so that they can be arranged in the appropriate category and defining this information and data based on the selected influencing factors.
- Investigating the resources that are available to the company, both internally and externally. If resources are scarce, it may be necessary to postpone or cancel projects, even if they meet the general requirements that the company sets for participation in projects.
- Narrowing the circle. Using influencing factors and other available information, for example, relating to resources, to reduce the number of projects that will be examined further.
- Arranging each set of tasks within each category of projects in relation to their relative importance and/or how appropriate they are.
- Choosing the projects that will be continued and deciding which projects should be put on hold. Keep a balance between the categories – in other words, try to avoid putting all your eggs in one basket.
- Introducing the process so that everyone understands the rules and then starting the process.

The selection of projects (Figure 7.5) is based on numerous factors which are important to weigh and evaluate. Among these are the following:

- Is the project aligned with the strategy and values of the organisation?
- Will the project increase profits for the organisation?
- Will the project improve the utilisation of labour?

Figure 7.5

Project selection.

- Will the project improve the utilisation of equipment and facilities?
- Will the project maintain or increase market share?
- Will the project open up new markets?
- Is the time to market acceptable?
- Will the project have any unforeseen impact on the present market?
- Will the project affect the image of the organisation?
- Will the project meet the needs of key stakeholders?
- Does the project fulfil all Health, Security, Safety and Environment (HSSE) requirements?
- Is the risk acceptable?
- Is the necessary knowledge and expertise available?
- Will the project cause unacceptable disruption in the regular operations of the organisation?
- Is the investment cost within given limits and acceptable?
- Does the project comply with all relevant standards, laws, and regulations?

The factors that form the basis for the selection of projects can be many or few. The list above is not actually an exhaustive list of what is important, but it gives a good overview. It is vital to build a systematic method to select projects on the basis of the criteria that have been determined. It is common to use the methods of *cost benefit analysis* or a *discounted cash flow analysis* to guide such decisions. Such methods based on financial calculations are certainly common and can be widely appropriate. However, it is often not enough to base a decision solely on such calculations. This applies, for example, when it is not possible to assess the consequences of decisions in financial terms. Further details will be discussed in the following sections as to which methods can be applied to make the final selection of projects.

What is the best solution for deciding on the selection of projects? To a large extent, this depends on the range of variables between different project options, both known and unknown. If these are simple, then a straightforward analysis of benefits and risks can be carried out and a decision made. A simple example would be our previously mentioned painting and decorating company deciding that it is best to carry out an indoor project and an outdoor project simultaneously (provided this fits in with the wishes of their customers) so that the overall workload won't be affected by adverse weather conditions. The majority of projects, however, are a lot more complex, and the different known and unknown variables involved can be analysed using a selection model that may be based more on theory, with a number of in-built assumptions, or more on empirically derived experience. Usually, it would be a blend of both, and the more realistic it becomes, the more complex the elements within it become. Typically, there would be a compromise so that the model is not too complex and is able to simplify selection decisions to a form that is properly understood by management.

The selection model needs to fulfil certain requirements. It is required, for example, to reflect the different solutions on offer, prioritise the most important influencing factors, and to be able to compare results with regard to risk. In addition, the model must be able to reflect realistic situations and needs to be flexible to account for the changes that may occur over time, for example, due to changes in the internal and external environment of the project, such as market price shifts or an altered tax environment. Last but not least, it needs to be easy to use.

Meredith et al. (2016) categorised decision models into three main groups, according to how the information and assumptions are laid out. In the first category, there is a choice that is not necessarily made based on measured criteria. In the second category, there are models based on financial considerations, and in the third, there are models that are not necessarily based on financial considerations but on some other measured criteria.

Selections that are not necessarily based on measured criteria

- Discretionary or emotionally influenced selections made by the top executives/management – often taken without the existence of a clear sense of logic. A kind of "sacred cow" that subordinates do not dare to question.
- Selections deemed essential to keep operations going, for example, when the government changed the diesel tax regime in Iceland in the summer of 2005. The fuel companies were then faced with the following "choice" – to implement changes to their equipment and work processes in order to respond to this new environment or to stop operating.
- Selections deemed necessary for competition. Sometimes, it may be considered important to initiate a project, even though the project is not necessarily likely to be effective. It is done in the context of the movements of others. An example of this might be the competition in the airline industry where an airline decides to start a scheduled flight to a specific airport because its main competitor offers trips there.
- Selections can be made where a business can see advantages in developing a new product or service which alone will not necessarily deliver profits

but is considered a necessary complement to the existing products or services of the company.

- Selections based on a non-quantitative comparison of benefits.

Selection models based on financial criteria

Financial selection models can be simplified so that they can be more easily understood, although this process may not fully reflect different realities. They can also be made more complex, with more realistic outputs, but are then more difficult to understand. They can also be made extremely complex to fully reflect the time value of money for large projects that involve many different elements and can also take account of the potential financial risks of a project, such as fluctuating interest rates, exchange rates, and market pricing over its life cycle. While there is a wide range of models used by different entities of varying sophistication, we outline below the main types of financial selection model, together with a brief explanation of each:

- The *payback period* is the time it takes a project's product to return the initial investment of margin from operations. For example, if a company invests 1 million GBP in new machinery, and the return on the operation of the machinery is 0.5 million GBP per year, the repayment period is two years. While very straightforward to understand, the payback period is considered a method of analysis with serious limitations and qualifications for its use, because it does not account for the time value of money, risk, financing, or other important considerations, such as the opportunity cost.
- The *return on investment (ROI)* reflects the amount of cash flow from operating the product compared to the money that was invested. The net profit for a given period of interest is divided by the amount of the initial investment, and this is multiplied by a hundred to give a percentage value.
- The *net present value (NPV)* is used when the profit of the investment is evaluated in the long term by using a time value of money. The initial investment amount is subtracted from the sum of the future net operation cash flows that are discounted at a chosen representative percentage rate for the period of analysis. If this value ends up as below zero, then the investment is not financially beneficial, and other options for the money that would otherwise have been invested in the proposed project may be found.
- The *internal rate of return (IRR)* is a method closely related to NPV that also accounts for the time value of money. It is said that the project constitutes a good investment if the internal rate of return is higher than what can be gained by putting the money that would otherwise have been invested to other uses, such as sitting in an interest-bearing deposit account. The internal rate of return of the project is therefore defined as

the discount interest rate that makes the net present value of the project zero over a given period.

The concepts of net present value and internal rate of return can be explained through a simple example. In a certain project, the cash flow is such that the initial cost of the project is 1 million GBP. After that, the operation of the product of the project starts to return fixed 0.3 million GBP profits every year, in the first five years of operations. The return threshold set by the investors is 10% in this example, as these are the best rates they could get if the money was used for other purposes. With the appropriate discount calculations, it is possible to calculate both the net present value (NPV) and internal rate of return (IRR) on the basis of the available information. In this example, using an IRR of 15% puts the NPV above 0 GBP for the five-year period, so the investment is therefore better than the alternatives.

Selection models that are not necessarily based on financial criteria, but also on other measured criteria

Like the aforementioned purely financial models, these can either be simple or complex to extremely complex and are an attempt to allow selection modelling under a wider range of categories, encompassing the full scope of a project and its effects. Some of the main types are listed below:

- Models with "either or" evaluations. Here a simple checklist is set up of all the influencing factors that the company considers as the basis for selecting projects. For each potential project, the list is gone through and an assessment is taken under each influencing factor, so that it is either "fulfilled" or "not fulfilled." The results in the filled matrix are then analysed, and the most favourable project is chosen according to a set of predetermined criteria.
- Models based on numerical rating under a number of different categories. It is very common to set up a checklist, as described above, but to go a step further in the execution. The influencing factors can be given different weightings, and it is also possible to give a rating for "either or" factors, for example from 0 (not fulfilled) to 1 (fulfilled). Certain assumptions and conceptual models will lie behind the different weightings and, for this, one can take advantage of useful methods that have been developed by others, such as the Analytics Hierarchy Process (AHP) (Saaty, 1990). The utilisation of the AHP in project management has been the topic of many academic publications. For example, Al-Harbi (2001) showed how AHP can be applied in the selection of contractors in tendering.
- Simple calculation models that can take into account both financial factors and other factors. For example, the Pareto Priority Index (PPI) as explained by Gryna (2001) represents a simple method for selecting from multiple improvement projects. The analysis takes into account four main

factors: savings resulting from the project (s), the probability of success (p), the cost of the project (c), and the time it takes to complete it (t). The PPI coefficient is calculated according to the formula:

$$PPI = \frac{s \times p}{c \times t}$$

The PPI coefficient is calculated for all the projects/tasks under consideration, and the one that has the highest PPI values gets priority. It should be borne in mind that the quality of the assessment is only as good as the input assumptions that are made under each heading.

An example of a potential scenario that can be assessed using the PPI selection tool may be a business that is faced with having to choose from the following four improvement projects. In Project A, the estimated saving is 10 million, the chances of success are measured at 70%, the cost of the project is 3 million, and the time to complete it is two years. In project B, the saving is estimated at 3 million, the chances of success are 80%, the cost is 500,000, and the time taken to complete the programme is six months. In project C, the estimated saving is 500,000, the chances of success are measured at 80%, the cost is 200,000, and the time taken to complete the project is three months. In project D, the estimated saving is 1 million, the chances of success are 90%, the cost is 300,000, and the time needed to complete the project is one year. How can the company prioritise these projects?

If the PPI coefficient is used, then quite decisive results can be seen. In project A, the coefficient is 1.2, in project B it is 9.6, in project C it is 8.0, and in project D it is 3.0. Accordingly, the company should start on project B, because there the PPI coefficient is highest. The next project would then be project C.

More complex selection models than those outlined above are often needed to select from competing projects, and a common method in this regard is the cost-benefit analysis (CBA). This is a common project selection tool and is an attempt to model the comparative differences between the expected balance of benefits and costs of new projects to all stakeholders – the risks of failure, an account of opportunity costs, and the risks of staying with the *status quo*. If necessary, it also includes external effects of the project, including those experienced by the wider public and the environment. Usually, all the different criteria would be given a weighting, a numerical score for candidate projects would be given under the different categories, and these would then be added up at the end for comparison with the alternatives. Below is the sequence of steps that comprise a generic cost-benefit analysis (Boardman et al., 2006):

- List alternative projects/programmes.
- List stakeholders.

- Select measurement(s) and measure all cost/benefit elements.
- Predict outcome and benefits over relevant time period.
- Convert all costs and benefits into a common currency.
- Apply discount rate.
- Calculate net present value of project options.
- Perform sensitivity analysis.
- Adopt recommended choice.

An example of the use of such methods is the process undertaken by Rannis (a publicly funded body that oversees the allocation of the Technology Development Fund in Iceland) in regard to selecting research projects that will receive public grants. Its role is to support innovation in the Icelandic economy by supporting research and development work in the area of technology development and industry. To be eligible to receive support from the fund, projects need to be novel and based on a well-formed idea of practical value that is likely to provide benefits above a certain threshold.

In the initial evaluation process, if applications do not meet these requirements, they are rejected. If these requirements are met, the application then goes to an expert panel which will conduct a form of CBA. There are four main components to this. Novelty (N) is defined as a change in known criteria, which leads to increased value creation in the market. The probability of success (L) is the total probability of the project succeeding as candidates have declared, and that the products reach the market. The value (V) in this case reflects the turnover resulting from the project outcome, as well as the value for the local users of the outcome. The expert panel also takes into account other factors (G), such as knowledge value, values for partnership/partnerships between research institutes and the economy, international co-operation, start-up business development, export potential, and other interests such as national interests. All these influencing factors are evaluated subjectively and get an individual rating. The overall rating of the assignment is finally calculated. In 2014, the following equation was used for project grant applications assessed for eligibility for the Technology Development Fund.

$$\text{Total grade} = \left(0{,}3\ N + 0{,}4\ V + 0{,}3\ G\right)\cdot\left(1 + L\right)$$

The expert panel will then prioritise projects in each sectoral category according to these results, and this priority list will be used for guidance in decision-making by Rannis in their final selections (Rannis, n.d.).

Reflection points

- Review Herbert Simon's simple three-step model for decision-making. Do you think this is a good model? If we take this as a representation of reality, what do you think is the weakest link in the decision-making process and why?

- Do you have personal experience of any of the selection models that are not based on measured criteria? Explain your case.
- It is said that Einstein stated that "not everything that counts can be counted, and not everything that can be counted counts." What kind of a project selection model could be chosen to deal with this reality? Why?

Bibliography

Al-Harbi, K.M.A.S. (2001). Application of the AHP in project management. *International Journal of Project Management, 19*(1), 19–27.

APM. (2004). *Project Risk Analysis and Management Guide.* High Wycombe: APM Publishing Limited.

Boardman, A.E., Greenberg, D.H., Vining, A.R., & Weimer, D.L. (2006). *Cost-Benefit Analysis, Concepts and Practice* (3rd ed.). Upper Saddle River: Prentice Hall.

BSI. (2010). Project management. Principles and guidelines for the management of projects (BS 6079-1:2010).

Chapman, C., & Ward, S. (2003). *Project Risk Management: Processes, Techniques, and Insights.* Chichester: Wiley.

Cooper, R.G., Edgett, S.J., & Kleinschmidt, E.J. (1999). New product portfolio management: Practices and performance. *Journal of Product Innovation Management, 16*(4), 333–351.

Forman, E.H., & Selly, M.A. (2001). *Decision by Objectives: How to Convince Others That You Are Right.* River Edge: World Scientific.

Gryna, F.M. (2001). *Quality Planning and Analysis: From Product Development through Use* (4th ed.). Boston, MA: McGraw-Hill.

Knight, F.H. (1921). *Risk, Uncertainty, and Profit.* Boston, MA: Hart, Schaffner & Marx; Houghton Mifflin Company.

Lichtenberg, S. (2000). *Proactive Management of Uncertainty Using the Successive Principle: A Practical Way to Manage Opportunities and Risks.* Copenhagan: Polyteknisk Press.

Meredith, J.R., Shafer, S.M., Mantel Jr, S.J., & Sutton, M.M. (2016). *Project Management in Practice.* Hoboken: Wiley Global Education.

Rannis. (n.d.). Tækniþróunarsjóður – leiðbeiningar 2014 fyrir umsækjendur. Retrieved from www.rannis.is/media/taeknithrounarsjodur/TS_Reglur_V14.pdf.

Russo, J.E., Schoemaker, P.J., & Russo, E.J. (1989). *Decision Traps: Ten Barriers to Brilliant Decision-Making and How to Overcome Them.* New York: Doubleday/Currency.

Saaty, T.L. (1990). How to make a decision: The analytic hierarchy process. *European Journal of Operational Research, 48*(1), 9–26.

Ward, S., & Chapman, C. (2003). Transforming project risk management into project uncertainty management. *International Journal of Project Management, 21*(2), 97–105.

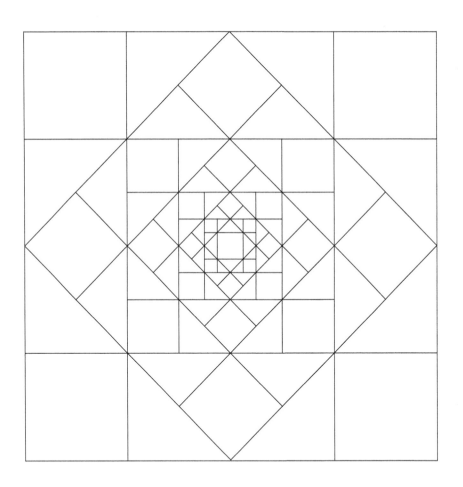

8 The project manager and the project team

······························

Methods of execution

Execution methods are those methods, tools, and processes that are used in the management of projects. The discussion of these methods can be divided into three main parts: (1) quality management within the project, including work processes and the quality assurance that is to be provided, (2) methods that involve the solving of specific work parts or the project as a whole, and (3) facilities.

Quality management within project management

We will talk about quality management within project management by referring to the quality trilogy devised by the famous guru of quality management, Joseph Juran. The quality trilogy consists of quality planning, quality control, and quality improvement (Gryna, 2001). As defined in the opening chapters, projects are temporary operations. In most cases, however, they are not isolated phenomena, and new projects will be worked on as others are underway and being completed. A project-orientated company that has built up a management system (quality planning) according to international standards such as ISO 9001 or ISO 14001 will have designed a process to deal with the preparation and execution of a stream of projects. Many of the methods that are used within projects are, by nature, established processes, even though projects are temporary. Various work parts that are performed in projects can therefore be described as processes that are repeated again and again whilst the project is in operation, and it is possible to monitor, refine, and improve efficiency for the next project if necessary. Examples of this are (a) processes for the preparation, execution, and follow-up of meetings and (b) processes relating to the handling and storage of information. These are both important operations within projects requiring considered and disciplined approaches that will benefit from lessons learned from previous experience.

In projects, quality control of different sorts takes place, whereby the products are monitored, and it is ensured that they meet agreed standards. This has been discussed already in Chapter 2. The third part of the trilogy, quality improvement, deals with continuously improving the practice of project management in the organisation. This includes assessing, benchmarking, and improving the organisational project management competences. The benchmarking can be carried out against projects and project management practices within the organisation or against external projects or organisations, or even against acknowledged excellence models such as the Project Excellence Baseline (IPMA, n.d.). This calls for keeping an open mindset and maintaining an overview of what are accepted as good project management practices. In continuation, the project management practices can be changed and improved. Such management of change can be revolutionary and happen over a shorter period of time. In other cases, it may be evolutionary and happen slowly. The reality is that people and organisations often have limited capacity and willingness to change. There are various reasons for this; sometimes the need for the change is not perceived, the change somehow goes against the culture of the organisation, there is a lack of energy or drive within the organisation to change, or any one of a multitude of other reasons. Experienced managers know that people – and thereby organisations – will change when they believe that this is in their best interest. Here lies the key to a successful change project, but the first step is to assess the adaptability and will to change.

Another important concept related to quality management is quality assurance, which involves providing customers, the work buyer, or stakeholders with the confidence that their expectations will be met. Depending on the nature of the project, there are various ways in which this can be approached which will be most appropriate. One way, certainly, is to follow established work procedures and assessment criteria that give customers confidence in the final result. A more obvious example would be testing new products according to current published standards within a particular sector, e.g. the fatigue performance of car tyres. Other examples would be the ability to produce detailed records of the life cycle of a project, including the minutes taken during meetings and details about decision-making criteria. This involves the organised storage of project data that can be easily accessed. Such a system can be certified according to the ISO 9001 standard, and there are international quality standards that deal with the application of quality management in projects, such as the ISO 10006 and the ISO 21500 standard, which contain guidelines that relate to best practice in project management. Another procedural method in project management that has become increasingly popular is PRINCE2. The original PRINCE (*PRoject IN Controlled Environments*) method first appeared in 1989 and is essentially a collection of templates and processes that reflect specific methods of preparation, planning, execution, and completion in projects. The method was developed in the UK for the UK Government as a standard of project management for projects related to information and telecommunication technologies. It did not take long, however, before the methodology was adopted in other areas of project management. PRINCE2 was released in 1996 as a generic project management methodology and built on the foundation of PRINCE. Since then, its popularity has grown considerably, particularly in the UK, but it has also gained a foothold in 50 additional countries around the world, and especially in the public sector. The 1996 version was revised in 2009 to reflect its now much broader scope, but the most recent version to date is Prince2 2017. Prince2 has, since 2013, been owned by Axelos Ltd (Axelos, n.d.).

Agile project management

"Agile" management is a project management approach that has become established in the engineering and software industries. The term is synonymous with a couple of techniques that have common characteristics. The main focus is on the outcomes of the project rather than the process that is used. The methods are simple and are designed to make execution easy. Little emphasis is placed on documentation, as rapid changes are expected, and the evaluation of the project often takes place with the participation of all the parties concerned, and great emphasis is put on co-operation. Here, there is a significant difference between Agile and more traditional methods, such as PRINCE2 and the use of standards such as ISO 9001.

One of the methods that fall into the Agile category is the so-called "Scrum" method that was developed by Ken Schwaber and Jeff Sutherland around 1990 (Schwaber, 2004). Scrum contains a set of principles regarding procedures and work in projects, and also defines a few key roles. The main reason for adopting the Scrum method is that it is impossible to predict the outcome in a large software project (or other particular types of project) far into the future. It is, therefore, impossible to use a routine set of procedures in the execution of such projects. Scrum is based on iterative advances called sprints and progressive delivery, i.e. the final product is delivered in stages, not in one piece at the end of the project. Each sprint can take two to four weeks and is worked on according to a list (*sprint goals*) that is derived from a product *backlog* or list of requirements, which the Scrum team and a representative of the owner have agreed upon. A work package in a software project includes a description of the work to be performed, the objectives, cost, resources needed, and duration, and a work package is typically referred to as a user story. Every day, there is a brief meeting – the Scrum meeting – where the team discusses what happened during the last 24 hours, and what will happen during the next 24 hours. The structure of the Scrum method, with its time-bound sprints, represents effective scope configuration management and alignment with the stakeholder's needs and requirements, and it helps to minimise errors, deficiencies, and unintended scope creep.

In terms of people involved in a project, there are a few key divisional roles in Scrum that distinguish between those that are committed to a project, those that are involved, and those that have ancillary roles. The representative of the owner is called the *product owner*. His role is to ensure that the views of the work buyer get delivered in the work of the team and that the

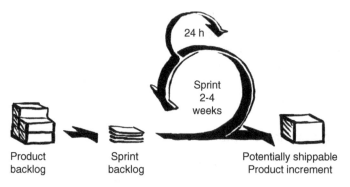

Figure 8.1

Simple representation of the Scrum method in project management.

work is in accordance with the overall objectives that the work buyer has set and is reflected in the product backlog. Another role in the Scrum method is the so-called Scrum master, who keeps track of the team itself and ensures, amongst other things, that they work according to the agreed principles. Figure 8.1 shows a visualisation of the Scrum method and outlines some of its key terms.

Schwaber (2004) explains that there is a fundamental difference between the traditional project management role and the role of the Scrum master, where he defines the Scrum master as a coach and mentor – someone who guides and explains, removes barriers, facilitates creativity, and empowers the team. In practice, the role of the Scrum master can be quite different from one organisation to another, and there are some similarities between the Scrum master role and the traditional role of a project manager, although the project manager typically takes responsibility for the outcome of the project as a whole.

Strategies/methods for solving work phases

There are many types of projects, as discussed at the beginning of the book, and there are just as many methods for solving work phases as there are projects. Owing to this wide variety, there is no way to describe, in a general manner, the technical methods that should be used in the execution of projects, as they must take into account the nature of each project. It is, however, possible to talk in general terms about the interaction between the client and the contractor. The client often gives a specific individual or party responsibility for the execution of work phases or the project as a whole, and these can either be departments or employees within a company or an external party, i.e. a contractor. The client has to decide whether, and to what extent, they are going to use a contractor and, if so, whether a single or multiple contractors are required. It also needs to be determined how negotiations with contractors and suppliers will be handled, what type of payment arrangements will be used, and what contract terms are to be used as guidelines. Subsequently, there is a need to decide who coordinates the work of the contractors and who will manage them. The client may want to do this themselves, but they might also want to be free from the management requirements that come with this. In this case, for example, they may get the largest contractor to manage and coordinate the activities of all the other contractors. This is related to the discussion of the selection of contractors and tendering arrangements, and in public projects over a certain size, there is an obligation to follow the formal tendering process. If the client is a private party, then they can negotiate directly with the contractor(s). In this process, it is necessary that a healthy business outlook governs the choice of contractors, whether private or public entities are involved.

Facilities

The need for facilities varies from one project to another. If the project is carried out by a group of people, then the requirement for a facility for the group needs to be evaluated. In small projects – with team members who meet regularly because of other matters and projects – it may be enough for the project group to be accommodated in the office of the project manager or in a meeting room when needed. In larger projects, where specific employees are employed, and one or more teams are generated that work together over variable time periods, it may be necessary to set up independent facilities for the project. In this case, it has to be ensured that the group has all the necessary facilities, premises, and technical equipment in order to carry out the work safely and efficiently. The project manager must define the needs at the beginning, evaluate the associated costs, and obtain approval from the steering group for the development of the necessary facilities. Figure 8.2 provides an overview of some elements that need to be considered in relation to the evaluation of the project's facilities.

The project manager

Many scholars have looked at the characteristics and ability factors that are needed to make an effective project manager, and this topic is discussed at length in our book *Project: Leadership*, which is part of this series and gives a good overview of leadership methodology and the personal attributes and development of the project manager, including emotions, thoughts, and general behaviour. Figure 1.1 at the beginning of this book divides essential skills in project management into strategic and organisational competences, personal and social competences, and methodical competences that relate to interaction with the environment.

There is a significant difference between traditional management and project management, and this is highlighted by a simple comparison in Table 8.1.

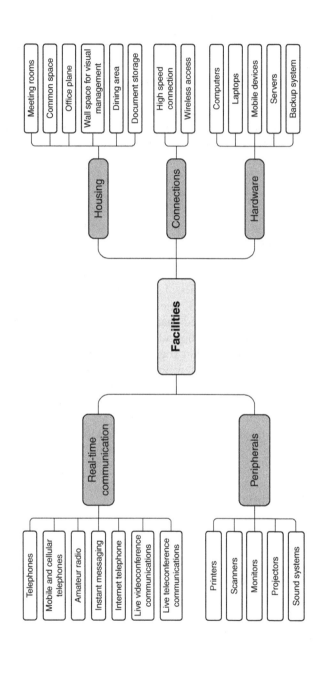

Figure 8.2

An overview of elements that need to be kept in mind in relation to the creation of facilities for projects.

Table 8.1 Differences between traditional management and project management

Traditional management	Project management
Tries to maintain the status quo and maximise success within a known system	Tries to achieve changes, often with new inventions of some sort
Authority and responsibility are defined depending on position on an organisation chart	Lines of authority can be unclear, and assignment of tasks can contradict the organisation plan
Assignments/tasks marked out and defined	Constant changes to assignments/tasks
Success defined regularly depending on how well targets are achieved	Success is determined by whether the project's objectives were attained or not
Degree of co-operation is known	Uncertainty in co-operation and potential disputes

It is not a given that a person who performs well as a department manager in a company is a good project manager. Those engaged in project management studies broadly agree about what characteristics are needed to make one an effective project manager and the level of application required. Among the most important roles of the project manager are to have an overview of the project at all times, to see the bigger context, and be aware of what is needed so that the professional objectives within the specified time frame and resources frame can be attained. He also needs to show positive leadership in the face of uncertain environments and demonstrate to the project team that they are able to promote the project amongst senior company management, if applicable, or to external investors. A good leader leads by example and should be able to make their team work in such a way that it works better than the sum of its parts. A football manager, for example, is a project manager of sorts, with each game representing a unique challenge. With limited resources at their disposal, they need to analyse the strengths and weaknesses of each opposing team and devise an effective plan to achieve a desirable result, as well as keep their eye on the longer-term targets.

A project manager is responsible for planning and organisation and will be required to make a range of decisions relating to projects. They will coordinate the work and delegate tasks, and are responsible for conveying information between employees of the project and ensuring that those in need of information will receive the right information – not too much or too little – at the right time. Communication skills are therefore important, and a substantial part of their daily duties is involved in controlling communication in the project. The project manager needs to ensure that all important stakeholders are engaged with the project in a productive manner, for example, by the provision of information to a steering group or a sponsor who needs to know about the current situation, including progress relative to stated objectives, dangers, and opportunities. These stakeholders may also be user groups, various institutes and opinion givers, and advisors who are important to the project.

It may be the case that the project manager needs to master various techniques and abilities to be able to fulfil their roles, and many job descriptions nowadays, for example, will mention competence in such and such management software. The need for technical expertise in the area of the project depends on the nature of the project. While it can be important in some roles, studies have shown that this is generally not the most important factor in the experience and knowledge bank of project managers. Attributes such as good judgement and people skills are particularly important, and project managers should have a firm grounding in ethics, which is the foundation of our societal structures. This involves having an understanding of the boundaries between right and wrong and the grey areas in between where disputes can arise. Many problems occur in projects, and it is the responsibility of the project manager to keep an overview of the problems, identify them as soon as possible, and understand the context, including the relevant stakeholders. A good problem resolution is founded on well-communicated values of stakeholders and on mutual understanding of various contexts. Many of the problems that arise within a project are likely to involve the scope, time frames, costs, and risks, or an interaction within any subset of all factors.

Conflicts of interest may crop up in the course of carrying out one's duties as a project manager and are more likely in a place like Iceland that has a small population, and where the same individuals may have multiple roles and interests. This situation, when it occurs, tests the moral awareness and professionalism of those involved. In other situations, the project manager will be required to act as a mediator and will need to perceive the nature of a conflict, the politics in a project, and how to resolve difficult and sensitive issues. They must have the drive and tenacity to deal with obstacles and be able to work under the pressure which accompanies most projects.

Reflection points

- Explain the quality trilogy in context with project management. Use a project-orientated organisation you know as a reference.
- Look up the Project Excellence Baseline. How can this model be used as a part of continuous improvement efforts of a project-orientated organisation?
- What are the key characteristics of the Scrum method, and what are its strengths (and weaknesses) as compared to a more conventional approach?
- It is stated that a good department manager will not necessarily be a good project manager. What do you think? Explain your view with a real example, if you can.

Teams and groups in projects

Project management is characterised by, among other things, the interaction of various types of groups and individuals in the project that need to communicate and work together so that the objectives of a project can be achieved.

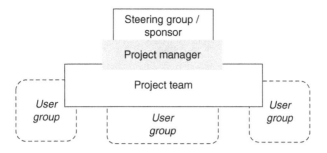

Figure 8.3

Main groups and key roles in projects.

Teamwork is therefore an important aspect of all projects where there are multiple groups working together, and it is possible to talk about some basic types and roles in this context. For example, it is common in projects to have a steering committee, a project team, and user groups working alongside each other. The interaction of these groups is shown graphically in Figure 8.3.

The structure shown in Figure 8.3 has been referred to in various chapters in this book, and the importance of effective communication between these main groups is vital, as is a clear understanding of decision-making roles. Without the consistent input of each of these groups, work can be carried out in a project that is later discarded when the opinions of a previously ignored group are found to be incompatible and necessitate a change of overall project direction. We also point out again that any given structure of the project organisation is valid only for a limited time, and changes in different contextual factors can call for adjustments or major changes to the project organisation.

The project team

A project team carries out the professional work in the project, led by the project manager. Within the project team, professional knowledge of the subject is required, and it is often preferable that participants have professional backgrounds of various types. Project management should, for example, comply with and utilise top professional project management standards such as listed in Chapter 1. Project teams can be one group or more, and sometimes it makes sense to have work parts of the project carried out by individuals working independently or as a combination of group and individual work. All of this depends on the nature and characteristics of projects as well as of the people who work on them. The manner in which the work of a project group is organised and how it evolves is very variable. Numerous factors influence this, and this has been a research topic in project management and related studies for many years. In our book *Project: Communication* in this book series, there is a detailed discussion about the origins of groups, their evolution and structure, and about communication and the decision-making process. Numerous factors can be outlined that influence whether a work group is effective or not, and below are some examples:

- Scope of a project.
- Complexity of a project.
- Composition of a group, including balance in their professional backgrounds.
- Shared vision of a group.
- Personalities of the individuals involved, particularly those with lead roles.
- Driving force and the motivation of those leading a group.
- Ambition of the participants.
- The level of respect shown for participants in a group by those with lead roles.

The level of knowledge about these factors in the planning stages of a project is variable, and some factors, such as the scope and complexity of a project, can usually be mapped out in advance. In this way, some factors are more controllable than others and can be tackled early by applying professional approaches in the preparation stages. This would include an analysis of the required professional background composition of a project team and implementing the necessary recruitment plan on the basis of this. Fair treatment of participants in all matters and opportunities given to engage with the project and put forward recommendations are far more likely to motivate people to work to the best of their abilities.

It is known that the happiness of participants in a project group and their alignment towards progress are important factors in success. It is also known that the characteristics of project groups are such that they often bring together people who have never worked together and only know each other slightly or not at all. This involves challenges that relate to human interaction and may have little or no effect on the material content of the project. These challenges also include opportunities, as we like to meet new people and take on new and exciting assignments. It can, therefore, be very interesting to look at ways in which it is possible to influence the workings of a project group, help it achieve maximum success, and deal with emerging problems.

The interactions between team members in a project group can take on different forms. There are many theories about the development of project groups that span their creation, progression through several development stages, and dissolution once they have completed their work. One such model is associated with Bruce Tuckman, who originally proposed it in 1965 (Tuckman & Jensen, 1977). This model focuses on the development of groups and assumes that they go through four development stages: *forming, storming, norming,* and *performing.* Later, a fifth stage, *adjourning,* was added. Tuckman believed that all of these development phases were necessary and unavoidable for a group to grow, deal with their challenges, resolve problems, find solutions, organise themselves, and finally provide the results that were

Figure 8.4

Development of project groups.

originally aimed for. These individual stages are discussed in turn below (see Figure 8.4).

Forming – At the initiation stage, a group is assembled, and its members meet and come to terms with what is required of them. They analyse what opportunities and challenges lie ahead and agree to participate and start the actual work. To begin with, it is normal that the work of a group consists of independent contributions, which may appear disjointed when viewed as a whole. Participants are most often enthusiastic and motivated but do not realise their own role well enough, and do not necessarily fully understand the content of the project. They are, therefore, somewhat self-centred, and it can be difficult to establish working relationships and effective communications. The formation stage is, however, important, as it is where conversations start between members of the team and they begin to get to know each other.

Storming – This stage is characterised by a considerable struggle for power and status, disputes in regard to what the content of the project should be, and what the role of each individual in a group should be. During the course of these battles, many different options on how to progress can be explored and, if there is a culture of independent thinking where people are not afraid to challenge the views of others, then it is likely that poor work choices are avoided before much time and resources are spent. In this way, this stage can be very beneficial to the project as a whole if carried out in the proper fashion. It is common for individuals to overlook things in their arguments or to promote a course of action that may only have select benefits. Groups, on the other hand, tend to have a form of collective wisdom and a wider perspective on things. An exception to this can be where groupthink is prevalent, and ideas put forward by certain contributors remain unchallenged either through fear of reprisal or otherwise. The danger in this stage is the development of wide rifts within a group, leading to a lack of success in achieving objectives, as people remain stuck in the battle phase, and little constructive work happens. For these reasons, the storming stage is important in the development phase of the group. It is often difficult, and much effort is needed. Some people handle such conflict badly, and it can be the case that some personality types just rub each other up the wrong way. In this case, a level-headed and decisive project manager is needed to control communications and aim to get the best results for a project.

Norming – Here, the group changes its rhythm, and team spirit and happiness can gradually form if outstanding issues are resolved in a satisfactory manner. Understanding of the project grows, and the role of participants becomes clearer. Relationships between participants are formed, and trust builds up, along with respect for different beliefs and values. The motivation of participants to achieve success is increasingly channelled in one direction.

Performing – A number of project teams manage to reach this point, but it is not always the case. If achieved, great efficiency and effectiveness in the work are realised, and a group works as a powerful team that finds ways to deliver the project as efficiently as possible without conflict and with minimal management intervention. Team members are very positive and encourage each other to maintain progress, and they have a good understanding of their roles and of the roles of others on the team. They are full of work energy and support each other, both within the group and outside it.

Adjourning – At this stage, the task of the group is being delivered, and the group is in the process of being dissolved. Here, new attitudes may arise, and the motivation to achieve the best results may be reduced. Erosion of close relationships with colleagues and worry about what will happen when the project ends can affect personal performance during the adjourning stage. An alternative development can be the channelling of peoples' willingness to work together to form new ventures, and this can be brought about quickly under the pressure of time and the prospect of being out of work in the near future.

Tuckman's model is simple in outline, but is useful for understanding the nature of group work, the problems that arise in communication within work groups, and how to deal with them. By being aware and understanding cooperation between people and the development of work groups, it is possible to gain success in developing effective work groups and creating a positive work spirit and work environment. Care should be taken to give the development stages described above sufficient time and to try not to force groups too quickly through the stages. The development stages will take different periods of time, and these will differ depending on a number of factors. For example, they can be short for people who have previously worked closely together and are used to dealing with each other. In all cases, however, it is important that stages do not drag on unnecessarily, and that momentum is maintained in projects.

Various other factors influence the results obtained in work groups. For example, there are often people in projects with different professional backgrounds and different status in the organisation of the company. Everyone is special and will act in his or her specific way – and apply his or her personal working style. It may, therefore, be necessary to deal with a variety of formal disputes before it is possible to direct attention and focus on material content and actual problems and solutions. In work groups, a contribution from all involved should be sought, and those who take part need to be willing to contribute. Most people can work in teams and enjoy the interaction with other people. There are, however, examples of individuals who work poorly in teams and find it difficult to accept the compromises that come with such co-operation. Nevertheless, these individuals may have important skills and knowledge needed for a project. In such cases, the project manager needs to look for ways to involve these individuals so that they can make a constructive contribution while still ensuring that they do not have a negative effect on the group as a whole. One way is not to let such a person participate in group activities. This can mean, for example, presenting the outcome of their work at meetings on their behalf, getting the feedback from other participants, and then going back to them if necessary. It is entirely normal for participants to look for consistency and fairness in their dealings with a project manager, and disputes are far more likely to be resolved if this is evident, and the manager is able to remain composed and decisive.

The project manager needs to help their team through difficulties, if encountered, and not interfere when the work is going well (see Figure 8.5). They need to ensure that suitable pressure is put on the team, yet not so much that it induces high stress levels and anxiety and becomes counterproductive. They need to help the team to understand the objectives of the project, direct

Figure 8.5

A project team.

attention to what is of most importance, and convey the needs of the work buyer and/or those that will receive the product and use it. It is beneficial if the team members in a project group have a basic knowledge of project management, as they all need to participate in understanding the nature of the management method which project management is, even though they are not all suitable or willing to take on the role of project manager.

The working method of a project group may vary in many ways, and the most appropriate working method should be selected to suit each group. Some general observations can be made, however, and it is not good, for example, to have work groups that are too large. Experience shows that if the number of group members exceeds six, then communication channels increase significantly and there is a risk that efficiency decreases and that imbalance between people emerges. Project groups are composed of people with extensive knowledge and experience in the subject areas of the project, and the work process that applies best to these people has to be found. Sometimes it makes sense to have the work take place at meetings, regular or irregular, over the project's lifetime. Sometimes it makes sense to divide the work between individuals, each one doing their jobs independently, and then the work is coordinated at meetings or by a project manager. Various things such as the location of team members affect what methods are selected. Sometimes groups are spread across countries, regions, and departments and do not have the opportunity to meet regularly or at all. Such groups are sometimes called dispersed project groups and will often use technologies such as video conferencing for communication. In all cases, it is necessary to ensure the flow of information between those working on the project, using whatever communication and information systems are most appropriate.

There are methods to analyse the strengths and weaknesses of people in group activities as well as the overall balance of a group. As an example, we can briefly mention the work of Meredith Belbin, who has defined a total of nine group roles (Belbin, 2010). These are shown below in italics (with our own short explanation given in each case):

- *Plant* – Creative and imaginative problem solver.
- *Resource Investigator* – Group networker and resource finder.
- *Coordinator* – Discussion controller, advocate of financial interests, and consensus finder.
- *Shaper* – Action lover keen to move things forward and not afraid of challenges and pressure.
- *Monitor/Evaluator* – Dispassionate critic who calmly reviews all options with bigger picture in mind.
- *Team Worker* – Maintains relationships within group and develops team spirit.
- *Implementer* – Practical thinker who understands systems and processes to achieve objectives.
- *Completer Finisher* – Detail person focused on quality and timelines.

- *Specialist* – Possessor of rare, much-needed expertise in specific, relevant areas.

According to the method, preferably all these characteristics need to be found in a group for optimal function, although some members may fulfil more than one role. The Belbin test is useful for reviewing the strengths and weaknesses of people in group activities, and it can be used as a reference when setting up a work group. The method can also be referred to when searching for reasons why it is difficult to get a particular working group to yield acceptable results. It is possible to read more about the Belbin method on the website www.belbin.com (Belbin, n.d.).

Project work is the actual process of creating the product of a project. A wide range of preparatory work that must be carried out before starting the actual execution can be included in this. The project management revolves around the key factors that were previously listed. Project work and project management should not be confused, even though one and the same person often handles the management of the project and part of the actual project work. This is actually more common than having a project manager whose sole role is management. Projects need to be very big to carry a full-time project manager, and few projects reach that size.

A common difficulty in maintaining a balance between project management and project work is the tendency to neglect the management component in favour of the project work. This tendency is reflected graphically in Figure 8.6.

Figure 8.6 shows a specific project with both project management and project work highlighted. The project management is situated above the project work, and the natural tendency in the diagram is for the focus to drift down towards the project work. Various explanations for this tendency exist, and three are most widely known. One is that it is in the nature of many people not to trust other people to carry out the actual project work. Many managers probably have the attitude that it simply takes too long to train a new person into a role, and that there is the risk that the outcome will not be as intended.

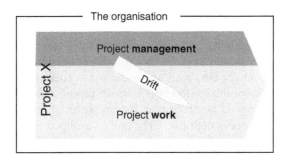

Figure 8.6

The tendency to neglect project management in favour of the project work.

It is, therefore, simpler just to do the work themselves. Another reason is that management is less tangible than the traditional norms of productivity, and many feel that there is little measurable success evident in their management work, whereas the physical work of the project is clearly obvious. Finally, it should be noted that many professionals consider management to be a rather dull subject, and that it is much more fun to be immersed in the project work and have their professional light shine there.

Morten Fangel (2013) has identified strategies to counteract these tendencies. Initially, a project is "started," which includes, among other things, initial preparation, the making and dissemination of a project plan, and other management works discussed in this book. At the end, a project is "closed," which includes, among other things, the outcome of the product of a project, and agreement and summarisation of how a project was managed and executed. Using this structure helps to delineate the management side of a project and encourages a project manager to set management goals and to record their progress, thus aiding prioritisation. It is rare that project managers only take care of project management – usually they need to conduct management alongside their professional material work. It is particularly important to make a distinction between project management and project work – the administrative tasks need to have priority in the endless priority list of the project manager nowadays – because, otherwise, there is a risk that the work of others in the team will be inefficient and erratic.

Disagreements of one type or another are an unavoidable consequence of human interaction, and it is the responsibility of the project manager to ensure that they do not become serious and impair the progress of a project. Disputes can be used in a constructive way to clear the air in a project and to resolve technical or other issues, provided they are handled correctly by all parties. An atmosphere of openness and trust that stems from the leaders in a project is very important in this regard. If people feel they are safe to express themselves so that a project can benefit from their opinions and suggestions, then that is likely to lead to a better outcome than a situation where fear and silence are the norm. One theory about disputes says that they belong to three main categories, and these are shown in Figure 8.7.

These categories are (1) misunderstandings and prejudices, (2) formal disputes, and (3) actual physical disputes. Their relative occurrence broadly corresponds to a so-called Pareto-principle, where 80% fall into the first category, 16% into the second, and 4% into the third. The numbers do not have to be taken too literally but, with an awareness of these general categories, the solutions to communication problems in projects can be found more quickly than they would be otherwise. By establishing a tradition and work method that encourages openness in the project group, it is possible to reveal and resolve misunderstandings and deal with any prejudices. This also has the effect of creating a more productive work environment where disputes are used to achieve better performance and favourable results, and to reveal interesting opportunities that would not otherwise have been discovered. For

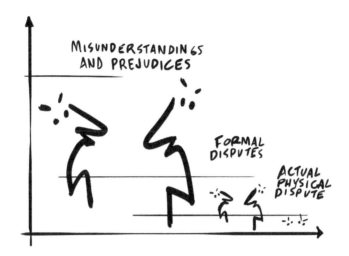

Figure 8.7

The three main categories for conflicts in projects.

these results to be obtained, it is necessary that all members of the working group adopt respect for the values of others, and this applies particularly to the project manager. Having respect for people's views and vision, not just within a project group, but in the wider community, is an essential characteristic of the project manager and those who work with them in the management of a project.

If a dispute is allowed to grow without anything being done, it may cause significant damage within a project team and in the group's communications with stakeholders. There are a couple of ways to deal effectively with conflict, and constructive discussion in order to understand the nature of the conflict and a search for solutions should be a top priority. It is advisable to try to find a compromise that is acceptable to both parties in a dispute. Failing this, a solution may have to be enforced, but it is important how this is actually managed. It is vital to demonstrate fairness in one's dealings as a project manager and to avoid situations where people may be humiliated in one way or another in front of others. As a project manager, one should be sensitive to the environment within the project and be able to spot potential flashpoints early. The next step may be to intervene to defuse situations where necessary or to organise work schedules so that incompatible work colleagues are kept apart.

User groups

User groups (sometimes referred to under the broad term of stakeholders) can vary widely between different types of project, for example, according to whether the project is public or private in nature. The former may include the building of a new public amenity, whereas the latter may include the development of a new consumer product. In either case, consultation with end users is an essential component of the project, and the formation of user groups and the conducting of consultations can direct the objective definitions in the most effective manner. Users will often set high standards or requirements – often higher than can be executed with limited resources – and expectation management can be important. These wishes or demands should be compiled as soon as possible so as to be able to realise their scope and evaluate them in light of the resources that are available. It is then perhaps possible to get a list of objectives that can be agreed upon, although the old adage that it is impossible to keep everyone happy will usually apply.

User groups are often defined and work in a systematic manner to collect information contained in the definition of the project. Sometimes, the user groups are not defined in a formal manner and, instead, information from users is collected through interviews and data collection or by other means. Unfortunately, there are many examples where users were not consulted, and this can have serious consequences. In the worst-case scenario, a large sum of money is invested to create a result that is ultimately unusable.

The construction of a new national hospital in Iceland is an example of a very large and complex project that affected the entire community, who all had direct and indirect interests related to the project. People had high expectations in regard to the benefits for the community, stakeholders, and the staff, and the project consultation was necessarily long and detailed. It was considered important to identify representative groups and individuals who were affected by the activities of the hospital and obtain information from them in a systematic way. In this process, a total of 50 user groups were recognised, and the scoping work involved about 300 workers from the National Hospital and the University of Iceland. Within these user groups, the main focus was on analysing the function and operation of the hospital and predicting its development and how the hospital work environment would have to change in the coming years so that the hospital could perform its role. Information and data obtained from the work of these user groups were used directly when it came to the needs analysis, and this became the basis for the preliminary design of the hospital.

Steering group/sponsor

The owners of a project appoint a steering group and their mandate is to protect the interests of the owners and ensure that the project is operated in accordance with the policies, priorities, and goals of the company, if applicable. Sometimes the role of the steering group is in the hands of one person who is then called a sponsor. The role of the sponsor includes an obligation to define, protect, and support the project from start to finish. The sponsor is usually a professional who is of a higher rank than the project manager and project team and is often an experienced director (Englund & Bucero, 2006).

The role of the sponsor (Figure 8.8) is very important and can be defined by three main dimensions – governance, support, and anchoring. If there is more

Figure 8.8

Project sponsor.

than one project owner, and/or if the project has a political aspect, and many people have to express their views and influence the project, then it is more appropriate to appoint a steering group. This group would have representatives of the owners to ensure that their attitudes and interests are championed when major and direction-affecting decisions are being made, and normally would include experienced external advisors or stakeholders. Such direction-affecting decisions, for example, may relate to the launch and completion of a project, in what way the tendering should be approached, or making decisions about disputes which arise in the project team and which the project manager does not feel able to tackle. The important aspect of a steering group is that it is a high-level consultative body that is there to discuss all the possible angles in a project and reach a consensus on the best way to proceed. This includes demarcating the main direction of a project, defining the objectives and prioritising them, and determining how the project should be executed.

The steering group is therefore charged with overseeing the project and setting the holistic objectives and expenditure framework. The steering group needs to have the time, interest, and sufficient knowledge and experience to support a project. This includes giving opinions on a range of important issues, participating in its preparation, securing necessary resources, promoting the progress of the project, and taking strategic decisions. The obvious advantage of having a steering group rather than a sponsor is that there are more points of view available, and important considerations are less likely to be overlooked. The main drawback, however, is that those who are chosen to sit on the steering group are generally busy people, and it may be a challenge to organise for them to meet together. A steering group needs to be able to come to a conclusion, even in difficult cases.

If the nature of a project is such that there is only one project owner – or if there is a strong consensus among different owners – then it is often agreeable to appoint a sponsor. The sponsor needs to be determined and self-motivated and above all needs to build a good relationship with both the project owner(s) and project manager and ensure their trust. The benefits of this arrangement are that the communication channels are short, and it is easier to meet and make important decisions. The potential risk is that the decisions are more likely to be homogeneous and based on the background and views of an individual instead of a group with a broad experience base. In complex projects, the likelihood of encountering unforeseen events can be much higher and may be outside of the experience base of an individual.

Reflection points

- Do you have personal experience of a project team that went off the rails? Explain the case, based on the factors that influence the effectiveness of a team, as listed in the chapter. Is anything missing from the list?
- Think about a project team you were a member of for any length of time. Mirror the development of this team in the model by Tuckman. Does the model help to explain the success or the problems encountered?
- Look at Belbin's team roles. Judging from the list, what do you think is your strongest role? Consider doing the assessment online and comparing the outcome to this self-image.
- Have you ever encountered the tendency to neglect project management in favour of the project work? What was the reason? What was the consequence?
- What happens in a project if a steering group does not have the necessary authority? Explain with an example.

Bibliography

Axelos. (n.d.). PRINCE2. Retrieved from www.axelos.com/best-practice-solutions/prince2.
Belbin. (n.d.). Retrieved from www.belbin.com.
Belbin, R. (2010). *Management Teams*. London: Routledge.
Englund, R.L., & Bucero, A. (2006). *Project Sponsorship: Achieving Management Commitment for Project Success*. New York: John Wiley & Sons.
Fangel, M. (2013). *Proactive Project Management – How to Make Common Sense Common Practice*. Hilleroed, Denmark: Fangel Consulting.
Gryna, F.M. (2001). *Quality Planning and Analysis: From Product Development through Use* (4th ed.). Boston: McGraw-Hill.
IPMA. (n.d.). IPMA project excellence baseline. Retrieved from www.ipma.world/projects/standard/.
Schwaber, K. (2004). *Agile Project Management with Scrum*. Redmond: Microsoft Press.
Tuckman, B.W., & Jensen, M.A.C. (1977). Stages of small-group development revisited. *Group & Organization Studies*, 2(4), 419–427.

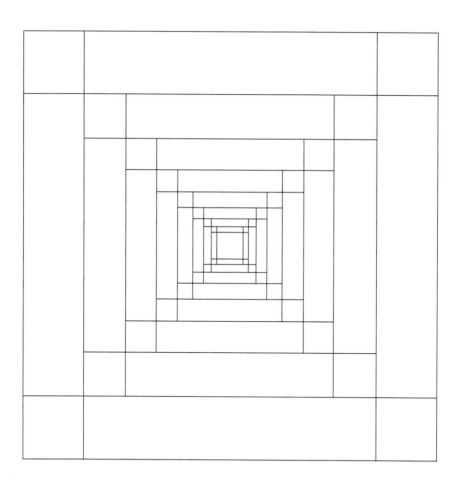

9 Project close-out

· ·

Organising the project close-out

The finishing stage of a project involves the delivery of the product of a project and agreement between the parties involved that all aspects of a project are satisfactorily completed (Figure 9.1). It also normally includes evaluation and documentation; the tying up of all loose ends in a project and the compilation of a report outlining key elements of the project delivery and other special undertakings.

This overall process is commonly referred to as close-out, and this term can also be applied to the finishing of the different phases in a project. It has two main elements, as shown in Figure 9.2.

Close-outs can occur in various ways. Sometimes they occur suddenly, e.g. when the project owner decides for some reason to stop the project, or when the main objectives are attained at some point, and the project is finished, perhaps sooner than intended. Sometimes, it is difficult to realise when a project is finished, and this is commonly due to the fact that project managers do not realise the importance of a formal close-out, and so do not carry one out. It can be tempting to continue directly onto the next project and neglect the closure of the last one. In this case, opportunities can be missed in regard to learning from the experience, in addition to the fact that not carrying out a formal finishing of a project can lead to uncertainty and cause difficulties for the different stakeholders involved. To counteract this, it should be recognised in the preparation phase of a project that it will be finished with a formal close-out. It is then ensured that the resources needed for the close-out are available. These resources include the time that the project manager and the key participants need to complete the full process.

As shown in Figure 9.2, two kinds of results come out of a close-out, and in both cases, they are based on a project plan that is made at the beginning of a project and is worked on throughout the project life cycle. One is the actual product (or products) of a project that emerges from a project on completion and has a life of its own after that. The other result is the knowledge that the participants in a project gain from carrying out a project. That experience will remain with those that were involved and is often documented in a special

Figure 9.1

Reaching the final gate.

report described later. In this way, even projects that were never successful in producing a product for whatever reason can still prove immensely valuable because of the experience gained.

It is said that project close-outs can be difficult because they often relate to difficult settlements and disagreements about finances, timing, and

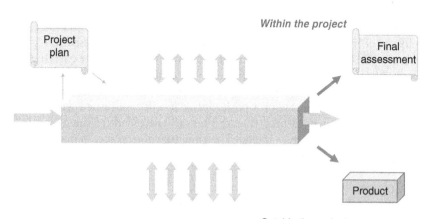

Within the project

Project plan

Final assessment

Product

Outside the project

Figure 9.2

Core elements of project close-out.

characteristics of products. They are often complex – for example, if there has been a lengthening of the project duration and it needs to be decided who is to pay additional costs. This, and other types of circumstances, should be anticipated and prepared for in a conscious and effective manner.

In small projects, close-out can occur rapidly, and it may even be carried out with modest preparation along with a formal close-out meeting if information has been well maintained during the project. In larger projects, the close-out is a more extensive phase that requires a lot of special preparation and coordination effort, as well as a considerable amount of interventional management by the project manager and the steering committee or sponsor.

Product delivered

The part of the close-out of a project that revolves around the delivery of the project's product to the project client and transfer of responsibilities often follows procedures which were defined in a contract at the beginning, often on the basis of tender documents. In such cases, the close-out also includes production of "as built" documentation, training of personnel who will operate the project outcome, and the commencement of the warranty period as well as final payments. If the product of the project is a structure or a software solution, then, presumably, technical conditions have been defined in the contract which the solution must meet. The close-out then involves a test period where the work buyer and contractors look at the characteristics of the project product together and ensure that they meet the set criteria. If they do not appear to meet the standards, then the contractor may need to make adjustments before final delivery and acceptance take place. In the building industry, for example, it is normal for an initial viewing of a new construction by the buyer to lead to the drawing up of a snag list that outlines items that they are not satisfied with. This is then systematically taken care of by the contractor. It is possible that the buyer retains some final payments for their own reasons, which may cause friction with the contractor. In a worst-case scenario, the contractor and the client may seek solutions through arbitration or in court if they cannot come to an agreement themselves. In other types of projects, warranties can be given by the contractor to reassure the buyer of the quality of the product and to provide recourse in the case of poor performance.

In some cases, it is not possible or feasible to assess whether a specific objective has been met or not, or the degree to which this objective has been met. One example of this could be the anticipated value gained from the project deliverable – this can be difficult to measure and verify during the project close-out. In such cases, validation may be a good way to determine the value gained from the project outcome. Validation can, in such cases, create a formal acceptance by the client.

The ambition of those charged with delivering a project must be to stick with what they have promised, within the specified time limit and compared to the agreed quality. Reliability of this kind is what develops good reputations and the prospect of repeat business in the future. It is good practice to seek out the views of the client, regardless of whether this is covered by contract or not, and check with them if they were satisfied with the product as well as the interaction with the project team throughout the project's duration. From this, valuable lessons can be drawn that can be useful for the future. This can be done by providing the client with a satisfaction questionnaire or, better still, at a special close-out meeting where the above items are looked at.

A large construction project in Iceland is the musical and conference centre, Harpa, situated prominently on the waterfront in Reykjavik (see Figure 9.3). This building became widely known, even in international circles, as its construction was interrupted for a time by the deep recession that hit Iceland in 2008. It had originally been part of a very ambitious development plan hatched during the boom years and had been led by a consortium headed by the Icelandic bank Landsbanki, which was nationalised along with the other major Icelandic banks in 2008. Half-finished and with construction halted for a long period, it became a symbol of the financial crash and a major source of debate in Iceland as to whether it should be finished with scarce public funds. After a lengthy period of deliberation, the new government installed after the financial crash made the decision to finish the construction.

The exterior design was developed by Ólafur Elíasson, an artist with Icelandic parents who grew up in Denmark, and Henning Larsen Architects. It was a highly ambitious glass façade, influenced by structures found in Icelandic nature. This exterior glasswork was originally put to tender in 2007

Figure 9.3

Harpa, musical, and conference centre (Harpa, n.d.) (photograph by Vigfús Birgisson).

and received only one bid in relation to the final design, manufacturing, and installation. This was submitted by a company called Lingyun, headquartered in Wuhan in China. When the installation of the glass structure was finally initiated in March 2010, the internal quality control unit of the principal Icelandic contractors, IAV, found a crack in the corner of some steel framework. This discovery led to an extensive check on all the units that were in the process of being installed. Flaws in the steel blocks were identified, and the outcome of this was that IAV had no choice but to dismantle the structure on the south side of the building for safety reasons. This was a difficult problem superimposed on an already politically sensitive project, but the sub-contractor of IAV in China, Lingyun and its sub-contractors, took full responsibility and agreed to rectify the manufacturing mistakes that had been made in China.

Officially opened for concerts in May 2011 while the exterior was unfinished, Harpa has since had its exterior finished and is fully operational as a venue. It has multiple facilities, including a large concert hall that is renowned for its acoustics, and can accommodate an audience of up to 1,800 people. It has remained a very busy venue since opening and won the 2013 EU Prize for Contemporary Architecture/Mies van der Rohe Award. A wealth of experience was gained from the management of this project that can be referenced for future projects in Iceland.

Learning from the experience

Project management is a discipline where much emphasis is placed on consciously learning from experience. As an example of this, we can point to the international certification system of project managers that was mentioned earlier in this book. It is largely based on the idea that applicants can demonstrate that they have experience in managing projects and that they have consciously worked at improving their knowledge and skills. By being aware of this important part of project management, project managers can, throughout the duration of the projects they are involved in, keep their eyes open for various things that occur, both positive and negative, with the aim of drawing experience from them. A number of aspects that have been discussed in this book should help to facilitate this process. Analysis of the environment, which is an essential element for planning, shines a light on things that particularly need to be kept in mind in a project. Plans are made with this information in mind, followed through, and are adapted and modified as needed. Information on progress, decisions, communications, and more are recorded and used by the project manager at the end to determine what can be learnt from the project. These findings are then documented for future reference.

Evidently, the way chosen for the carrying out of this aspect of the close-out has little effect on the quality associated with a project – whether that is the quality related to a project's product or regarding the methods employed during a project. The reason is that the project is more or less finished. The close-out does, on the other hand, have a significant effect on the views concerning the project and the experience, knowledge, and ability of the project team and those that are involved in the project during its lifetime. Extensive knowledge in particular areas can be built up over many years in organisations, and these become repositories of information.

An example of this in Iceland is the Government Construction Contracting Agency (GCCA, or FSR in Icelandic) that has the role of administering government construction projects and carrying out consultation on technical matters, procurement, and preparation of projects. Its role is to develop specialist knowledge about construction in the public sector, which ensures that it can perform its role to a high standard and deliver quality output (Government Construction Contracting Agency, n.d.). An important aspect of their work is the carrying out of a delivery evaluation of the projects they are involved in, in order to learn from experience. Advanced use of information technology means that this information can be easily accessed as a reference in future projects. The following information is usually recorded:

- *Preparation: A general description of, among other things, what is involved in an execution, who the buyer is, and what the main parameters are.*
- *Practical execution: An explanation of the tendering of the execution, contracts with contractors, and progress of the project, as well as any major changes in the project schedule and of the execution supervision.*
- *Account settlement: Documentation of the voted expenditure for the execution of a project, along with its actual costs. Deviations shall be explained.*
- *Summary and conclusions: Overall evaluation put forward in regard to how successful the execution was. This may compare the cost of the execution to other similar executions.*

It is stated in the regulations that the GCCA is obliged to compile figures from each project delivery about the actual costs and to make them available for those that are working on the preparation of public projects. It is possible then for companies submitting bids on public works to use these figures in their preparation work. The following elements that relate to the recording of progress and outcomes of projects should be considered:

- It is important at the beginning of a project to pay close attention to how information shall be gathered about a project and how best to use it.
- After completing the above preparation, it is necessary to collect all accessible and tangible information about the project, which enables the comparison of actual progress to the objectives and key performance indicators defined at the beginning. If a plan has been made with an emphasis on numerical representations, then the follow-up during the lifetime of the project should be a straightforward task based on measurement.

- There are various elements in projects that cannot be measured but are still important, such as the various experiences and feelings of those people that participate in a project in a direct or indirect way. To garner such information, it is possible, for instance, to hold a meeting to bring together members of the project team that may also include other stakeholders. At these meetings, the format should be such that people can express their views in a succinct manner, outlining what they thought went well and what could have been done better in a project.
- When all the information is gathered and, if applicable, data processed, a document may be prepared to disseminate the results by the most suitable means. This could include compiling presentation material or a brief report.
- Finally, it needs to be ensured that the results are delivered to those that most need them. This ensures that the experience from a completed project will be useful for the next project.

The meeting that was mentioned in the above list is called a close-out meeting. This is where various issues related to the delivery of the product and summaries of the experiences of the project work are discussed. At such a meeting, a simple skeleton of a programme, as shown in Figure 9.4, can be useful.

Prior to the meeting, a *post-implementation review* may be initiated which seeks out the views of participants and stakeholders. The meeting itself begins with a general introduction by the project manager and a comparison of the set objectives with the results obtained. Depending on circumstances, a more accurate report about the results can be made, particularly if some aspects deviated from what was originally planned. It is appropriate to review the assessment of customer satisfaction, and there is an option that a representative of the customer(s) can be called into the meeting to give their opinion. The performance of participants needs to be looked at in order to recognise good work, where appropriate, or poor work, if required, to prevent the repetition of problems in later projects. There should also be an assessment of whether the project has been a profitable undertaking and whether it was beneficial in the end to those that worked on it. The status of the project should be gone over at the end, i.e. whether it is necessary to tie up loose ends, who should do this, and how it should be conducted.

It is appropriate to review the project management carefully by looking at the methodology that was used, discussing its advantages and disadvantages, what worked and what needs improvement. The project work is a factor that may be looked at in specific detail in a close-out meeting – the different work processes and interaction in the work groups, difficulties that arose, and how they were addressed. It is also possible to discuss the various appliances and tools that were used in the project work – information technology, conferencing systems, networking and communication systems, and more. Under this general heading, it may be advisable to allow the working group members to express themselves and relate their opinions. In doing this, it is necessary to

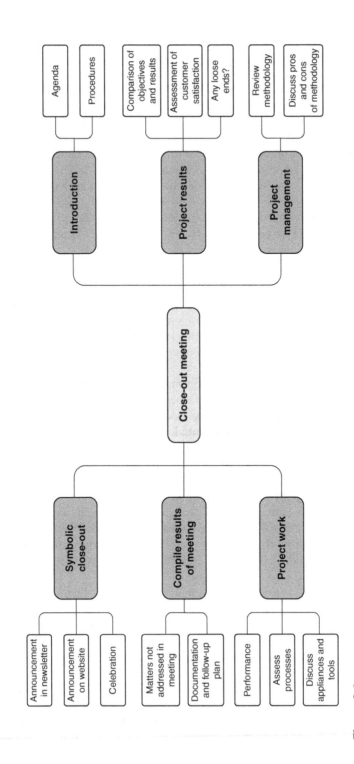

Figure 9.4

A framework for a schedule of a project close-out meeting.

Figure 9.5

Project close-out.

allow an open discussion whilst still staying focused and directing the emphasis on the project. The framework for this discussion could, on the one hand, include discussing what was done well and, on the other hand, what could have been done better. We want to understand what was done well so that it can be repeated in the next project. We also want to understand what was not done well in order to be able to do better in the next project.

The results of the close-out need to be compiled in a formal manner and made available to those that need it – participants of the project and people in the company that use project management and could learn from this experience. The report that comes out of this is often called the *project delivery report*, and its key elements and metrics can be stored in a *lessons learnt database* or *project repository*. A part of the start-up of a project can thus be to check the lessons learnt database and gather experience from previous projects that are considered relevant, both projects where the newly formed project team were participants, and also other projects from the organisation, or even from the wider community. The keeper of the lessons learnt database could, for example, be the company project management office (PMO), or the quality management function of the organisation.

Last, but not least, it is good to celebrate the close-out milestone in a symbolic manner and show people that their work is valued). This can be done by an announcement in the company's newsletter or on the website and/or with a celebration of one sort or another that does not need to cost a lot relative to the overall budget of the project. This can make a big difference to morale and team spirit and provide encouragement for the project group to tackle new challenges in other projects in the future.

Reflection points

- Have you participated in a project where there was no formal close-out or a poorly managed close-out? What were the consequences for some of the stakeholders, such as the project team, the project manager, the project sponsor, the client, the organisation – and yourself?

- How can validation in project close-down work in practice? Explain this with an example you know or create a simple story to explain this.
- What are the main challenges regarding knowledge management in a project-orientated organisation, and how can they be dealt with?

Bibliography

Government Construction Contracting Agency. (n.d.). Role of GCCA. Retrieved from www.fsr.is/um-fsr/hlutverk-fsr/.

Harpa. (n.d.). Harpa. Retrieved from https://en.harpa.is.

Index

•••

Page numbers in **bold** denote tables, in *italic* denote figures

activity 20, **22**, 23, *29*, 32–33, 38, 47, 56, **101**, 127, 131, 133, 172, 190; on Arc (AOA) 137, *139–140*; on Node (AON) 137, *139*, 139; *see also* task
actual cost (AC) 190–193, 244
agile: project management 42, 219; practice 7
agreements 49, 94, 106, 125, 152, 157, 163, 166, 172–175, 232, 239, 241
Analytics Hierarchy Process (AHP) 211
Association of Cost Engineers 150
associations: project management 2, 4–5, 8; professional 4, 6, 85
Axelos Ltd. 219

Barnes, M. 111
Bechtel 60–61
Belbin, M. 230–231, 236
benefits 16, 20, 48, 52, 55, 57, 79, 110, 120, 212, 213, 234, 236
Boehm, B.W. 42
budget at completion (BOC) 191–193
Build–Operate–Transfer (BOT) 175

cash flow 26, 64, 84, **103**, **105**, 149, 157, **160**, 161, 190, 208, 210–211
change control 74, 187–188, *189*, 190, 194
Chapman, C. 198, 200, 204
Chartered Association for Project Management (APM) 5–8, *7*, 122, 200
Cheops Pyramid 15, *15*, 23, 66
codes of conduct 83, 85
Cold War 23

communication: channels 30, 178, *178*, 184, 230, 236; formal 177, 179–182, 194; informal 177, 180, 182–183, 194; international 157; plan 96; skills 1, 162, 223; tele- 66, 85, 218
complexity: analysis **105**, 106, *130*; organisational 88–89, **89**, 90; of a project 88, **89**, 226; resource 88–89, **89**, 90; technical 88–89, **89**, 90
conflict management 174
contingency 153, 154, *158*, 161; fund 157, 191; plan 97, 100, 127, 200
contract 36, 60, 63, 93, **102**, **104**, 106, 113, 116, **121**, 125, 127, 131, *132*, 134, 154, *156*, 159, 164, 173–177, 188, 241–242, 244; negotiations 49, 63, 65, **101**; parties 174–175; temporary 56; terms 174–175, 187, 221
Cooper, R.G. 45, 206
cost: benefit analysis (CBA) 208, 212–213; breakdown structure (CBS) 154, *156*, 157
critical path 18, 24, 27, 133, 140–142, **140**, *141–142*, 147, 202–203, *204*; Method (CPM) 23–25, 140, 202
culture 16, 28, 45, 46, 58, 66, 83, 84, 88, 162, 184, 218, 227

Darwin, C. 187
decision-making **22**, 55, 81, 91, 96, 123, 126, 204–206, 213, 218, 225
delegate 223
diatomite 39–41

documentation 58, 79, 94, 131, *133*, 173, 177, *182*, 219, 239, 241, 244, *246*
Dvir, D. 187

earned value (EV) 177, 190–194, *193*; management (EVM) 190
Eimskip 65
Einstein, A. 214
estimate at completion (EAT) 192–193
European Union (EU) 174
execution: actual 35–36, 41, 48, 92, 125, 135, 231; period 36, **97**, 147, 159, 190; phase 36, 38, 41, 50, 125–126, 136, 147–148, 157, 171; of projects 1, 64, 68, 174, 198, 220; skills 1, 9; stage 38, 149, 187, 197
expert/expertise 40, 47, 54–55, 63–64, 92, 112, 130, 149, 162, 184, 207–208, 224, 231; panel 213
Eyjólfsson, H. 25–26, 31

Fangel, M. 74–75, 115, 232
FIDIC terms 174
FIFA World Cup 120, **120–121**, 122
financial control 191
Flyvberg, B. 50
Forman, E. 205–206
Fridgeirsson, T.V. 50
functional organisation 69

Gaddis, P.O. 24
Gantt, H. 24, 136; chart 24, 136n137, *137–138*
goal 5, 9, 13–14, 20, 23, 30, *32*, 39, 60, 68, 74, 109–115, 119, 172–173, 186–187, 191, 207, 219, 232, 234; hierarchy 118; project 20, 30, 49, 118–119, *119*, 172; setting 26, 28, 30, 82, 86, 109–110, 112–114, *119*, 121, 206; *see also* strategic
Government Construction Contracting Agency (GCCA) 244
Gryna, F.M. 211, 217

Al-Harbi, K.M.A.S. 211
Harpa concert and conference hall 19–20, 242–243, *242*
Hauksson, T. 31
Health, Security, Safety and Environment (HSSE) 59–61, 208

herring factory 25–26, 204
Hof Cultural and Conference Center 188–190, *189*
HydroPower Coop 79, **80**

IAV (Icelandic company) 17, 19–20, *21*, 22, 61, 243
Icelandic Alloys Ltd. 117–118
information: available 42, 197, 205, 207, 211; gathering 26, 81, *81*, 117, **150**, 171, 184, *185*, 207; management 177; personal 92; system 131, 178–179, 183, 230
Information and Communication Technology (ICT) 53
interested parties 33, 79, 91, 177
internal rate of return (IRR) 210–211
International Federation of Consulting Engineers 174
International Organization for Standardization (ISO) 13, 22, 47, 66, 157, 217–218
International Project Management Association (IPMA) 2, 4–8, 13, 16, 18, 22, 27, 122, 218; Certified Projects Director (IPMA Level A) 5; Certified Senior Project Manager (IPMA Level B) 4; Certified Project Manager (IPMA Level C) 5; Certified Project Management Associate (IPMA Level D) 5
International Project Management Association's Competence Baseline (ICB4) 2, 3, 4, 6, 9, 13, 16, 18, 27
International Standards Office 14
iterative *32*, 42, 68, **89**, 111, 219; approach *32*, 43, 124

Johnson, G. 68
Juran, J. 217

Kaldi 67
Kárahnjúkavirkjunar, V. 16–18
Kerzner, H. 74, 150
Key Performance Indicators (KPI) 244
Knight, F. 197
knowledge: base 27, 57; basic 230; management 248; modern 27;

necessary 76, **76**, 208; professional 225; specialist 179, 244; technological 56
Kozak-Holland 66

Lake Myvatn 39, 45
leadership 18, 221, 223; skills 1–2, **22**, 31; style 31–32
lessons learned 9, 58, 98, 177, 217, 242, 247
Lenfle, S. 24
Lichtenberg, S. 197
Lim, C.S. 114–115
Lingyun 243
Lock, D. 111, 150

make or buy 147
Marel 45, 47
Mars Climate Orbiter 2, 8
Master of Project Management (MPM) 48
master plan 46, 122–124, 126, 130, 133
matrix organisation 58
mature 31, 78; enterprises 62
Meredith, J.R. 74, 128, 148, 206, 209
Mikkelsen, H. 74, 164
milestones 9, 38, 49, 64, 80, 110, 113, **118**, 122–126, 131, 137, 139, 142, 183, 247
monitor 26, 75, 77, 86, 217, 230
Morris, P. 24

National Power Company 17–18
net present value (NPV) 210–211, 213

Oberg, J. 4
opportunities 5, 30, 45, 52, 63, 66, 75–76, **76**, 81, 84, 91, 96–97, **97**, 100, 172, 182–183, 206, 223, 226–227, 232, 239
Össur 45

Pareto Priority Index (PPI) 211–212
partnership 82, 92, 172, 175, 213
Payne, J.H. 32
planned value (PV) 191–193
Political, Economic, Sociological, Technological, Legal, and Environmental (PESTLE) 83–85, 89, 90, 94, 98, **102**, **104**–105, 104
portfolio 5, 18–20, *19*, **22**, 22, 29, 37–38, *37*, *39*, 43, 48, 62, 68, 206;

management 6, 18, 20, 22, 48–49, 206; *see also* risk
practice: best 187, 218; good 6, 85, 174, 242; management 60, 218; work 60, 65, 83
Private Finance Initiative (PFI) 175–176
probability 96, 199, 202–203, *202*, 212–213; of success 43, 104, 109, 213
problems: potential 1, 177, 179, 204; serious 27, 56
procurement 8, 9, 35, 38, 147–148, 173, 244
Program Evaluation and Review Technique (PERT) 23–25, 202, 204, **204**
programme 5, 16–20, *19*, **22**, 22–24, 29, 37–38, *37*, 40, 48–49, 52–53, 62, 64–65, 68, **97**, 112, 212, 245; certification 6; computer 112; management 6, 18, 20, **22**, 49, 52–53, 57; research 5
progress 22, 44, 46, 96, 98, 112, 133, 162, 164, 167, 177, 182–183, 186–187, 192, 223, 226–228, 232, 243–244; meeting 177, *181*, 184, 186; project 30, 42, 44, 58, 61, 75, 78–79, 91, 93–94, **97**, **101**, 123, 180, 183–184, 190, 199, 206, 232, 235, 244
project: budget 42, 120, 191; change 41; charter 80, 118; close-out 239–241, *240*, *246*–247, 248; control 177; costs 50, 112, **118**, *156*; design 30, 33, **44**, 48, 145, 157, 162–163, 165, 175, 198; environment 82–83, 88–89, *101*, 106, *106*, 123, 152, 173, 199, 202, 204; handbook 179–181; lead 31, 33, 93; life cycle 31, 33–34, *34–35*, 36, *37*, *41*, 43, 51, 54, *61*, 74, 80, 96, 98, **105**, 122–124, *124–125*, 146, 159, 187, 194, 197, 200, 239; objectives 14, 112, 116–117, 119–120, *119*, *121*, 122, 177, 179, 183, 188; organisation 19, 33–34, 56, 57–58, 91, 126, 165, *166*, 225; -orientated organisation 54, 69, 217, 224, 248; outcomes 92, **101**, 106; phase 124, **126**, 142, 147, 172, 187, 192; planning 4, 73–74, *75*, 79, 84–86, 91, 93, 106, 112, 150, 162; review 47, 64, 75, 94, 112, 122, 130, 172, 187, 245, *246*; start up 171–172, *172*, 176; *see also* execution, progress

project deliverables 122
Project Excellence Baseline 218, 224
project finance 64, 125
PRoject IN Controlled Environments
   (PRINCE) 218–219; PRINCE2 218–219
project management: plan 172; proactive
   73, 78; success 41, 49, 112–113;
   see also agile
Project Management Book of Knowledge
   (PMBOK) 5, 7, 8
project management competence 4, 28,
   58, 59, 120, 218
Project Management Institute (PMI)
   5, 7–8
project management office (PMO)
   57–58, 247
project management professional (PMP)
   1, 5, 7
project owner 49, 60, 115, 190, 235,
   236, 239
Project, Programme and Portfolio (PPP)
   management 13, 27, 53, 62, 68
Public–Private Partnership (PPP) 175

quality: control 2, 187, 217, 243;
   improvement 217–218; management
   112, 217–218, 247; requirements 1, 112,
   187; standards 1, 112, 122, 218; trilogy
   217, 224
quality assurance 112, 217, 218

recycling 106, 146; aluminium dross
   101–102, 104–105, 106–107, *106*
reporting 9, 54, 58, 60, 64, 187, 190
request: for information (RFI) 174; for
   proposal (RFP) 174; for quotation
   (RFQ) 174
requirements 1–2, 8, 13–14, 17, 26, 53,
   60–61, 63, 74–75, 79, 84–86, **89**, 92–
   93, **101**, 110–113, 122, 126, 134, 147,
   154, 157, 162, 164, 173, 187, 207–209,
   213, 219, 221, 234; financial 145, 159;
   labour 36, 53, *54*, 152
resources: available 68, 147; financial
   34, 65, 157; human (HR) 44, 46,
   53, 56, 69; levelling 147; limited
   20, 84, 147, 223, 234; necessary
   19, 24, 74, 77, 147, 149, 198, 235;
   see also complexity

responsibility 2, 5, 33, 38, 46, 49, 57, 58,
   59, 63, 127, 148, 162, 163, 165, 166, 167,
   168, 182, 220, 224, 232, 243
risk 20, 33, 47–48, 52, 55–56,
   59–60, 62–65, 67–68, 75–76, **76**,
   83–84, 96–98, **97**, 98–99, 100,
   101, 104, *106*, 127, 134, 152, 173–175,
   182–183, 187, 190, 197–201, *200*,
   204–209, 212, 224, 230–232, 236;
   factors 45, 78, 98; financial 210;
   measurement 22, 197; portfolio 18;
   security 59
risk analysis 100, 174
risk management 74, 98, 197, 200–201,
   201, 206–207; framework 98, 200;
   process of 200–201
role/task division 57, 161, 172, 177

schedule 20, 22, **22**, 24, 26, 42, 54, 66,
   74, 113, 115, 131, 133, 145, 161, 179,
   183, 186, 192–193, 197–198, 209, 233,
   244, *246*; time 74, 96, 100, 123–124,
   133–134, 136–137, 190
schedule performance index (SPI) 192
schedule variance (SV) 192–193
Schoper, Y.G. 34, 51, 65
Schriever, B. 24
Schwaber, K. 219–220
Science Department of the University of
   Iceland 47
scope: creep 79, 219; of delivery 20, **22**; of
   the project 30, 79, 84, 86, 88, 126–127,
   152, 171, 187, 199, 211, 226
scrum: master 220; method 219–220,
   220, 224
Shenhar, A.J. 64, 115
Simon, H. 204, 206, 213
social: dimension 48; disaster **44**, 48;
   projects **44**, 48
society 27, 48, 59, 85, 86, *101*, **102–103**,
   105, *106*
specifications 22, 111–113, 119–120, *119*,
   173, 177, 187
sponsor 47, 66, 86, 91, **103**, **120**, 163–164,
   164, *166*, 166–167, *168*, *178*, 179, **180**,
   183, 188, 199, 223, *225*, 234–236, *235*,
   241, 248
stakeholder 20, **22**, 30, 33, 49, 59, 68, 74,
   86, 91–94, *91*, *95*, 96, *101*, 104, 106,

106, 113, 119, 123, 130, *130*, 162, 164, 171–172, 177, 180, 183–184, 187–188, 190, 198, 208, 212, 218–219, 223–224, 233–235, 239, 245, 248
stakeholder analysis 102
steering committee 163, *164*, 199, 225, 241
Stephenson, A. 2, 4
strategic: change 16, 20; decision 38, 68, 142, 235; goals 9, 16–18, 20, 52, 68; management 52, 68; objectives **22**, 68; planning 26, 78, 84; skills 1
strategy 16, 18, 24, 46, 54, 67–68, 69, 77, 78, 83, 94, 96, 147, 162
success criteria 112
suppliers 38, 46, 56, 64–65, 84, 92, **101**, **104**, 142, 147, 152–153, 164, *164*, 173–174, 187, 199, 220
sustainability 7, 69
Sydney Opera House 50–51, *51*, 122

task: duration 142, **204**; sequence 2, 24
team 5, 33, 38, 42, 55, 56, 59, 66, 78, 81, 117, 120, 121, 164, 181, 183, 187, 194, 199, 219, 220, 221, 223, 225, 226, 227, 228, 229, 230, 232, 233, 234, 235, 236, 242, 244, 245, 247, 248
teamwork 81, 255
technology 23–25, 47, 52, 56, 66, 83–86, 85, 92, *101*, **102–105**, 106, *106*, 181, 198, 200, 213, 218, 230; information

(IT) 157, 183–184, 244–245; *see also* complexity, knowledge
Technology Development Fund 213
temporary organisation 14, 16, 33, 52, 162
Tracy, B. 109
transformation 16, 46
Tuckman, B. 226, 228, 236
Turner, J.R. 30, 41, 115

uncertainty 9, 24, 73, 86, 96–98, **97**, 100, **101**, **104**, 106, *106*, 110, 112, 130, *130*, 134, 145, 152, **152**, 157, 159, 161, 171–172, 197–202, 204, 206, **223**, 239
United Nations 174
users 49, 77, 92–93, 110, 115, 164, 189, 213, 219, 223, 225, *225*, 233–234

values 69, 94, 109, 162, 193, 203, 213, 224, 228, 233

Ward, S. 198, 200, 204
waterfall model 42
work breakdown *81*, 124, *128*, 137, 142; structure (WBS) 122–123, *130*, 142
workforce 47, 66, **89**, 117, 148, **150**, *151*, 184
work packages 22, 122–123, 126–127, 130–131, 135, 149, 153, 219

Zurich Insurance Group 32

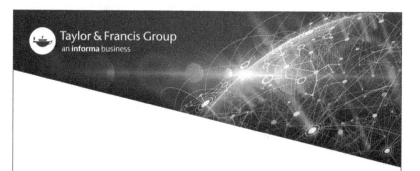